Jesus.
His Words.
Translated into today.

Copyright © 2025 by Golden Rule Publishing
All rights reserved.

No part of this publication may be reproduced, stored in a retrieval system, or transmitted in any form or by any means without prior written permission from the publisher, except for brief quotations used in reviews or scholarly works.

This book presents a modern-language interpretation of the red-letter words of Jesus Christ as recorded in the King James Version of the Bible. Every effort has been made to maintain the integrity, spirit, and accuracy of His original message. The author makes no representations or warranties regarding theological interpretation, doctrinal alignment, or denominational approval.

The content is provided "as is" for spiritual insight and personal reflection. It is not intended to replace scripture, provide religious instruction, or serve as legal, psychological, or medical advice. Readers are encouraged to seek guidance from qualified spiritual leaders, biblical scholars, or licensed professionals.

Due to the size and scope of this work, not every modernized verse includes the full KJV text above it. However, readers can access the complete list of Jesus' red-letter verses in the King James Version at www.JesusHisWords.com for study and reference.

The author and publisher disclaim any liability for errors, omissions, or consequences resulting from the use or interpretation of this material. All responsibility for how this book is used or understood lies with the reader. Scripture quotations are taken from the King James Version of the Bible, which is in the public domain.

First Edition
Golden Rule Publishing
Modern-language interpretations ("Jesus: Today") © 2025 by Golden Rule Publishing
ISBN: 979-8-218-67104-4

GOLDEN RULE PUBLISHING

For my grandparents,
the roots beneath it all.
Cornelius J. Mears and Mary A. Mears.
Donal A. Williams and Emma J. Williams.
Your names still echo through time.
This is for your honor.
Eternally remembered.

For my children,
Ruby West and Abel Saint Levant.
You are my legacy, and theirs.
The story continues in you.
When the world grows loud,
may you always recognize His voice.

For my mom and dad,
Janelle Wine and Terry Mears.
For every prayer whispered,
for every unseen sacrifice,
this is a piece of your love made visible.

For my siblings,
Jessica, Cody, and Heidi.
The ones who know where I came from,
and still remind me who I am.

For my friend, ***Diane Sweet.***
Even without sharing my faith,
you have shared your heart.
This belongs to you too.

And for those who have heard of Him,
but never heard from Him.
He is still speaking.
Always has been.
Always will.

-TJM

Introduction

The world got loud.
So loud that His voice, the one that once calmed storms, started to sound like a whisper.

Everyone had something to say.
Everyone had an answer.
But I didn't need answers.
I needed Him.

So I opened the Bible and went straight to the red letters.
The words that changed everything.
The words that still pulse with power if we can quiet down long enough to hear them.

But some of them felt far away.
Holy, but hard to reach.
Beautiful, but buried under centuries of language and translation.

So I started to listen differently.
To write what I heard.
Not to change His message, but to let it speak in the heartbeat of now.

Every line in this book began as a whisper between me and God.
His words, as written in the King James, restated in today's language—clear, faithful, and alive.

No commentary.
No filter.
No noise.
Just Jesus, speaking again.

This is not a replacement for Scripture.
It is a bridge back to His voice.
A way to recognize the same tone that called fishermen to follow, that told the storm to be still, that spoke life into the dead.

If even one heart hears Him through this, the purpose is complete.

Let every page lead you closer.
Let every word point back to Him.

Notes to the Reader

You may have heard about *Jesus*.
You might have been told who He is, what He said, or what He meant.
But this book is not someone else explaining Him to you.
This is Him. Speaking.

From Matthew to Revelation, the red-letter words record what Jesus said. In many Bibles, His words are printed in red so they stand out. In these pages, those words are presented in the language of today, clear, direct, and alive.

The red-letter books include ***Matthew, Mark, Luke, John, Acts,*** *and* ***Revelation***. Each was written originally in Greek between about AD 60 and 100.

Matthew was a tax collector before Jesus called him to follow. Leaving his old life behind, he became one of the twelve disciples. His account highlights Jesus as the promised Messiah and often points back to the Hebrew Scriptures.

Mark, also called John Mark, was not one of the twelve disciples but was a close companion of Peter. His Gospel reflects Peter's eyewitness memories and is known for being the earliest and most action-packed account of Jesus' life.

Luke was a physician and historian, and a close friend of Paul the apostle. He carefully investigated the stories of Jesus and wrote them down in an orderly way. Luke also wrote ***Acts***, which tells how the good news spread from Jerusalem into the wider world through the apostles and the early church.

John was one of the twelve disciples, known as "the beloved disciple." He was especially close to Jesus, present at the Last Supper and at the cross. His Gospel emphasizes who Jesus truly is, the Son of God, and gives long, deep teachings not found in the other Gospels. John also wrote **Revelation** while exiled on the island of Patmos, recording the visions God gave him about the final victory of Christ.

Each book gives a unique perspective, yet together they carry one voice: the voice of ***Jesus Christ.***

He is closer than you think. And He is still speaking.
Let these words interrupt you. Heal you. Find you.
Just Jesus.
Still speaking Still saving.
Still turning hearts back to life.

Table of Contents

Introduction	i
Notes to Reader	ii
Matthew	1
Mark	126
Luke	177
John	262
Acts	325
Revelation	328

All are welcome at His table.
There is room for every heart that seeks truth,
and grace enough for all who come.

Matthew

Matthew 11:28 (KJV)
"Come unto me, all ye that labour and are heavy laden, and I will give you rest."
Jesus (Today):
Come to Me. If you're exhausted and carrying too much, I will give you rest.

"Kingdom Revealed"
His first words of promise. Heaven touches earth as He calls ordinary lives into extraordinary purpose.

Matthew 3

Matthew 3:15 (KJV)
"Suffer it to be so now: for thus it becometh us to fulfil all righteousness. Then he suffered him."
Jesus (Today):
Let it happen now. This is the way it has to be,
so we can complete everything the Father set in motion.

Matthew 4

Matthew 4:4 (KJV)
"It is written, Man shall not live by bread alone, but by every word that proceedeth out of the mouth of God."
Jesus (Today):
It's written, you don't live on bread alone.
You live on every word that God speaks.

Matthew 4:7 (KJV)
"It is written again, Thou shalt not tempt the Lord thy God."
Jesus (Today):
It's written again, don't put God to the test. Ever.

Matthew 4:10 (KJV)
"Get thee hence, Satan: for it is written, Thou shalt worship the Lord thy God, and him only shalt thou serve."
Jesus (Today):
Get out of here, Satan. It says, worship the Lord your God, and

serve Him alone. That's final.

Matthew 4:17
" Repent: for the kingdom of heaven is at hand."
Jesus (Today):
Turn your life around today. Repent, because heaven's kingdom is here.

Matthew 4:19
"Follow me, and I will make you fishers of men."
Jesus (2025):
Follow me. I'll teach you how to reach people and bring them in.

Matthew 5

Matthew 5:3 (KJV)
"Blessed are the poor in spirit: for theirs is the kingdom of heaven."
Jesus (Today):
Blessed are those who know they need Me. Heaven is theirs.

Matthew 5:4 (KJV)
"Blessed are they that mourn: for they shall be comforted."
Jesus (Today):
Blessed are they who are grieving, you're not forgotten. You will be comforted.

Matthew 5:5 (KJV)
"Blessed are the meek: for they shall inherit the earth."
Jesus (Today):
Blessed are those who are gentle. The world might not notice you, but the earth will belong to you.

Matthew 5:6 (KJV)
"Blessed are they which do hunger and thirst after righteousness: for they shall be filled."
Jesus (Today):
Blessed are those starving for what's right, because you'll be satisfied you until you're overflowing with life.

Matthew 5:7 (KJV)
"Blessed are the merciful: for they shall obtain mercy."
Jesus (Today):
Blessed are those who give mercy freely,
because you'll find mercy waiting for you too.

Matthew 5:8 (KJV)
"Blessed are the pure in heart: for they shall see God."
Jesus (Today):
Blessed are the ones who keep their hearts pure,
they will see God.

Matthew 5:9 (KJV)
"Blessed are the peacemakers: for they shall be called the children of God."
Jesus (Today):
Blessed are the ones who carry peace wherever they go.
They'll be called children of God.

Matthew 5:10 (KJV)
"Blessed are they which are persecuted for righteousness' sake: for theirs is the kingdom of heaven."

Jesus (Today):
Blessed are you when you're hated for doing what's right, because the kingdom of heaven already belongs to you.

Matthew 5:11 (KJV)
"Blessed are ye, when men shall revile you, and persecute you, and shall say all manner of evil against you falsely, for my sake."

Jesus (Today):
Blessed are you when people tear you down, lie about you, and push you away, all because of Me.

Matthew 5:12 (KJV)
"Rejoice, and be exceeding glad: for great is your reward in heaven: for so persecuted they the prophets which were before you."

Jesus (Today):
Don't let it break you. Be exceedingly glad. Heaven is waiting. They did the same thing to every prophet before you.

Matthew 5:13 (KJV)
"Ye are the salt of the earth: but if the salt have lost his savour, wherewith shall it be salted? it is thenceforth good for nothing, but to be cast out, and to be trodden under foot of men."

Jesus (Today):
You are the salt of the earth. But if the salt loses its flavor, it's no good. People just throw it out and walk over it.

Matthew 5:14 (KJV)
"Ye are the light of the world. A city that is set on an hill cannot be hid."

Jesus (Today):

You're the light of the world. You're built to shine,
like a city set high on a hill where no one can miss you.

Matthew 5:15 (KJV)
"Neither do men light a candle, and put it under a bushel, but on a candlestick; and it giveth light unto all that are in the house."
Jesus (Today):
No one lights a lamp just to hide it. They lift it high, so it fills the whole house with light, and everyone can see.

Matthew 5:16 (KJV)
"Let your light so shine before men, that they may see your good works, and glorify your Father which is in heaven."
Jesus (Today):
So let your light shine boldly. Let them see the beauty of your life, and when they do, they'll see your Father too.

Matthew 5:17 (KJV)
"Think not that I am come to destroy the law, or the prophets: I am not come to destroy, but to fulfil."
Jesus (Today):
Don't think I came to tear everything down.
I didn't come to destroy the law,
I came to complete it, every word.

Matthew 5:18 (KJV)
"For verily I say unto you, Till heaven and earth pass, one jot or one tittle shall in no wise pass from the law, till all be fulfilled."
Jesus (Today):
Truth is, until heaven and earth disappear, *not one detail* of God's law will vanish, every letter will come true.

Matthew 5:19 (KJV)
"Whosoever therefore shall break one of these least commandments, and shall teach men so, he shall be called the least in the kingdom of heaven:"

Jesus (Today):
If you ignore even the smallest command and teach others to do the same, you'll be called least in heaven.

Matthew 5:20 (KJV)
"For I say unto you, That except your righteousness shall exceed the righteousness of the scribes and Pharisees, ye shall in no case enter into the kingdom of heaven."

Jesus (Today):
I tell you the truth, unless your way of living is more genuine than that of the teachers of the law and the religious influencers of today, you won't enter the Kingdom of Heaven.

Matthew 5:21 (KJV)
"Ye have heard that it was said by them of old time, Thou shalt not kill; and whosoever shall kill shall be in danger of the judgment:"

Jesus (Today):
You've heard it said long ago, "don't murder."
And if you do, you'll face judgment.

Matthew 5:22 (KJV)
"But I say unto you, That whosoever is angry with his brother without a cause shall be in danger of the judgment: and whosoever shall say to his brother, Raca, shall be in danger of the council: but whosoever shall say, Thou fool, shall be in danger of hell fire."

Jesus (Today):
But I say even *rage* puts you on trial. If you hold anger in your heart, if you insult your brother or call him worthless, you're risking judgment. You'll answer for it. And if you keep going, if you let your heart go dark, you're in danger of hell fire.

Matthew 5:23 (KJV)
"Therefore if thou bring thy gift to the altar, and there rememberest that thy brother hath ought

against thee;"
Jesus (Today):
So if you're bringing an offering to God, and you remember someone has something against you, stop right there.

Matthew 5:24 (KJV)
"Leave there thy gift before the altar, and go thy way; first be reconciled to thy brother, and then come and offer thy gift."
Jesus (Today):
Leave the gift. Go make it right with them first.
Then come back and bring your offering.

Matthew 5:25 (KJV)
"Agree with thine adversary quickly, whiles thou art in the way with him; lest at any time the adversary deliver thee to the judge, and the judge deliver thee to the officer, and thou be cast into prison."
Jesus (Today):
Settle things quickly with the one who's against you.
If you drag it out, they might take you to court, and next thing you know, you're standing before a judge and being locked up.

Matthew 5:26 (KJV)
"Verily I say unto thee, Thou shalt by no means come out thence, till thou hast paid the uttermost farthing."
Jesus (Today):
Because I'm telling you, you won't be free until you've paid every last cent.

Matthew 5:27 (KJV)
"Ye have heard that it was said by them of old time, Thou shalt not commit adultery:"
Jesus (Today):
You've heard it said, "Do not commit adultery."

Matthew 5:28 (KJV)
"But I say unto you, That whosoever looketh on a woman to lust after her hath committed adultery with her already in his heart."

Jesus (Today):
But I'm telling you, if you're fantasizing about them like that, you've already cheated in your heart. If your heart crosses the line, your body already has.

Matthew 5:29 (KJV)
"And if thy right eye offend thee, pluck it out, and cast it from thee: for it is profitable for thee that one of thy members should perish, and not that thy whole body should be cast into hell."

Jesus (Today):
If your eye is leading you into darkness,
tear your gaze away. It's better to lose one part of yourself than to lose your whole soul.

Matthew 5:30 (KJV)
"And if thy right hand offend thee, cut it off, and cast it from thee: for it is profitable for thee that one of thy members should perish, and not that thy whole body should be cast into hell."

Jesus (Today):
If your own hand drags you into sin, cut it off. It's better to lose one part than let your whole life be destroyed. Get rid of whatever is killing your soul.

Matthew 5:31 (KJV)
"It hath been said, Whosoever shall put away his wife, let him give her a writing of divorcement:"

Jesus (Today):
You've heard it said, "If you want to leave your wife,
just hand her divorce papers."

Matthew 5:32 (KJV)
"But I say unto you, That whosoever shall put away his wife, saving for the cause of fornication,

causeth her to commit adultery: and whosoever shall marry her that is divorced committeth adultery."

Jesus (Today):
But I'm telling you, if you divorce your wife for anything other than unfaithfulness, you're causing her to commit adultery. And if someone marries a woman who was divorced that way, he's committing adultery too.

Matthew 5:33 (KJV)
"Again, ye have heard that it hath been said by them of old time, Thou shalt not forswear thyself, but shalt perform unto the Lord thine oaths:"

Jesus (Today):
You've also heard, don't break your promises. Mean what you say to God.

Matthew 5:34 (KJV)
"But I say unto you, Swear not at all; neither by heaven; for it is God's throne:"

Jesus (Today):
But I'm telling you, don't swear at all. Not by heaven, because that's God's throne.

Matthew 5:35 (KJV)
"Nor by the earth; for it is his footstool: neither by Jerusalem; for it is the city of the great King."

Jesus (Today):
Don't swear by the earth, because it's God's footstool. And don't swear by Jerusalem, because it's the city of the great King.

Matthew 5:36 (KJV)
"Neither shalt thou swear by thy head, because thou canst not make one hair white or black."

Jesus (Today):
And don't swear by your own head, because you can't make a single hair white or black.

Matthew 5:37 (KJV)
"But let your communication be, Yea, yea; Nay, nay: for whatsoever is more than these cometh of evil."
Jesus (Today):
Just let your "yes" be yes, and your "no" be no.
Anything more than that is coming from the wrong place.

Matthew 5:38 (KJV)
"Ye have heard that it hath been said, An eye for an eye, and a tooth for a tooth:"
Jesus (Today):
You've heard, "Eye for an eye. Tooth for a tooth."

Matthew 5:39 (KJV)
"But I say unto you, That ye resist not evil: but whosoever shall smite thee on thy right cheek, turn to him the other also."
Jesus (Today):
But I'm telling you, don't fight back with revenge. If someone hits you on one cheek, offer them the other.

Matthew 5:40 (KJV)
"And if any man will sue thee at the law, and take away thy coat, let him have thy cloak also."
Jesus (Today):
If someone takes you to court to get your shirt, give them your jacket too.

Matthew 5:41 (KJV)
"And whosoever shall compel thee to go a mile, go with him twain."
Jesus (Today):
If someone makes you go one mile, go the extra mile with them.

Matthew 5:42 (KJV)
"Give to him that asketh thee, and from him that would borrow of thee turn not thou away."
Jesus (Today):
If someone needs something, give. And if someone needs to borrow from you, don't turn them away.

Matthew 5:43 (KJV)
"Ye have heard that it hath been said, Thou shalt love thy neighbour, and hate thine enemy."
Jesus (Today):
You've heard, "Love your neighbor, hate your enemy."

Matthew 5:44 (KJV)
"But I say unto you, Love your enemies, bless them that curse you, do good to them that hate you, and pray for them which despitefully use you, and persecute you;"
Jesus (Today):
But I tell you, love your enemies. Bless those who curse you, do good to those who hate you, and pray for those who mistreat and persecute you.

Matthew 5:45 (KJV)
"That ye may be the children of your Father which is in heaven: for he maketh his sun to rise on the evil and on the good, and sendeth rain on the just and on the unjust."
Jesus (Today):
Do this, and you'll be showing the world who your Father is. He makes the sun rise on both the evil and the good, and He sends rain on the just and the unjust alike.

Matthew 5:46 (KJV)
"For if ye love them which love you, what reward have ye? do not even the publicans the same?"
Jesus (Today):

If you only love people who love you back, what's special about that? Even corrupt people know how to do that.

Matthew 5:47 (KJV)
"And if ye salute your brethren only, what do ye more than others? do not even the publicans so?"
Jesus (Today):
If you're only kind to people in your circle, how are you any different? Everybody does that.

Matthew 5:48 (KJV)
"Be ye therefore perfect, even as your Father which is in heaven is perfect."
Jesus (Today):
So aim higher. Be complete. Be perfect like your Father in heaven. Whole and holy in how you love.

Matthew 6

Matthew 6:1 (KJV)
"Take heed that ye do not your alms before men, to be seen of them: otherwise ye have no reward of your Father which is in heaven."
Jesus (Today):
Be careful not to turn your generosity into a performance. If that's your goal you've already lost your reward from your Father.

Matthew 6:2 (KJV)
"Therefore when thou doest thine alms, do not sound a trumpet before thee, as the hypocrites do in the synagogues and in the streets, that they may have glory of men. Verily I say unto you, They have their reward."
Jesus (Today):

When you give, don't make a show of it,
like the ones who blow their own horns in the streets, chasing the applause of people. I'm telling you the truth,
that applause is all the reward they'll ever get.

Matthew 6:3 (KJV)
"But when thou doest alms, let not thy left hand know what thy right hand doeth:"
Jesus (Today):
When you give, do it so quietly that your left hand doesn't even know what your right is doing.

Matthew 6:4 (KJV)
"That thine alms may be in secret: and thy Father which seeth in secret himself shall reward thee openly."
Jesus (Today):
Give in secret, and your Father, who sees every hidden thing, will make sure the reward shows up where everyone can see.

Matthew 6:5 (KJV)
"And when thou prayest, thou shalt not be as the hypocrites are: for they love to pray standing in the synagogues and in the corners of the streets, that they may be seen of men. Verily I say unto you, They have their reward."
Jesus (Today):
When you pray, don't put on a show like the ones who love to be seen. They already have their reward,
the applause of people. But that's all they'll get.

Matthew 6:6 (KJV)
"But thou, when thou prayest, enter into thy closet, and when thou hast shut thy door, pray to thy Father which is in secret; and thy Father which seeth in secret shall reward thee openly."
Jesus (Today):
When you pray, go somewhere quiet. Shut the door. Speak to the

Father in secret, and He who sees every hidden thing will reward you openly.

Matthew 6:7 (KJV)
"But when ye pray, use not vain repetitions, as the heathen do: for they think that they shall be heard for their much speaking."
Jesus (Today):
And when you pray, don't use empty, repetitive words like people who don't know God. They think long prayers get more attention.

Matthew 6:8 (KJV)
"Be not ye therefore like unto them: for your Father knoweth what things ye have need of, before ye ask him."
Jesus (Today):
Don't be like them. Your Father already knows what you need, even before you ask.

Matthew 6:9 (KJV)
"After this manner therefore pray ye: Our Father which art in heaven, Hallowed be thy name."
Jesus (Today):
So pray like this:
Father in heaven, Your name is holy.

Matthew 6:10 (KJV)
"Thy kingdom come, Thy will be done in earth, as it is in heaven."
Jesus (Today):
Let Your kingdom come.
Let Your will be done here on earth, just like it is in heaven.

Matthew 6:11 (KJV)
"Give us this day our daily bread."
Jesus (Today):
Give us what we need today.

Matthew 6:12 (KJV)
"And forgive us our debts, as we forgive our debtors."
Jesus (Today):
And forgive us our debts, as we also forgive those who owe us.

Matthew 6:13 (KJV)
"And lead us not into temptation, but deliver us from evil: For thine is the kingdom, and the power, and the glory, for ever. Amen."
Jesus (Today):
Don't let us fall into temptation. Deliver us from evil. The kingdom, the power, and the glory all belong to You. Forever. Amen.

Matthew 6:14 (KJV)
"For if ye forgive men their trespasses, your heavenly Father will also forgive you:"
Jesus (Today):
If you forgive others, your Father in heaven will forgive you.

Matthew 6:15 (KJV)
"But if ye forgive not men their trespasses, neither will your Father forgive your trespasses."
Jesus (Today):
But if you don't forgive others for their wrongs, your Father won't forgive your wrongs either.

Matthew 6:16 (KJV)
"Moreover when ye fast, be not, as the hypocrites, of a sad countenance: for they disfigure their

faces, that they may appear unto men to fast. Verily I say unto you, They have their reward."
Jesus (Today):
When you fast, don't walk around looking miserable to prove a point. If you're just putting on a show, that's your whole reward.

Matthew 6:17 (KJV)
"But thou, when thou fastest, anoint thine head, and wash thy face;"
Jesus (Today):
When you fast, clean yourself up. Look like nothing's different.

Matthew 6:18 (KJV)
"That thou appear not unto men to fast, but unto thy Father which is in secret: and thy Father, which seeth in secret, shall reward thee openly."
Jesus (Today):
You're not doing it for people to see anyway. Do it for your Father, who sees what happens in secret. And He'll reward you in the open.

Matthew 6:19 (KJV)
"Lay not up for yourselves treasures upon earth, where moth and rust doth corrupt, and where thieves break through and steal:"
Jesus (Today):
Don't stack your treasures on earth, where moths can eat them, rust can ruin them, and thieves can take them away.

Matthew 6:20 (KJV)
"But lay up for yourselves treasures in heaven, where neither moth nor rust doth corrupt, and where thieves do not break through nor steal:"
Jesus (Today):
Instead, build treasure in heaven, where nothing can touch it, nothing can rot it, and no one can take it from you.

Matthew 6:21 (KJV)
"For where your treasure is, there will your heart be also."
Jesus (Today):
Wherever your treasure is, your heart will follow.

Matthew 6:22 (KJV)
"The light of the body is the eye: if therefore thine eye be single, thy whole body shall be full of light."
Jesus (Today):
The eye is the lamp of the body. If your eye is healthy, your whole body will be full of light.

Matthew 6:23 (KJV)
"But if thine eye be evil, thy whole body shall be full of darkness. If therefore the light that is in thee be darkness, how great is that darkness!"
Jesus (Today):
But if your eye is bad, your whole body will be full of darkness. And if the light in you is darkness, how deep that darkness is.

Matthew 6:24 (KJV)
"No man can serve two masters: for either he will hate the one, and love the other; or else he will hold to the one, and despise the other. Ye cannot serve God and mammon."
Jesus (Today):
You can't serve two masters. You'll either love one and hate the other, or stay loyal to one and reject the other.
You cannot serve both God and money.

Matthew 6:25 (KJV)
"Therefore I say unto you, Take no thought for your life, what ye shall eat, or what ye shall drink; nor yet for your body, what ye shall put on. Is not the life more than meat, and the body than raiment?"
Jesus (Today):
So hear Me, stop stressing about your life.

What you'll eat, what you'll drink, what you'll wear.
Isn't life more than food? Isn't your body more than clothes?

Matthew 6:26 (KJV)
"Behold the fowls of the air: for they sow not, neither do they reap, nor gather into barns; yet your heavenly Father feedeth them. Are ye not much better than they?"

Jesus (Today):
Look at the birds flying free. They don't plant, they don't harvest, they don't stockpile anything. But your Father feeds them. Aren't you worth more than that?

Matthew 6:27 (KJV)
"Which of you by taking thought can add one cubit unto his stature?"

Jesus (Today):
Which of you can add even an inch to your height by worrying?

Matthew 6:28 (KJV)
"And why take ye thought for raiment? Consider the lilies of the field, how they grow; they toil not, neither do they spin:"

Jesus (Today):
And why are you worrying about clothes? Look at the lilies growing wild, they don't work, they don't spin thread, they simply grow.

Matthew 6:29 (KJV)
"And yet I say unto you, That even Solomon in all his glory was not arrayed like one of these."

Jesus (Today):
I'm telling you, even Solomon in all his royal splendor wasn't dressed as beautifully as one of these.

Matthew 6:30 (KJV)
"Wherefore, if God so clothe the grass of the field, which to day is, and to morrow is cast into the oven, shall he not much more clothe you, O ye of little faith?"

Jesus (Today):
If God takes care of the grass, which is alive today and thrown out tomorrow, don't you think he'll take even better care of you? Where's your faith?

Matthew 6:31 (KJV)
"Therefore take no thought, saying, What shall we eat? or, What shall we drink? or, Wherewithal shall we be clothed?"

Jesus (Today):
So stop saying, "What will we eat?" or "What will we wear?"

Matthew 6:32 (KJV)
"(For after all these things do the Gentiles seek:) for your heavenly Father knoweth that ye have need of all these things."

Jesus (Today):
People who don't know God chase after all those things. But your Father already knows what you need, before you even ask.

Matthew 6:33 (KJV)
"But seek ye first the kingdom of God, and his righteousness; and all these things shall be added unto you."

Jesus (Today):
Run after the kingdom first, chase His heart, His goodness, His ways, and everything else you need will find its way to you.

Matthew 6:34 (KJV)
"Take therefore no thought for the morrow: for the morrow shall take thought for the things of itself. Sufficient unto the day is the evil thereof."

Jesus (Today):
Stop worrying about tomorrow. Tomorrow will worry about

itself. Today has enough to deal with.

Matthew 7

Matthew 7:1 (KJV)
"Judge not, that ye be not judged."
Jesus (Today):
Don't judge other people, or you'll be judged the same way.

Matthew 7:2 (KJV)
"For with what judgment ye judge, ye shall be judged: and with what measure ye mete, it shall be measured to you again."
Jesus (Today):
The way you judge others is how you'll be judged. And the measure you use to give out judgment is the same measure that will be used on you.

Matthew 7:3 (KJV)
"And why beholdest thou the mote that is in thy brother's eye, but considerest not the beam that is in thine own eye?"
Jesus (Today):
Why are you focused on the tiny flaw in someone else's life, while ignoring the massive one in your own?

Matthew 7:4 (KJV)
"Or how wilt thou say to thy brother, Let me pull out the mote out of thine eye; and, behold, a beam is in thine own eye?"
Jesus (Today):
How can you say, "Let me help fix you," when you haven't dealt with what's blinding you?

Matthew 7:5 (KJV)
"Thou hypocrite, first cast out the beam out of thine own eye; and then shalt thou see clearly to cast out the mote out of thy brother's eye."
Jesus (Today):
You hypocrite. First deal with your own mess. Then you'll see clearly enough to help someone else.

Matthew 7:6 (KJV)
"Give not that which is holy unto the dogs, neither cast ye your pearls before swine, lest they trample them under their feet, and turn again and rend you."
Jesus (Today):
Don't hand what's sacred to those who won't treasure it. Don't toss your pearls to those who'll only trample them, then turn and tear you apart. They'll stomp them and come for you next.

Matthew 7:7 (KJV)
"Ask, and it shall be given you; seek, and ye shall find; knock, and it shall be opened unto you:"
Jesus (Today):
Ask, and it'll be given. Seek, you'll find. Knock, and the door will be open.

Matthew 7:8 (KJV)
"For every one that asketh receiveth; and he that seeketh findeth; and to him that knocketh it shall be opened."
Jesus (Today):
Everyone who asks, receives. Everyone who searches, finds. And for the one who knocks? That door's opening.

Matthew 7:9 (KJV)
"Or what man is there of you, whom if his son ask bread, will he give him a stone?"

Jesus (Today):
If your child asks for bread, are you handing him a rock?

Matthew 7:10 (KJV)
"Or if he ask a fish, will he give him a serpent?"
Jesus (Today):
Or if he wants fish, would you hand him a snake?

Matthew 7:11 (KJV)
"If ye then, being evil, know how to give good gifts unto your children, how much more shall your Father which is in heaven give good things to them that ask him?"
Jesus (Today):
If you, messed up as you are, still know how to give your kids good stuff, how much more will your Father in heaven give good things to anyone who asks?

Matthew 7:12 (KJV)
"Therefore all things whatsoever ye would that men should do to you, do ye even so to them: for this is the law and the prophets."
Jesus (Today):
Treat people how you want to be treated. That's the heart of everything God's ever asked.

Matthew 7:13 (KJV)
"Enter ye in at the strait gate: for wide is the gate, and broad is the way, that leadeth to destruction, and many there be which go in thereat:"
Jesus (Today):
Take the narrow road. The wide road looks easy, but it leads to destruction, and many will take it.

Matthew 7:14 (KJV)
"Because strait is the gate, and narrow is the way, which leadeth unto life, and few there be that find it."
Jesus (Today):
The gate that leads to life is narrow, and the path is difficult and only a few will ever find it.

Matthew 7:15 (KJV)
"Beware of false prophets, which come to you in sheep's clothing, but inwardly they are ravening wolves."
Jesus (Today):
Watch out for fake prophets, they dress like sheep, but they're really wolves.

Matthew 7:16 (KJV)
"Ye shall know them by their fruits. Do men gather grapes of thorns, or figs of thistles?"
Jesus (Today):
You'll know who they are by their fruit. You don't get grapes from a thornbush.

Matthew 7:17 (KJV)
"Even so every good tree bringeth forth good fruit; but a corrupt tree bringeth forth evil fruit."
Jesus (Today):
In the same way, every good tree produces good fruit, but a bad tree produces bad fruit.

Matthew 7:18 (KJV)
"A good tree cannot bring forth evil fruit, neither can a corrupt tree bring forth good fruit."
Jesus (Today):
A good tree can't produce bad fruit, and a bad tree can't produce good fruit.

Matthew 7:19 (KJV)
"Every tree that bringeth not forth good fruit is hewn down, and cast into the fire."
Jesus (Today):
Every tree that doesn't produce good fruit is cut down and thrown into the fire.

Matthew 7:20 (KJV)
"Wherefore by their fruits ye shall know them."
Jesus (Today):
That's how you know them, by their fruit.

Matthew 7:21 (KJV)
"Not every one that saith unto me, Lord, Lord, shall enter into the kingdom of heaven; but he that doeth the will of my Father which is in heaven."
Jesus (Today):
Not everyone who says to me, "Lord, Lord," will enter the kingdom of heaven, but only the one who does the will of my Father in heaven.

Matthew 7:22 (KJV)
"Many will say to me in that day, Lord, Lord, have we not prophesied in thy name? and in thy name have cast out devils? and in thy name done many wonderful works?"
Jesus (Today):
Many will come to Me then and say, "Lord, didn't we preach in Your name, cast out demons in Your name, and perform miracles in Your name?"

Matthew 7:23 (KJV)
"And then will I profess unto them, I never knew you: depart from me, ye that work iniquity."
Jesus (Today):
Then I will say to them plainly, "I never knew you. Leave My presence, you who chose to live in disobedience."

Matthew 7:24 (KJV)
"Therefore whosoever heareth these sayings of mine, and doeth them, I will liken him unto a wise man, which built his house upon a rock:"

Jesus (Today):
If you hear My words and live them,
you're like a wise builder, laying your house down on solid rock.

Matthew 7:25 (KJV)
"And the rain descended, and the floods came, and the winds blew, and beat upon that house; and it fell not: for it was founded upon a rock."

Jesus (Today):
The rain poured down, the floods rose, and the wind slammed against that house; but it didn't fall, because it was built on the rock.

Matthew 7:26 (KJV)
"And every one that heareth these sayings of mine, and doeth them not, shall be likened unto a foolish man, which built his house upon the sand:"

Jesus (Today):
But anyone who hears My words and ignores them is like a foolish man who built his house on sand.

Matthew 7:27 (KJV)
"And the rain descended, and the floods came, and the winds blew, and beat upon that house; and it fell: and great was the fall of it."

Jesus (Today):
The rain came, the floods rose, and the winds pounded that house and it collapsed completely. Its fall was great.

Matthew 8

Matthew 8:3 (KJV)
"I will; be thou clean. And immediately his leprosy was cleansed."
Jesus (Today):
I will. Be healed and made whole.

Matthew 8:4 (KJV)
"See thou tell no man; but go thy way, shew thyself to the priest, and offer the gift that Moses commanded, for a testimony unto them."
Jesus (Today):
Don't tell anyone right now. Just go show the priest and do what Moses instructed. Let *that* be your proof.

Matthew 8:7 (KJV)
"I will come and heal him."
Jesus (Today):
I'll come. I'll heal him.

Matthew 8:10 (KJV)
"Verily I say unto you, I have not found so great faith, no, not in Israel."
Jesus (Today):
Truth is, I haven't seen faith like this anywhere in Israel.

Matthew 8:13 (KJV)
"Go thy way; and as thou hast believed, so be it done unto thee."
Jesus (Today):
Go. Because you believed it's already done.

Matthew 8:20 (KJV)
"The foxes have holes, and the birds of the air have nests; but the Son of man hath not where to

lay his head."
Jesus (Today):
Foxes have dens, birds have nests, but Me? I've got no place to lay my head.

Matthew 8:22 (KJV)
"Follow me; and let the dead bury their dead."
Jesus (Today):
Follow Me. Let the dead bury the dead.

Matthew 9

Matthew 9:2 (KJV)
"Son, be of good cheer; thy sins be forgiven thee."
Jesus (Today):
Take heart, son. Your sins are forgiven.

Matthew 9:4 (KJV)
"Wherefore think ye evil in your hearts?"
Jesus (Today):
Why are you thinking such evil thoughts?

Matthew 9:5 (KJV)
"For whether is easier, to say, Thy sins be forgiven thee; or to say, Arise, and walk?"
Jesus (Today):
What's easier to say, your sins are forgiven, or get up and walk?

Matthew 9:6 (KJV)
"Arise, take up thy bed, and go unto thine house."
Jesus (Today):
Get up. Grab your bed. Go home.

Matthew 9:9 (KJV)
"Follow me."
Jesus (Today):
Follow Me.

Matthew 9:12 (KJV)
"They that be whole need not a physician, but they that are sick."
Jesus (Today):
Healthy people don't need a doctor, sick ones do.

Matthew 9:13 (KJV)
"But go ye and learn what that meaneth, I will have mercy, and not sacrifice: for I am not come to call the righteous, but sinners to repentance."
Jesus (Today):
Go and learn what this means. I desire mercy, not sacrifice. I didn't come to call the righteous, I came to call sinners to repent and turn back to God.

Matthew 9:15 (KJV)
"Can the children of the bridechamber mourn, as long as the bridegroom is with them? but the days will come, when the bridegroom shall be taken from them, and then shall they fast."
Jesus (Today):
Can the wedding guests mourn while the groom is still with them? No, but the time is coming when the groom will be taken away, and then they will fast.

Matthew 9:22 (KJV)
"Daughter, be of good comfort; thy faith hath made thee whole."
Jesus (Today):
Daughter, take heart. Your faith healed you.

Matthew 9:24 (KJV)
"Give place: for the maid is not dead, but sleepeth."
Jesus (Today):
Make room. She's not dead, she's just asleep.

Matthew 9:28 (KJV)
"Believe ye that I am able to do this?"
Jesus (Today):
Do you believe that I am able to do this?

Matthew 9:29 (KJV)
"According to your faith be it unto you."
Jesus (Today):
Let it be done for you according to your faith.

Matthew 9:30 (KJV):
"See that no man know it."
Jesus (Today):
See to it that no one knows about this.

Matthew 9:37 (KJV):
"The harvest truly is plenteous, but the labourers are few;"
Jesus (Today):
The harvest truly is huge, but the workers are few.

Matthew 9:38 (KJV)
"Pray ye therefore the Lord of the harvest, that he will send forth labourers into his harvest."
Jesus (Today):
So pray to the Lord in charge of the harvest to send more workers out into His fields.

Matthew 10

Matthew 10:5 (KJV)
"Go not into the way of the Gentiles, and into any city of the Samaritans enter ye not:"
Jesus (Today):
Don't go in the direction of the Gentiles or enter any Samaritan town.

Matthew 10:6 (KJV)
"But go rather to the lost sheep of the house of Israel."
Jesus (Today):
Go to the lost sheep of Israel first.

Matthew 10:7 (KJV)
"And as ye go, preach, saying, The kingdom of heaven is at hand."
Jesus (Today):
As you go, tell them: Heaven's kingdom is here.

Matthew 10:8 (KJV)
"Heal the sick, cleanse the lepers, raise the dead, cast out devils: freely ye have received, freely give."

Jesus (Today):
Heal the sick. Cleanse those with disease. Raise the dead. Cast out demons. You received all of this freely. Now give it freely.

Matthew 10:14 (KJV)
"And whosoever shall not receive you, nor hear your words, when ye depart out of that house or city, shake off the dust of your feet."

Jesus (2025):
If anyone refuses to welcome you or listen to what you say, just leave that house or town and shake the dust off your feet.

Matthew 10:16 (KJV)
"Behold, I send you forth as sheep in the midst of wolves: be ye therefore wise as serpents, and harmless as doves."

Jesus (Today):
I'm sending you out like sheep surrounded by wolves. So be wise like a snake, but harmless like a dove.

Matthew 10:19-20 (KJV)
"But when they deliver you up, take no thought how or what ye shall speak: for it shall be given you in that same hour what ye shall speak. For it is not ye that speak, but the Spirit of your Father which speaketh in you."

Jesus (Today):
When they hand you over, don't worry about what to say. The right words will be given to you in that very moment. It won't even be you speaking, it will be the Spirit of your Father which speaks through you.

Matthew 10:22 (KJV)
"And ye shall be hated of all men for my name's sake: but he that endureth to the end shall be saved."

Jesus (Today):

You'll be hated by everyone because of Me. But if you hold on till the end, you'll be saved.

Matthew 10:26 (KJV)
"Fear them not therefore: for there is nothing covered, that shall not be revealed; and hid, that shall not be known."
Jesus (Today):
Don't be afraid of them. Everything hidden will be revealed. Everything secret will be brought into the light.

Matthew 10:27 (KJV)
"What I tell you in darkness, that speak ye in light: and what ye hear in the ear, that preach ye upon the housetops."
Jesus (Today):
What I whisper to you in the dark, shout it out in the light. What you hear quietly in your ear, proclaim it from the rooftops.

Matthew 10:28 (KJV)
"And fear not them which kill the body, but are not able to kill the soul: but rather fear him which is able to destroy both soul and body in hell."
Jesus (Today):
Don't fear the ones who can kill your body but can't touch your soul. Fear the One who holds both your body and soul in His hands.

Matthew 10:29 (KJV)
"Are not two sparrows sold for a farthing? And one of them shall not fall on the ground without your Father seeing."
Jesus (Today):
Aren't two sparrows sold for almost nothing?
And yet not one of them falls without your Father seeing.

Matthew 10:30 (KJV)
"But the very hairs of your head are all numbered."
Jesus (Today):
God even knows the exact number of hairs on your head.

Matthew 10:31 (KJV)
"Fear ye not therefore, ye are of more value than many sparrows."
Jesus (Today):
So don't be afraid, you're worth far more to Him than many sparrows.

Matthew 10:32 (KJV)
"Whosoever therefore shall confess me before men, him will I confess also before my Father which is in heaven."
Jesus (Today):
If you speak up for Me here, I'll speak up for you in front of My Father in heaven.

Matthew 10:33 (KJV)
"But whosoever shall deny me before men, him will I also deny before my Father which is in heaven."
Jesus (Today):
But if you deny Me, I'll deny you in front of Him too.

Matthew 10:34 (KJV)
"Think not that I am come to send peace on earth: I came not to send peace, but a sword."
Jesus (Today):
Don't think I came to bring peace to the earth. I didn't come to bring peace, but a sword.

Matthew 10:35 (KJV)
"For I am come to set a man at variance against his father, and the daughter against her mother, and the daughter in law against her mother in law."

Jesus (Today):
I came to turn a man against his father, a daughter against her mother, and a daughter-in-law against her mother-in-law.

Matthew 10:36 (KJV)
"And a man's foes shall be they of his own household."

Jesus (Today):
Sometimes your biggest enemies will come from inside your own home.

Matthew 10:37 (KJV)
"He that loveth father or mother more than me is not worthy of me: and he that loveth son or daughter more than me is not worthy of me."

Jesus (Today):
Anyone who loves their father or mother more than me is not worthy of me. Anyone who loves their son or daughter more than me is not worthy of me.

Matthew 10:38 (KJV)
"And he that taketh not his cross, and followeth after me, is not worthy of me."

Jesus (Today):
If you won't pick up your cross and follow Me, you're not ready for Me.

Matthew 10:39 (KJV)
"He that findeth his life shall lose it: and he that loseth his life for my sake shall find it."

Jesus (Today):

If you try to keep your life, you'll lose it. But if you give it up for Me, you'll truly find it.

Matthew 10:40 (KJV):
"He that receiveth you receiveth me, and he that receiveth me receiveth him that sent me."
Jesus (Today):
If they welcome you, they're welcoming Me. And if they welcome Me, they're welcoming Him who sent Me.

Matthew 10:41 (KJV):
"He that receiveth a prophet in the name of a prophet shall receive a prophet's reward; and he that receiveth a righteous man in the name of a righteous man shall receive a righteous man's reward."
Jesus (Today):
Anyone who welcomes a prophet because they are a prophet will receive a prophet's reward. And anyone who welcomes a righteous person because they are righteous will receive a righteous person's reward.

Matthew 10:42 (KJV):
"And whosoever shall give to drink unto one of these little ones a cup of cold water only in the name of a disciple, verily I say unto you, he shall in no wise lose his reward."
Jesus (Today):
And if anyone gives even a cup of cold water
to one of the least of these because they belong to Me,
I promise you, they will never lose their reward.

Matthew 11

Matthew 11:4-5 (KJV)
"Go and shew John again those things which ye do hear and see: "The blind receive their sight, and the lame walk, the lepers are cleansed, and the deaf hear, the dead are raised up, and the poor have the gospel preached to them."

Jesus (Today):
Go tell John what's happening:
The blind see. The crippled walk. Those suffering from incurable disease are clean. The deaf hear. The dead are rising. And the poor are finally hearing the gospel.

Matthew 11:6 (KJV)
"And blessed is he, whosoever shall not be offended in me."

Jesus (Today):
Blessed are the ones who don't get offended by Me.

Matthew 11:7 (KJV)
"And as they departed, Jesus began to say unto the multitudes concerning John, What went ye out into the wilderness to see? A reed shaken with the wind?"

Jesus (Today):
What did you go out into the wilderness to see?
A fragile reed swaying in the wind?

Matthew 11:8 (KJV)
"But what went ye out for to see? A man clothed in soft raiment? behold, they that wear soft clothing are in kings' houses."

Jesus (Today):
Or were you looking for a man dressed in luxury?
Those who wear soft clothes live in royal palaces.

Matthew 11:9 (KJV)

"But what went ye out for to see? A prophet? yea, I say unto you, and more than a prophet."
Jesus (Today):
Then what did you go to see? A prophet?
Yes, and even more than a prophet.

Matthew 11:10 (KJV)
"For this is he, of whom it is written, Behold, I send my messenger before thy face, which shall prepare thy way before thee."
Jesus (Today):
This is the one the Scriptures were talking about: I'm sending my messenger ahead of you to get things ready.

Matthew 11:11 (KJV)
"Verily I say unto you, Among them that are born of women there hath not risen a greater than John the Baptist: notwithstanding he that is least in the kingdom of heaven is greater than he."
Jesus (Today):
Truly I tell you, of all who have ever been born of, no one has been greater than John the Baptist. But even the least person in the Kingdom of Heaven is greater than he is.

Matthew 11:12 (KJV)
"And from the days of John the Baptist until now the kingdom of heaven suffereth violence, and the violent take it by force."
Jesus (Today):
From the time of John the Baptist until now, the kingdom of heaven has been under attack, and forceful people are trying to seize it.

Matthew 11:13 (KJV):
"For all the prophets and the law prophesied until John."
Jesus (Today):
All the prophets and the law pointed forward until John came.

Matthew 11:14 (KJV):
"And if ye will receive it, this is Elias, which was for to come."
Jesus (Today):
And if you're willing to believe it, John is Elijah, the one who was promised to come.

Matthew 11:15 (KJV)
"He that hath ears to hear, let him hear."
Jesus (Today):
If you've got ears, listen up.

Matthew 11:16 (KJV):
"But whereunto shall I liken this generation? It is like unto children sitting in the markets, and calling unto their fellows,"
Jesus (Today):
What can I even compare this generation to? They're like children sitting in the marketplace, shouting back and forth at each other.

Matthew 11:17 (KJV):
"We have piped unto you, and ye have not danced; we have mourned unto you, and ye have not lamented."
Jesus (Today):
We played music, but you didn't dance. We cried, but you didn't cry with us.

Matthew 11:18–19 (KJV)
"For John came neither eating nor drinking, and they say, He hath a devil. The Son of man came eating and drinking, and they say, Behold a man gluttonous, and a winebibber, a friend of

publicans and sinners. But wisdom is justified of her children."

Jesus (Today):
John didn't eat or drink, and people said, "He's possessed." Then the Son of Man came eating and drinking, and they said, "He's a glutton, a drunk, and friends with all the wrong people." But in the end, wisdom is shown by the results.

Matthew 11:21 (KJV)
"Woe unto thee, Chorazin! woe unto thee, Bethsaida! for if the mighty works, which were done in you, had been done in Tyre and Sidon, they would have repented long ago in sackcloth and ashes."

Jesus (Today):
Chorazin. Bethsaida. You're in trouble. If Tyre and Sidon had seen what you've seen, they would've dropped everything and turned to God.

Matthew 11:22 (KJV)
"But I say unto you, It shall be more tolerable for Tyre and Sidon at the day of judgment, than for you."

I'm telling you, it will be easier for Tyre and Sidon on judgment day than it will be for you.

Matthew 11:23 (KJV)
"And thou, Capernaum, which art exalted unto heaven, shalt be brought down to hell: for if the mighty works, which have been done in thee, had been done in Sodom, it would have remained until this day."

Jesus (Today):
And you, Capernaum, you think you're lifted up to heaven, but you'll be brought down to hell. If the miracles done here had been done in Sodom, it would still be standing today.

Matthew 11:24
"But I say unto you, That it shall be more tolerable for the land of Sodom in the day of judgment, than for thee."

Jesus (Today):
But I'm telling you, it will be easier for Sodom on judgment day than it will be for you.

Matthew 11:25 (KJV)
"I thank thee, O Father, Lord of heaven and earth, because thou hast hid these things from the wise and prudent, and hast revealed them unto babes."

Jesus (Today):
Thank You, Father, Lord of heaven and earth, for hiding these deep truths from the proud and revealing them to the humble.

Matthew 11:26 (KJV)
"Even so, Father: for so it seemed good in thy sight."

Jesus (Today):
Yes, Father, because that's what You wanted.

Matthew 11:27 (KJV)
"All things are delivered unto me of my Father: and no man knoweth the Son, but the Father; neither knoweth any man the Father, save the Son, and he to whomsoever the Son will reveal him."

Jesus (Today):
All things have been given to me by my Father. No one truly knows the Son except the Father, and no one truly knows the Father except the Son and those to whom the Son chooses to reveal Him.

Matthew 11:28 (KJV)
"Come unto me, all ye that labour and are heavy laden, and I will give you rest."

Jesus (Today):
Come to Me. If you're exhausted and carrying too much, I will give you rest.

Matthew 11:29 (KJV)
"Take my yoke upon you, and learn of me; for I am meek and lowly in heart: and ye shall find rest unto your souls."
Jesus (Today):
Come walk with Me. Let Me teach you how to live, because I'm gentle with you, and humble in heart. And when you do, you'll find rest for your soul.

Matthew 11:30 (KJV)
"For my yoke is easy, and my burden is light."
Jesus (Today):
The way I give you to live is easy, and the weight I put on you is light.

Matthew 12

Matthew 12:3 (KJV)
"Have ye not read what David did, when he was an hungred, and they that were with him;"
Jesus (Today):
Haven't you read what David did when he was hungry, and those who were with him?

Matthew 12:4
"How he entered into the house of God, and did eat the shewbread, which was not lawful for him to eat, neither for them which were with him, but only for the priests?"
Jesus (Today):
He went into God's house and ate the sacred bread. That bread

wasn't even lawful for him or his men to eat. It was only meant for the priests.

Matthew 12:5
"Or have ye not read in the law, how that on the sabbath days the priests in the temple profane the sabbath, and are blameless?"
Jesus (Today):
Or haven't you read in the law that on the Sabbath the priests in the temple break the Sabbath rules yet they're not guilty?

Matthew 12:6 (KJV)
"But I say unto you, That in this place is one greater than the temple."
Jesus (Today):
I'm telling you, *someone greater than the temple* is standing right here.

Matthew 12:7 (KJV)
"But if ye had known what this meaneth, I will have mercy, and not sacrifice, ye would not have condemned the guiltless."
Jesus (Today):
But if you had understood what it means, "I desire mercy, not sacrifice," you would not have condemned the innocent.

Matthew 12:8 (KJV)
"For the Son of man is Lord even of the sabbath day."
Jesus (Today):
The Son of Man is Lord even of the Sabbath.

Matthew 12:11 (KJV)
"What man shall there be among you, that shall have one sheep, and if it fall into a pit on the

sabbath day, will he not lay hold on it, and lift it out?"
Jesus (Today):
If any of you has a sheep and it falls into a pit on the Sabbath, wouldn't you reach in and pull it out?"

Matthew 12:12 (KJV)
"How much then is a man better than a sheep? Wherefore it is lawful to do well on the sabbath days."
Jesus (Today):
So how much more valuable is a person? It's always right to do good, even on the Sabbath.

Matthew 12:13 (KJV)
"Stretch forth thine hand."
Jesus (Today):
Reach out your hand.

Matthew 12:25 (KJV)
"Every kingdom divided against itself is brought to desolation; and every city or house divided against itself shall not stand:"
Jesus (Today):
Every kingdom divided against itself will be ruined, and every city or household divided against itself will not stand.

Matthew 12:26 (KJV)
"And if Satan cast out Satan, he is divided against himself; how shall then his kingdom stand?"
Jesus (Today):
And if Satan drives out Satan, he is divided against himself. How then can his kingdom stand?

Matthew 12:27 (KJV)
"And if I by Beelzebub cast out devils, by whom do your children cast them out? therefore they shall be your judges."
Jesus (Today):
And if I drive out demons by Satan, by whom do your own people drive them out? They will be your judges.

Matthew 12:28
"But if I cast out devils by the Spirit of God, then the kingdom of God is come unto you."
Jesus (2025):
But if I'm driving out demons by the Spirit of God, then God's kingdom has already arrived here among you.

Matthew 12:29
"Or else how can one enter into a strong man's house, and spoil his goods, except he first bind the strong man? and then he will spoil his house."
Or how can someone break into a strong man's house and take his belongings unless he first ties up the strong man? Only then can he take over his house.

Matthew 12:30 (KJV)
"He that is not with me is against me; and he that gathereth not with me scattereth abroad."
Jesus (Today):
If you're not with Me, you're against Me. If you're not helping Me gather, you're scattering.

Matthew 12:31 (KJV)
"Wherefore I say unto you, All manner of sin and blasphemy shall be forgiven unto men: but the

blasphemy against the Holy Ghost shall not be forgiven unto men."
Jesus (Today):
I'm telling you every kind of sin and insult against God can be forgiven but speaking against the Holy Spirit will never be forgiven.

Matthew 12:32 (KJV)
"And whosoever speaketh a word against the Son of man, it shall be forgiven him: but whosoever speaketh against the Holy Ghost, it shall not be forgiven him, neither in this world, neither in the world to come."
Jesus (Today):
Anyone who speaks against Me can be forgiven but anyone who speaks against the Holy Spirit will never be forgiven not in this life or in the life to come.

Matthew 12:33 (KJV)
"Either make the tree good, and his fruit good; or else make the tree corrupt, and his fruit corrupt: for the tree is known by his fruit."
If you say the tree is good then its fruit has to be good. If you say the tree is bad then its fruit is bad. A tree is always known by the fruit it produces.

Matthew 12:34 (KJV)
"O generation of vipers, how can ye, being evil, speak good things? for out of the abundance of the heart the mouth speaketh."
Jesus (Today):
You snakes. How can evil people speak anything good? Your mouth spills whatever your heart is full of.

Matthew 12:35 (KJV)
"A good man out of the good treasure of the heart bringeth forth good things: and an evil man out of the evil treasure bringeth forth evil things."

Jesus (Today):
A good person brings good things out of the good stored in their heart, and an evil person brings evil things out of the evil stored there.

Matthew 12:36 (KJV)
"But I say unto you, That every idle word that men shall speak, they shall give account thereof in the day of judgment."
Jesus (Today):
I'm telling you the truth; every careless word people speak, they will have to answer for it on the day of judgment.

Matthew 12:37 (KJV)
"For by thy words thou shalt be justified, and by thy words thou shalt be condemned."
Jesus (Today):
Your words will either clear you or condemn you.

Matthew 12:39-40 (KJV)
"An evil and adulterous generation seeketh after a sign; and there shall no sign be given to it, but the sign of the prophet Jonas: "For as Jonas was three days and three nights in the whale's belly; so shall the Son of man be three days and three nights in the heart of the earth."
Jesus (Today):
An evil and unfaithful generation keeps looking for a sign. But no sign will be given to them except the sign of the prophet Jonah. Just as Jonah spent three days and three nights in the belly of a whale, the Son of Man will be in the heart of the earth for three days and three nights.

Matthew 12:43 (KJV)
"When the unclean spirit is gone out of a man, he walketh through dry places, seeking rest, and findeth none."

Jesus (Today):
When an unclean spirit leaves a person it wanders through empty, barren places looking for rest but doesn't find any.

Matthew 12:44 (KJV)
"Then he saith, I will return into my house from whence I came out; and when he is come, he findeth it empty, swept, and garnished."
Jesus (Today):
Then it says, "I'll go back to the person I came from." When it returns it finds that life empty, cleaned up, and put in order.

Matthew 12:45 (KJV)
"Then goeth he, and taketh with himself seven other spirits more wicked than himself, and they enter in and dwell there: and the last state of that man is worse than the first. Even so shall it be also unto this wicked generation."
Jesus (Today):
Then it goes and brings seven other spirits even more wicked than itself and they all move in and live there. That person ends up worse off than before. That's exactly how it will be with this wicked generation.

Matthew 12:48-50 (KJV)
"Who is my mother? and who are my brethren? "Behold my mother and my brethren! For whosoever shall do the will of my Father which is in heaven, the same is my brother, and sister, and mother."
Jesus (Today):
You want to know who My real family is?
Right here. Anyone who does the will of My Father in heaven, that's My family. You are my family.

Matthew 13

Matthew 13:3 (KJV)
"Behold, a sower went forth to sow;"
Jesus (Today):
Picture this, a farmer heads out to plant some seeds...

Matthew 13:4 (KJV):
"And when he sowed, some seeds fell by the way side, and the fowls came and devoured them up:"
Jesus (Today):
Some of the seed fell along the path, and birds came and ate it up.

Matthew 13:5 (KJV):
"Some fell upon stony places, where they had not much earth: and forthwith they sprung up, because they had no deepness of earth:"
Jesus (Today):
Some fell on rocky ground where there wasn't much soil. It sprang up quickly, but there was no depth.

Matthew 13:6 (KJV):
"And when the sun was up, they were scorched; and because they had no root, they withered away."
Jesus (Today):
When the sun rose, it scorched the plants, and since they had no roots, they withered away.

Matthew 13:7 (KJV):

"And some fell among thorns; and the thorns sprung up, and choked them:"
Jesus (Today):
Some seeds fell among thorns, and the thorns grew up and choked them.

Matthew 13:8 (KJV):
"But other fell into good ground, and brought forth fruit, some an hundredfold, some sixtyfold, some thirtyfold."
Jesus (Today):
But some fell on good soil and it produced a harvest. Some a hundredfold, some sixty, some thirty.

Matthew 13:9 (KJV)
"Who hath ears to hear, let him hear."
Jesus (Today):
If you've got ears, listen up.

Matthew 13:10 (KJV)
"Because it is given unto you to know the mysteries of the kingdom of heaven, but to them it is not given."
Jesus (Today):
You've been given the ability to understand the secrets of heaven's kingdom but they haven't been given that.

Matthew 13:11 (KJV)
"For whosoever hath, to him shall be given, and he shall have more abundance: but whosoever hath not, from him shall be taken away even that he hath."
Jesus (Today):
Whoever already has will be given even more and they'll have

more than enough. But whoever doesn't have will lose even what little they do have.

Matthew 13:12 (KJV)
"Therefore speak I to them in parables: because they seeing see not; and hearing they hear not, neither do they understand."

Jesus (Today):
That's why I speak to them in parables, because though they see, they do not really see, and though they hear, they do not understand.

Matthew 13:13 (KJV)
"And in them is fulfilled the prophecy of Esaias, which saith, By hearing ye shall hear, and shall not understand; and seeing ye shall see, and shall not perceive:"

Jesus (Today):
This is exactly what Isaiah's prophecy was about: You'll keep on hearing but won't understand, you'll keep on seeing and not perceiving.

Matthew 13:14 (KJV)
"For this people's heart is waxed gross, and their ears are dull of hearing, and their eyes they have closed; lest at any time they should see with their eyes and hear with their ears, and should understand with their heart, and should be converted, and I should heal them."

Jesus (2025):
These people's hearts have become hard. Their ears can barely hear and they've shut their eyes. If they really saw with their eyes, heard with their ears, and understood in their hearts, they would turn to Me and I would heal them.

Matthew 13:16 (KJV)
"But blessed are your eyes, for they see: and your ears, for they hear."

Jesus (Today):

But your eyes, they see. Your ears? They actually *hear*. That's a blessing.

Matthew 13:17 (KJV)
"For verily I say unto you, That many prophets and righteous men have desired to see those things which ye see, and have not seen them; and to hear those things which ye hear, and have not heard them."

Jesus (Today):
Truly I tell you, many prophets and righteous people longed to see what you see but did not see it, and to hear what you hear but did not hear it.

Matthew 13:18-19 (KJV)
"Hear ye therefore the parable of the sower. When any one heareth the word of the kingdom, and understandeth it not, then cometh the wicked one, and catcheth away that which was sown in his heart. This is he which received seed by the way side."

Jesus (Today):
Listen then to the parable of the sower. When anyone hears the message about the kingdom and does not understand it, the enemy comes and snatches away what was sown in their heart. This is the seed sown along the path.

Matthew 13:20 (KJV)
"But he that received the seed into stony places, the same is he that heareth the word, and anon with joy receiveth it;"

Jesus (Today):
The one who receives the seed on rocky ground is the person who hears the word and immediately receives it with joy.

Matthew 13:21 (KJV)
"Yet hath he not root in himself, but dureth for a while: for when tribulation or persecution ariseth because of the word, by and by he is offended."

Jesus (Today):
He has no root in himself, so he lasts only a short time. When trouble or persecution comes because of the word, he quickly falls away.

Matthew 13:22 (KJV)
"He also that received seed among the thorns is he that heareth the word; and the care of this world, and the deceitfulness of riches, choke the word, and he becometh unfruitful."
Jesus (Today):
The one who receives the seed among the thorns is the person who hears the word but the worries of life and the lies of wealth choke it out, and it doesn't produce anything.

Matthew 13:23 (KJV)
"But he that received seed into the good ground is he that heareth the word, and understandeth it; which also beareth fruit, and bringeth forth, some an hundredfold, some sixty, some thirty."
Jesus (Today):
But the good soil? That's the one who hears it, gets it, and lets it grow. And what comes out? A return...thirty, sixty, even a hundred times more.

Matthew 13:25 (KJV)
"But while men slept, his enemy came and sowed tares among the wheat, and went his way."
Jesus (Today):
But while everyone was asleep the enemy came and scattered weeds among the wheat and then left.

Matthew 13:26 (KJV)
"But when the blade was sprung up, and brought forth fruit, then appeared the tares also."

Jesus (Today):
When the plants started to grow and produce grain the weeds showed up right alongside them.

Matthew 13:27 (KJV)
"So the servants of the householder came and said unto him, Sir, didst not thou sow good seed in thy field? from whence then hath it tares?"
Jesus (Today):
The owner's servants came and asked him Didn't you plant good seed in your field? Where did all these weeds come from?

Matthew 13:28
"He said unto them, An enemy hath done this. The servants said unto him, Wilt thou then that we go and gather them up?"
Jesus (Today):
He told them an enemy did this. The servants asked Do you want us to go pull the weeds out?

Matthew 13:29 (KJV)
"But he said, Nay; lest while ye gather up the tares, ye root up also the wheat with them."
Jesus (Today):
No he answered because if you pull up the weeds now you might uproot the wheat with them.

Matthew 13:30 (KJV)
"Let both grow together until the harvest: and in the time of harvest I will say to the reapers, Gather ye together first the tares, and bind them in bundles to burn them: but gather the wheat into my barn."
Jesus (Today):
Let both grow together until harvest. When it's time I'll tell the

workers: Gather the weeds first and tie them up to be burned then bring the wheat into my barn.

Matthew 13:33 (KJV)
"The kingdom of heaven is like unto leaven, which a woman took, and hid in three measures of meal, till the whole was leavened."
Jesus (Today):
God's kingdom is like yeast that a woman mixed into a large batch of flour until it spread through the whole dough.

Matthew 13:37 (KJV)
"He that soweth the good seed is the Son of man;"
Jesus (2025):
The one who plants the good seed is the Son of Man.

Matthew 13:38 (KJV)
"The field is the world; the good seed are the children of the kingdom; but the tares are the children of the wicked one;"
Jesus (Today):
The field is the world. The good seed stands for the people of God's kingdom. The weeds are the people who belong to the wicked one.

Matthew 13:39 (KJV)
"The enemy that sowed them is the devil; the harvest is the end of the world; and the reapers are the angels."
Jesus (Today):
The enemy who planted them is the devil. The harvest is the end of the world, and the workers harvesting are the angels.

Matthew 13:40 (KJV)
"As therefore the tares are gathered and burned in the fire; so shall it be in the end of this world."
Jesus (Today):
Just like the weeds are pulled up and burned, that's how it will be at the end of the world.

Matthew 13:41–42 (KJV)
"As therefore the tares are gathered and burned in the fire; so shall it be in the end of this world. The Son of man shall send forth his angels, and they shall gather out of his kingdom all things that offend, and them which do iniquity; And shall cast them into a furnace of fire: there shall be wailing and gnashing of teeth."
Jesus (Today):
As the weeds are pulled up and burned in the fire, so it will be at the end of the age. The Son of Man will send out his angels, and they will gather out of his kingdom everything that causes sin and all who do evil. They will throw them into the blazing furnace, where there will be crying and grinding of teeth.

Matthew 13:43 (KJV)
"Then shall the righteous shine forth as the sun in the kingdom of their Father. Who hath ears to hear, let him hear."
Jesus (Today):
Then the ones who live right will shine like the sun in their Father's kingdom. If you've got ears, pay attention.

Matthew 13:44 (KJV):
"Again, the kingdom of heaven is like unto treasure hid in a field; the which when a man hath found, he hideth, and for joy thereof goeth and selleth all that he hath, and buyeth that field."
Jesus (Today):
Again, the kingdom of heaven is like a treasure hidden in a field. When someone finds it, they hide it again, and in joy, sell everything they own to buy that field.

Matthew 13:45 (KJV)
"Again, the kingdom of heaven is like unto a merchant man, seeking goodly pearls".
Jesus (Today)
The Kingdom of Heaven is like a merchant searching for fine pearls.

Matthew 13:46 (KJV)
"Who, when he had found one pearl of great price, went and sold all that he had, and bought it."
Jesus (Today)
When he finds one priceless pearl, he sells everything he has to buy it.

Matthew 13:47 (KJV)
"Again, the kingdom of heaven is like unto a net, that was cast into the sea, and gathered of every kind."
Jesus (Today)
The Kingdom of Heaven is like a net thrown into the sea that gathers all kinds of fish.

Matthew 13:48 (KJV)
"Which, when it was full, they drew to shore, and sat down, and gathered the good into vessels, but cast the bad away."
Jesus (Today)
When it is full, the fishermen pull it to shore, sit down, collect the good fish in baskets, and throw the bad ones away.

Matthew 13:49 (KJV)
"So shall it be at the end of the world the angels shall come forth, and sever the wicked from among the just."

Jesus (Today)
That is how it will be at the end of the world. The angels will come and separate the wicked from the righteous.

Matthew 13:50 (KJV)
"And shall cast them into the furnace of fire there shall be wailing and gnashing of teeth."
Jesus (Today)
They will throw them into the blazing furnace where there will be crying and grinding of teeth.

Matthew 13:51 (KJV)
"Have ye understood all these things?
Jesus (Today)
Have you understood all of this?

Matthew 13:52 (KJV)
"Therefore every scribe which is instructed unto the kingdom of heaven is like unto a man that is an householder, which bringeth forth out of his treasure things new and old."
Jesus (Today):
Every teacher of the law who has been instructed about the kingdom of heaven is like a homeowner who brings out of his storeroom treasures both new and old.

Matthew 13:57 (KJV):
"A prophet is not without honour, save in his own country, and in his own house."
Jesus (Today):
A prophet is honored everywhere except in his own town and in his own home.

Matthew 14

Matthew 14:16 (KJV)
"They need not depart; give ye them to eat."
Jesus (Today):
They don't need to leave. Give them something to eat.

Matthew 14:18 (KJV):
"Bring them hither to me."
Jesus (Today):
Bring them here to Me.

Matthew 14:27 (KJV)
"Be of good cheer; it is I; be not afraid."
Jesus (Today):
Take courage. It's Me. Don't be afraid.

Matthew 14:29 (KJV)
"Come."
Jesus (Today):
Come.

Matthew 14:31 (KJV)
"O thou of little faith, wherefore didst thou doubt?"
Jesus (Today):
You have so little faith. Why did you doubt?

Matthew 15

Matthew 15:3 (KJV)
"But he answered and said unto them, Why do ye also transgress the commandment of God by your tradition?"

Jesus (Today):
Why is it that you break God's actual commands just to hold on to your traditions?

Matthew 15:4 (KJV)
"For God commanded, saying, Honour thy father and mother: and, He that curseth father or mother, let him die the death."

Jesus: (Today):
God's command is this: Respect your father and mother. And He also said, anyone who curses their parents deserves death.

Matthew 15:5 (KJV)
"But ye say, Whosoever shall say to his father or his mother, It is a gift, by whatsoever thou mightest be profited by me;"

Jesus (Today):
But you say that if someone tells their father or mother, "What I would have given to help you is now a gift to God,'" that is enough.

Matthew 15:6 (KJV)
"And honour not his father or his mother, he shall be free. Thus have ye made the commandment of God of none effect by your tradition."

Jesus (Today):
So they don't honor their parents, and you say that's fine. By

your traditions you've canceled out God's command.

Matthew 15:7–8 (KJV)
"Ye hypocrites, well did Esaias prophesy of you, saying, This people draweth nigh unto me with their mouth, and honoureth me with their lips; but their heart is far from me."

Jesus (Today):
You hypocrites. Isaiah was talking about you. These people say all the right things, but their hearts are nowhere near Me.

Matthew 15:9 (KJV)
"But in vain they do worship me, teaching for doctrines the commandments of men."

Jesus (Today):
Their worship means nothing because they've replaced My truth with their own man-made teachings.

Matthew 15:10 (KJV):
"Hear, and understand:"

Jesus (Today):
Listen up, and understand this.

Matthew 15:11 (KJV)
"Not that which goeth into the mouth defileth a man; but that which cometh out of the mouth, this defileth a man."

Jesus (Today):
It is not what goes into a person's mouth that makes them unclean, but what comes out of their mouth. That is what makes them unclean.

Matthew 15:13 (KJV)
"Every plant, which my heavenly Father hath not planted, shall be rooted up."

Jesus (Today):
Anything My Father didn't plant, it's getting pulled up by the roots.

Matthew 15:14 (KJV)
"Let them alone: they be blind leaders of the blind. And if the blind lead the blind, both shall fall into the ditch."

Jesus (Today):
Leave them alone. They're blind guides leading the blind, and when one blind person leads another, they'll both fall into the ditch.

Matthew 15:16 (KJV)
"Are ye also yet without understanding?"

Jesus (Today):
Are you still not getting it?

Matthew 15:17 (KJV)
"Do not ye yet understand, that whatsoever entereth in at the mouth goeth into the belly, and is cast out into the draught?"

Jesus (Today):
Don't you see that what you eat just goes into your stomach and then out of your body?

Matthew 15:18 (KJV):
"But those things which proceed out of the mouth come forth from the heart; and they defile the man."

Jesus (Today):
But what comes out of your mouth comes from your heart.

That's what makes you unclean.

Matthew 15:19 (KJV):
"For out of the heart proceed evil thoughts, murders, adulteries, fornications, thefts, false witness, blasphemies:"
Jesus: (Today):
Because the heart is where evil thoughts come from, things like murder, adultery, sexual sin, stealing, lying, and blasphemy.

Matthew 15:20 (KJV):
"These are the things which defile a man: but to eat with unwashen hands defileth not a man."
Jesus (Today):
These are the things that make a person unclean. But eating with unwashed hands does not make anyone unclean.

Matthew 15:24 (KJV):
" I am not sent but unto the lost sheep of the house of Israel."
Jesus: (Today):
I was sent only to the lost sheep of Israel.

Matthew 15:26 (KJV):
"It is not meet to take the children's bread, and to cast it to dogs."
Jesus: (Today):
It's not right to take the children's bread and throw it to the dogs.

Matthew 15:28 (KJV):
"O woman, great is thy faith: be it unto thee even as thou wilt."

Jesus: (Today):
Woman, your faith is great. What you're asking for is done.

Matthew 15:32 (KJV)
"Then Jesus called his disciples unto him, and said, I have compassion on the multitude, because they continue with me now three days, and have nothing to eat: and I will not send them away fasting, lest they faint in the way."
Jesus (Today):
I feel compassion for this crowd. They've been with Me for three days and have nothing to eat. I'm not sending them away hungry; they'll collapse on the way home.

Matthew 15:34 (KJV)
"How many loaves have ye?"
Jesus (Today):
How many loaves do you have?

Matthew 16

Matthew 16:2-3 (KJV)
"When it is evening, ye say, It will be fair weather: for the sky is red. And in the morning, It will be foul weather to day: for the sky is red and lowring. O ye hypocrites, ye can discern the face of the sky; but can ye not discern the signs of the times?"
Jesus (Today):
When evening comes you say the weather will be good because the sky is red. And in the morning you say today's going to be stormy because the sky is red and overcast.
You hypocrites. You know how to read the sky but you can't recognize the signs of the times.

Matthew 16:4 (KJV)
"A wicked and adulterous generation seeketh after a sign; and there shall no sign be given unto it, but the sign of the prophet Jonas. And he left them, and departed."

Jesus (Today):
You're part of a wicked and unfaithful generation, always chasing after signs. But the only sign you'll get is the one Jonah gave.

Matthew 16:6 (KJV)
"Take heed and beware of the leaven of the Pharisees and of the Sadducees."

Jesus (Today):
Watch out and be on guard against the teaching of the Pharisees and the Sadducees.

Matthew 16:8 (KJV)
"O ye of little faith, why reason ye among yourselves, because ye have brought no bread?"

Jesus (Today):
You have such little faith. Why are you worried about not bringing bread?

Matthew 16:9 (KJV)
"Do ye not yet understand, neither remember the five loaves of the five thousand, and how many baskets ye took up?"

Jesus (Today):
Don't you understand yet? Don't you remember the five loaves that fed five thousand, and how many baskets you had left over?

Matthew 16:10 (KJV)
"Neither the seven loaves of the four thousand, and how many baskets ye took up?"

Jesus (Today):

Or the seven loaves that fed four thousand. Do you remember how many baskets you picked up afterward?

Matthew 16:11 (KJV)
"How is it that ye do not understand that I spake it not to you concerning bread, that ye should beware of the leaven of the Pharisees and of the Sadducees?"

Jesus (Today):
How do you still not understand that I wasn't talking about bread? I said to watch out for the leaven of the Pharisees and Sadducees.

Matthew 16:13 (KJV)
"Whom do men say that I the Son of man am?"

Jesus (Today):
Who do people say that I, the Son of Man, am?

Matthew 16:15 (KJV)
"But whom say ye that I am?"

Jesus (Today):
But who do you say I am?

Matthew 16:17 (KJV)
"Blessed art thou, Simon Barjona: for flesh and blood hath not revealed it unto thee, but my Father which is in heaven."

Jesus (Today):
You are blessed, Simon, son of Jonah. You didn't figure this out on your own. My Father in heaven showed it to you.

Matthew 16:18 (KJV)
"And I say also unto thee, That thou art Peter, and upon this rock I will build my church; and the

gates of hell shall not prevail against it."
Jesus (Today):
And now I tell you, you are Peter, and on this rock I will build My church, and the gates of hell will not be able to stop it.

Matthew 16:19 (KJV)
"And I will give unto thee the keys of the kingdom of heaven: and whatsoever thou shalt bind on earth shall be bound in heaven: and whatsoever thou shalt loose on earth shall be loosed in heaven."
Jesus (Today):
I'm giving you the keys to God's kingdom. What you lock on earth will be locked in heaven, and what you unlock on earth will be unlocked in heaven.

Matthew 16:23 (KJV)
"Get thee behind me, Satan: thou art an offence unto me: for thou savourest not the things that be of God, but those that be of men."
Jesus (Today):
Get behind me, Satan. You are an offense to me. You are thinking not of God's ways but of human ways.

Matthew 16:24 (KJV)
"If any man will come after me, let him deny himself, and take up his cross, and follow me."
Jesus (Today):
If anyone wants to follow Me, they must deny themselves, take up their cross, and follow me.

Matthew 16:25 (KJV)
"For whosoever will save his life shall lose it: and whosoever will lose his life for my sake shall find it."
Jesus (Today):
If you try to keep your life, you'll lose it. But if you lose it for Me? That's where real life starts.

Matthew 16:26 (KJV)
"For what is a man profited, if he shall gain the whole world, and lose his own soul? or what shall a man give in exchange for his soul?"
Jesus (Today):
What's the point of gaining the whole world… if it costs you your soul? What's worth trading that for?

Matthew 16:27 (KJV):
"For the Son of man shall come in the glory of his Father with his angels; and then he shall reward every man according to his works."
Jesus: Today (Today):
The Son of Man will come in His Father's glory, with His angels, and He'll reward everyone based on what they've done.

Matthew 16:28 (KJV):
"Verily I say unto you, There be some standing here, which shall not taste of death, till they see the Son of man coming in his kingdom."
Jesus: (Today):
I'm telling you the truth, some of you standing here won't die before you see the Son of Man coming in His kingdom.

Matthew 17

Matthew 17:7 (KJV)
"Arise, and be not afraid."
Jesus (Today):
Get up. Don't be afraid.

Matthew 17:9 (KJV)
"Tell the vision to no man, until the Son of man be risen again from the dead."

Jesus (Today):
Don't tell anyone what you saw on that mountain until after I rise from the dead.

Matthew 17:11 (KJV)
"Elias truly shall first come, and restore all things."

Jesus (Today):
Elijah is coming, to reset and restore everything.

Matthew 17:12 (KJV)
"But I say unto you, That Elias is come already, and they knew him not, but have done unto him whatsoever they listed. Likewise shall also the Son of man suffer of them."

Jesus (Today):
I'm telling you the truth. Elijah has already come, and they didn't recognize him. They did whatever they wanted to him. The same thing is going to happen to the Son of Man. I will suffer at their hands.

Matthew 17:17 (KJV)
"O faithless and perverse generation, how long shall I be with you? how long shall I suffer you? bring him hither to me."

Jesus (Today):
You faithless, perverse generation, how long do I have to deal with this? Bring him to me.

Matthew 17:20 (KJV)
"Because of your unbelief: for verily I say unto you, If ye have faith as a grain of mustard seed, ye shall say unto this mountain, Remove hence to yonder place; and it shall remove; and nothing shall be impossible unto you."

Jesus (Today):

You couldn't do it because of your lack of faith. I'm telling you, if you had faith even as small as a mustard seed, you could tell this mountain, "Move from here to there," and it would move. Nothing would be impossible.

Matthew 17:22 (KJV)
"The Son of man shall be betrayed into the hands of men:"
Jesus (Today):
The Son of Man is going to be betrayed and handed over to men.

Matthew 17:23 (KJV)
"And they shall kill him, and the third day he shall be raised again."
Jesus (Today):
They will kill Me. But on the third day, I will rise again.

Matthew 18

Matthew 18:3 (KJV)
"Verily I say unto you, Except ye be converted, and become as little children, ye shall not enter into the kingdom of heaven."
Jesus (Today):
Listen, unless you change and become like a child, you're not getting into heaven's kingdom.

Matthew 18:4 (KJV)
"Whosoever therefore shall humble himself as this little child, the same is greatest in the kingdom of heaven."
Jesus (Today):
Whoever humbles themselves like this child will be the greatest in heaven's kingdom.

Matthew 18:5 (KJV)
"And whoso shall receive one such little child in my name receiveth me."

Jesus (Today):
And if you welcome a child like this in My name, you're welcoming Me.

Matthew 18:6 (KJV)
"But whoso shall offend one of these little ones which believe in me, it were better for him that a millstone were hanged about his neck, and that he were drowned in the depth of the sea."

Jesus (Today):
If you cause even one of these little ones who believe in Me to fall, it would be better for you to have a stone tied around your neck and be thrown into the deepest part of the sea.

Matthew 18:7 (KJV)
"Woe unto the world because of offences! for it must needs be that offences come; but woe to that man by whom the offence cometh!"

Jesus (Today):
This world is full of things that trip people up, and yes, they're going to come. But woe to the person out there causing them.

Matthew 18:8 (KJV)
"Wherefore if thy hand or thy foot offend thee, cut them off, and cast them from thee: it is better for thee to enter into life halt or maimed, rather than having two hands or two feet to be cast into everlasting fire."

Jesus (Today):
If your hand or your foot causes you to sin, cut it off and throw it away. It's better to walk into eternal life missing a part of you than to be whole and thrown into the fire forever.

Matthew 18:9 (KJV)
"And if thine eye offend thee, pluck it out, and cast it from thee: it is better for thee to enter into

life with one eye, rather than having two eyes to be cast into hell fire."
Jesus (Today):
And if your eye leads you into sin, take it out and throw it away. It's better to step into life with one eye than to be fully intact and thrown into hell's fire.

Matthew 18:10 (KJV)
"Take heed that ye despise not one of these little ones; for I say unto you, That in heaven their angels do always behold the face of my Father which is in heaven."
Jesus (Today):
Be careful not to look down on even one of these little ones. I'm telling you, their angels are always standing before My Father in heaven.

Matthew 18:11 (KJV)
"For the Son of man is come to save that which was lost."
Jesus (Today):
The Son of Man came to save what was lost.

Matthew 18:12 (KJV)
"How think ye? if a man have an hundred sheep, and one of them be gone astray, doth he not leave the ninety and nine, and goeth into the mountains, and seeketh that which is gone astray?"
Jesus (Today):
What do you think? If a man has a hundred sheep and one wanders off, doesn't he leave the ninety-nine and go search for the one that's lost?

Matthew 18:13 (KJV)
"And if so be that he find it, verily I say unto you, he rejoiceth more of that sheep, than of the ninety and nine which went not astray."
Jesus (Today):

And if he finds it, I'm telling you the truth, he celebrates that one more than the ninety-nine that never wandered off.

Matthew 18:14 (KJV)
"Even so it is not the will of your Father which is in heaven, that one of these little ones should perish."

Jesus (Today):
Same with your Father, He doesn't want *even one* of these little ones to be lost.

Matthew 18:15 (KJV)
"Moreover if thy brother shall trespass against thee, go and tell him his fault between thee and him alone: if he shall hear thee, thou hast gained thy brother."

Jesus (Today):
If someone wrongs you, go talk to them privately. If they listen and hear you out, you've restored your relationship.

Matthew 18:16 (KJV)
"But if he will not hear thee, then take with thee one or two more, that in the mouth of two or three witnesses every word may be established."

Jesus (Today):
But if he won't listen, bring one or two others with you so there's clarity and accountability in what's being said.

Matthew 18:17 (KJV)
"And if he shall neglect to hear them, tell it unto the church: but if he neglect to hear the church, let him be unto thee as an heathen man and a publican."

Jesus (Today):
And if he still refuses to listen, take it to the community. And if he won't listen even then, treat him like someone who doesn't yet know God.

Matthew 18:18 (KJV)
"Verily I say unto you, Whatsoever ye shall bind on earth shall be bound in heaven: and whatsoever ye shall loose on earth shall be loosed in heaven."
Jesus (Today):
I'm telling you the truth. Whatever you bind on earth will be bound in heaven, and whatever you release on earth will be released in heaven.

Matthew 18:19 (KJV)
"Again I say unto you, That if two of you shall agree on earth as touching any thing that they shall ask, it shall be done for them of my Father which is in heaven."
Jesus (Today):
Let Me say it again. If two of you agree here on earth about anything you ask for, My Father in heaven will do it for you.

Matthew 18:20 (KJV)
"For where two or three are gathered together in my name, there am I in the midst of them."
Jesus (Today):
Because wherever two or three come together in My name, I am right there with them.

Matthew 18:22 (KJV)
"Jesus saith unto him, I say not unto thee, Until seven times: but, Until seventy times seven."
Jesus (Today):
I'm not telling you to forgive just seven times. I'm telling you to forgive seventy times seven.

Matthew 18:23 (KJV)
"Therefore is the kingdom of heaven likened unto a certain king, which would take account of his

servants."

Jesus (Today):
The kingdom of heaven is like a king who decided to settle accounts of his servants.

Matthew 18:32 (KJV)
"O thou wicked servant, I forgave thee all that debt, because thou desiredst me:"

Jesus (Today):
You wicked servant. I forgave your entire debt because you begged Me to.

Matthew 18:33 (KJV)
"Shouldest not thou also have had compassion on thy fellowservant, even as I had pity on thee?"

Jesus (Today):
Shouldn't you have shown the same mercy to your fellow servant that I showed to you?

Matthew 18:35 (KJV)
"So likewise shall my heavenly Father do also unto you, if ye from your hearts forgive not every one his brother their trespasses."

Jesus (Today):
That's exactly what My Father in heaven will do to you if you don't forgive your brother from your heart.

Matthew 19

Matthew 19:4 (KJV)
"Have ye not read, that he which made them at the beginning made them male and female,"

Jesus (Today):
Haven't you read that in the beginning, the Creator made them male and female?

Matthew 19:5 (KJV)
"For this cause shall a man leave father and mother, and shall cleave to his wife: and they twain shall be one flesh?"

Jesus (Today):
For this reason a man will leave his father and mother and be joined to his wife, and the two will become one.

Matthew 19:6 (KJV)
"Wherefore they are no more twain, but one flesh. What therefore God hath joined together, let not man put asunder."

Jesus (Today):
So they are no longer two, but one. And what God has joined together, no one should separate.

Matthew 19:8 (KJV)
"Moses because of the hardness of your hearts suffered you to put away your wives: but from the beginning it was not so."

Jesus (Today):
Moses allowed divorce because your hearts were hard. But that was never how it was meant to be.

Matthew 19:9 (KJV)
"And I say unto you, Whosoever shall put away his wife, except it be for fornication, and shall marry another, committeth adultery: and whoso marrieth her which is put away doth commit adultery."

Jesus (Today):
And I'm telling you this; whoever divorces his wife for any

reason other than adultery; and marries someone else is committing adultery. And whoever marries a divorced woman is doing the same.

Matthew 19:11 (KJV)
"All men cannot receive this saying, save they to whom it is given."

Jesus (Today):
Not everyone can accept this, only those it's been given to.

Matthew 19:12 (KJV)
"For there are some eunuchs, which were so born from their mother's womb: and there are some eunuchs, which were made eunuchs of men: and there be eunuchs, which have made themselves eunuchs for the kingdom of heaven's sake. He that is able to receive it, let him receive it."

Jesus (Today):
Some people are born unable to marry. Others are made that way by people. And some choose that life for the sake of the kingdom of heaven. If you can receive this, receive it.

Matthew 19:14 (KJV)
"Suffer little children, and forbid them not, to come unto me: for of such is the kingdom of heaven."

Jesus (Today):
Let the children come to Me. Don't stop them. The kingdom of heaven belongs to ones like these.

Matthew 19:17 (KJV)
"Why callest thou me good? there is none good but one, that is, God: but if thou wilt enter into life, keep the commandments."

Jesus (Today):
Why do you call Me good? There's only one who is truly good,

and that is God. But if you want to enter into life, keep the commandments.

Matthew 19:18 (KJV)
"Thou shalt do no murder, Thou shalt not commit adultery, Thou shalt not steal, Thou shalt not bear false witness,"
Jesus (Today):
Do not murder. Do not commit adultery. Do not steal. Do not lie about others.

Matthew 19:19 (KJV)
"Honour thy father and thy mother: and, Thou shalt love thy neighbour as thyself."
Jesus (Today):
Honor your father and mother. And love your neighbor the way you love yourself.

Matthew 19:21 (KJV)
"If thou wilt be perfect, go and sell that thou hast, and give to the poor, and thou shalt have treasure in heaven: and come and follow me."
Jesus (Today):
If you really want to go all in, sell your stuff, give it to the poor, and you'll have treasure in heaven. Then come follow Me.

Matthew 19:23 (KJV)
"Verily I say unto you, That a rich man shall hardly enter into the kingdom of heaven."
Jesus (Today):
I'm telling you the truth. It's hard for someone who is rich to enter the kingdom of heaven.

Matthew 19:24 (KJV)
"And again I say unto you, It is easier for a camel to go through the eye of a needle, than for a rich man to enter into the kingdom of God."

Jesus (Today):
I'm telling you, it's easier to squeeze a *camel* through a needle's eye than for a rich man to enter God's kingdom.

Matthew 19:26 (KJV)
"With men this is impossible; but with God all things are possible."

Jesus (Today):
With people? It's impossible.
But with God, *anything's possible*.

Matthew 19:28 (KJV)
"Verily I say unto you, That ye which have followed me, in the regeneration when the Son of man shall sit in the throne of his glory, ye also shall sit upon twelve thrones, judging the twelve tribes of Israel."

Jesus (Today):
I tell you the truth. When everything is made new and the Son of Man sits on His glorious throne, you who have followed Me will also sit on twelve thrones, judging the twelve tribes of Israel.

Matthew 19:29 (KJV)
"And every one that hath forsaken houses, or brethren, or sisters, or father, or mother, or wife, or children, or lands, for my name's sake, shall receive an hundredfold, and shall inherit everlasting life."

Jesus (Today):
And everyone who has left houses, brothers, sisters, father, mother, wife, children, or land for My name's sake will receive a hundred times as much and will inherit eternal life.

Matthew 19:30 (KJV)
"But many that are first shall be last; and the last shall be first."

Jesus (Today):
But many who are first now will be last then, and many who are last now will be first.

Matthew 20

Matthew 20:13 (KJV)
"Friend, I do thee no wrong: didst not thou agree with me for a penny?"

Jesus (Today):
Friend, I haven't wronged you. Didn't we agree on that amount?

Matthew 20:14 (KJV)
"Take that thine is, and go thy way: I will give unto this last, even as unto thee."

Jesus (Today):
Take your pay and go. I choose to give the one who came last the same as I gave you.

Matthew 20:15 (KJV)
"Is it not lawful for me to do what I will with mine own? Is thine eye evil, because I am good?"

Jesus (Today):
Don't I have the right to do what I want with what belongs to Me? Or are you jealous because I'm generous?

Matthew 20:16 (KJV)
"So the last shall be first, and the first last: for many be called, but few chosen."

Jesus (Today):

So the last will be first, and the first will be last. Many are called, but only a few are chosen.

Matthew 20:18-19 (KJV)
"Behold, we go up to Jerusalem; and the Son of man shall be betrayed unto the chief priests and unto the scribes, and they shall condemn him to death, And shall deliver him to the Gentiles to mock, and to scourge, and to crucify him: and the third day he shall rise again."

Jesus (Today):
We're going to Jerusalem. The Son of Man will be betrayed, handed over, beaten, mocked, and killed. But on the third day? He'll rise.

Matthew 20:20-23 (KJV)
"What wilt thou? Ye know not what ye ask. Are ye able to drink of the cup that I shall drink of, and to be baptized with the baptism that I am baptized with? Ye shall drink indeed of my cup, and be baptized with the baptism that I am baptized with: but to sit on my right hand, and on my left, is not mine to give, but it shall be given to them for whom it is prepared of my Father."

Jesus (Today):
What do you want? You don't know what you're asking. Can you drink the cup I'm about to drink and go through the baptism I'm about to face? You will drink My cup and you will share My baptism, but sitting at My right or My left isn't Mine to give. Those places belong to those My Father has prepared them for.

Matthew 20:25-28 (KJV)
"Ye know that the princes of the Gentiles exercise dominion over them, and they that are great exercise authority upon them. But it shall not be so among you: but whosoever will be great among you, let him be your minister; And whosoever will be chief among you, let him be your servant: Even as the Son of man came not to be ministered unto, but to minister, and to give his life a ransom for many."

Jesus (Today):
You know how rulers boss people around and leaders throw their weight around. But it's not supposed to be like that with you. If you want to be great, serve. If you want to lead, serve

even more. The Son of Man came not to be served, but to serve, and to give his life to free many.

Matthew 21

Matthew 21:2-3 (KJV)
"Go into the village over against you, and straightway ye shall find an ass tied, and a colt with her: loose them, and bring them unto me. And if any man say ought unto you, ye shall say, The Lord hath need of them; and straightway he will send them."
Jesus (Today):
Go into the village ahead of you and right away you'll find a donkey tied there with her colt beside her. Untie them and bring them to Me. If anyone asks you about it, say, The Lord needs them, and he will let you take them.

Matthew 21:13 (KJV)
"It is written, My house shall be called the house of prayer; but ye have made it a den of thieves."
Jesus (Today):
It's written, My house will be called a house of prayer. But you've turned it into a den of thieves.

Matthew 21:16 (KJV)
"Yea; have ye never read, Out of the mouth of babes and sucklings thou hast perfected praise?"
Jesus (Today):
Yes, I hear them. Haven't you read this? "From the mouths of children and infants You have called forth praise."

Matthew 21:19 (KJV)
"Let no fruit grow on thee henceforward for ever."

Jesus (Today):
You'll never grow fruit again.

Matthew 21:21 (KJV)
"Verily I say unto you, If ye have faith, and doubt not, ye shall not only do this which is done to the fig tree, but also if ye shall say unto this mountain, Be thou removed, and be thou cast into the sea; it shall be done. And all things, whatsoever ye shall ask in prayer, believing, ye shall receive."

Jesus (Today):
If you have faith without doubt, you'll not only do what I did to the fig tree. You'll tell a mountain to move and be thrown into the sea, and it will happen.

Matthew 21:22 (KJV)
"And all things, whatsoever ye shall ask in prayer, believing, ye shall receive."

Jesus (Today):
Whatever you ask for in prayer, *if you believe*, you'll receive it.

Matthew 21:24-25 (KJV)
"I also will ask you one thing, which if ye tell me, I in like wise will tell you by what authority I do these things. The baptism of John, whence was it? from heaven, or of men?"

Jesus (Today):
I'll ask you just one question. If you answer Me, I'll tell you by what authority I'm doing these things. John's baptism, was it from heaven, or was it from men?

Matthew 21:27 (KJV)
"Neither tell I you by what authority I do these things."

Jesus (Today):
Then I won't tell you by what authority I do these things.

Matthew 21:28 (KJV)

"But what think ye? A certain man had two sons; and he came to the first, and said, Son, go work to day in my vineyard."

Jesus (Today):

What do you think? A man had two sons. He went to the first and said, "Son, go work in the vineyard today."

Matthew 21:30 (KJV)

"And he came to the second, and said likewise. And he answered and said, I go, sir: and went not."

Jesus (Today):

Then he went to the second son and said the same thing. The son answered, "yes sir," but never went.

Matthew 21:31 (KJV)

"Jesus saith unto them, Verily I say unto you, That the publicans and the harlots go into the kingdom of God before you."

Jesus (Today):

Which of the two did what his father wanted? Listen, the tax collectors and prostitutes are getting into the kingdom before you.

Matthew 21:32 (KJV)

"For John came unto you in the way of righteousness, and ye believed him not: but the publicans and the harlots believed him: and ye, when ye had seen it, repented not afterward, that ye might believe him."

Jesus (Today):

John came showing you the way of righteousness and you didn't believe him. But the tax collectors and prostitutes did. And even after seeing that, you still refused to turn around and believe him.

Matthew 21:33–41 (KJV)

"Hear another parable: There was a certain householder, which planted a vineyard, and hedged it round about, and digged a winepress in it, and built a tower, and let it out to husbandmen, and went into a far country: And when the time of the fruit drew near, he sent his servants to the husbandmen, that they might receive the fruits of it. And the husbandmen took his servants, and beat one, and killed another, and stoned another. Again, he sent other servants more than the first: and they did unto them likewise. But last of all he sent unto them his son, saying, They will reverence my son. But when the husbandmen saw the son, they said among themselves, This is the heir; come, let us kill him, and let us seize on his inheritance. And they caught him, and cast him out of the vineyard, and slew him. When the lord therefore of the vineyard cometh, what will he do unto those husbandmen?"

Jesus (Today):

Listen to another story. There was a landowner who planted a vineyard. He put a wall around it, dug a winepress, and built a watchtower. Then he rented it to some farmers and went away. When harvest time came, he sent his servants to collect his share of the fruit. But the farmers grabbed his servants. They beat one, killed another, and stoned a third. Then he sent more servants than before, but they treated them the same way. Last of all he sent his son, thinking, They will respect my son. But when the farmers saw the son, they said to each other, This is the heir. Come on, let's kill him and take his inheritance. So they seized him, threw him out of the vineyard, and killed him. When the owner of the vineyard comes, what do you think he will do to those farmers?

Matthew 21:42 (KJV)

"Did ye never read in the scriptures, The stone which the builders rejected, the same is become the head of the corner: this is the Lord's doing, and it is marvellous in our eyes?"

Jesus (Today):

Have you never read the Scriptures?
The stone the builders rejected has become the cornerstone.
The Lord made it happen, and it's incredible in our eyes.

Matthew 21:43 (KJV)

"Therefore say I unto you, The kingdom of God shall be taken from you, and given to a nation bringing forth the fruits thereof."

Jesus (Today):
So hear this. The kingdom of God will be taken from you and handed to a people who will actually produce its fruit.

Matthew 21:44 (KJV)
"And whosoever shall fall on this stone shall be broken: but on whomsoever it shall fall, it will grind him to powder."
Jesus (Today):
Anyone who falls on this stone will be broken to pieces, but anyone on whom it falls will be crushed.

Matthew 22

Matthew 22:2-14 (KJV)
"The kingdom of heaven is like unto a certain king, which made a marriage for his son, And sent forth his servants to call them that were bidden to the wedding: and they would not come. Again, he sent forth other servants, saying, Tell them which are bidden, Behold, I have prepared my dinner: my oxen and my fatlings are killed, and all things are ready: come unto the marriage. But they made light of it, and went their ways, one to his farm, another to his merchandise: And the remnant took his servants, and entreated them spitefully, and slew them. But when the king heard thereof, he was wroth: and he sent forth his armies, and destroyed those murderers, and burned up their city. Then saith he to his servants, The wedding is ready, but they which were bidden were not worthy. Go ye therefore into the highways, and as many as ye shall find, bid to the marriage. So those servants went out into the highways, and gathered together all as many as they found, both bad and good: and the wedding was furnished with guests. And when the king came in to see the guests, he saw there a man which had not on a wedding garment: And he saith unto him, Friend, how camest thou in hither not having a wedding garment? And he was speechless. Then said the king to the servants, Bind him hand and foot, and take him away, and cast him into outer darkness; there shall be weeping and gnashing of teeth. For many are called, but few are chosen."
Jesus (Today):
The kingdom of heaven is like a king who prepared a wedding banquet for his son. He sent his servants to call those who had been invited, but they refused to come. Then he sent more servants, saying, tell those who were invited, Look, I've

prepared my dinner. My oxen and fattened cattle have been butchered, and everything is ready. Come to the wedding banquet. But they paid no attention and went off. One to his farm, another to his business. The rest seized his servants, mistreated them, and killed them. The king was furious. He sent his army to destroy those murderers and burn their city. Then he said to his servants, The wedding banquet is ready, but those I invited didn't deserve to come. Go out to the streets and invite everyone you find to the banquet. So the servants went out and gathered everyone they could find, both good and bad, and the wedding hall was filled with guests. But when the king came in to see the guests, he noticed a man there who wasn't wearing wedding clothes. He asked him, Friend, how did you get in here without wedding clothes? The man was speechless. Then the king told the servants, Tie him hand and foot, and throw him outside into the darkness, where there will be weeping and grinding of teeth. For many are invited, but few are chosen.

Matthew 22:18 (KJV)
"Why tempt ye me, ye hypocrites?"
Jesus (Today):
I see right through you. Why are you testing me, you hypocrites?

Matthew 22:19 (KJV)
"Shew me the tribute money."
Jesus (Today):
Show me the coin used for the tax.

Matthew 22:20 (KJV)
"Whose is this image and superscription?

Jesus (Today):
Whose face is this, and whose name is on it?

Matthew 22:21 (KJV)
"Render therefore unto Caesar the things which are Caesar's; and unto God the things that are God's."

Jesus (Today):
Then give Caesar what belongs to Caesar and give God what belongs to God.

Matthew 22:29 (KJV)
"Ye do err, not knowing the scriptures, nor the power of God."

Jesus (Today):
You're wrong, because you don't know Scriptures, or the power of God.

Matthew 22:30 (KJV)
"For in the resurrection they neither marry, nor are given in marriage, but are as the angels of God in heaven."

Jesus (Today):
When the dead rise, they won't marry or be given in marriage. They'll be like the angels in heaven.

Matthew 22:31 (KJV)
"But as touching the resurrection of the dead, have ye not read that which was spoken unto you by God,"

Jesus (Today):
And about the resurrection, haven't you read what God said to you?

Matthew 22:32 (KJV)
"I am the God of Abraham, and the God of Isaac, and the God of Jacob? God is not the God of the

dead, but of the living."
Jesus (Today):
I am the God of Abraham, the God of Isaac, and the God of Jacob. God is not the God of the dead, but of the living.

Matthew 22:37 (KJV)
"Thou shalt love the Lord thy God with all thy heart, and with all thy soul, and with all thy mind."
Jesus (Today):
Love the Lord your God with all your heart, all your soul, and all your mind.

Matthew 22:38 (KJV)
"This is the first and great commandment."
Jesus (Today):
This is the first and greatest commandment.

Matthew 22:39 (KJV)
"And the second is like unto it, Thou shalt love thy neighbour as thyself."
Jesus (Today):
And the second one is just as important. Love your neighbor like you love yourself.

Matthew 22:40 (KJV)
"On these two commandments hang all the law and the prophets."
Jesus (Today):
Everything in the Law and everything the prophets said, it all hangs on these two commands.

Matthew 22:42 (KJV)
"Saying, What think ye of Christ? whose son is he? They say unto him, The son of David."

Jesus (Today):
What do you think about Christ? Whose Son is He?

Matthew 22:43 (KJV)
"He saith unto them, How then doth David in spirit call him Lord,"
Jesus (Today):
Then how is it that David, speaking by the Spirit, calls Him "Lord"?

Matthew 22:44 (KJV)
"The Lord said unto my Lord, Sit thou on my right hand, till I make thine enemies thy footstool?"
Jesus (Today):
The Lord said to my Lord, "Sit at my right hand until I put your enemies under your feet."

Matthew 22:45 (KJV)
"If David then call him Lord, how is he his son?"
Jesus (Today):
So if David calls Him "Lord," how can He also be his son?

Matthew 23

Matthew 23:2 (KJV)
"The scribes and the Pharisees sit in Moses' seat:"
Jesus (Today):
The teachers of the law and the Pharisees sit in Moses' place of authority.

Matthew 23:3 (KJV)
"All therefore whatsoever they bid you observe, that observe and do; but do not ye after their works: for they say, and do not."

Jesus (Today):
So whatever they tell you to do, do it and keep it. But do not follow their example, because they do not practice what they preach.

Matthew 23:4 (KJV)
"For they bind heavy burdens and grievous to be borne, and lay them on men's shoulders; but they themselves will not move them with one of their fingers."

Jesus (Today):
They pile up heavy, crushing rules and put them on people's shoulders, but they won't lift a finger to help carry the weight.

Matthew 23:5 (KJV)
"But all their works they do for to be seen of men: they make broad their phylacteries, and enlarge the borders of their garments…"

Jesus (Today):
Everything they do is just for show. They make their prayer boxes big and their tassels long, so everyone notices.

Matthew 23:6 (KJV)
"And love the uppermost rooms at feasts, and the chief seats in the synagogues…"

Jesus (Today):
They love the best seats at the banquets and the front rows at the synagogue.

Matthew 23:7 (KJV)
"And greetings in the markets, and to be called of men, Rabbi, Rabbi."
Jesus (Today):
They love getting attention in public and being greeted with titles like, "Rabbi, Rabbi."

Matthew 23:8 (KJV)
"But be not ye called Rabbi: for one is your Master, even Christ; and all ye are brethren."
Jesus (Today):
But do not be called "Rabbi," for you have one Teacher, even Christ, and you are all brothers and sisters.

Matthew 23:9 (KJV)
"And call no man your father upon the earth: for one is your Father, which is in heaven."
Jesus (Today):
And don't call anyone on earth your spiritual father, because you have one Father, and He's in heaven.

Matthew 23:10 (KJV)
"Neither be ye called masters: for one is your Master, even Christ."
Jesus (Today):
Don't let people call you master. You only have one true Master, the Messiah.

Matthew 23:11 (KJV)
"But he that is greatest among you shall be your servant."
Jesus (Today):
The greatest one among you will be the one who serves everyone else.

Matthew 23:12 (KJV)
"And whosoever shall exalt himself shall be abased; and he that shall humble himself shall be exalted."

Jesus (Today):
If you lift *yourself* up, you'll be brought low. But if you humble yourself, God will raise you up.

Matthew 23:13 (KJV)
"But woe unto you, scribes and Pharisees, hypocrites! for ye shut up the kingdom of heaven against men: for ye neither go in yourselves, neither suffer ye them that are entering to go in."

Jesus (Today):
But woe to you, scribes and Pharisees, hypocrites! You shut the door of the kingdom of heaven in people's faces. You yourselves do not enter, nor do you allow those who are trying to enter to go in.

Matthew 23:14 (KJV)
"Woe unto you, scribes and Pharisees, hypocrites! for ye devour widows' houses, and for a pretence make long prayer: therefore ye shall receive the greater damnation."

Jesus (Today):
You take advantage of widows and then cover it up with long showy prayers. Because of that, your judgment will be even worse.

Matthew 23:15 (KJV)
"Woe unto you... ye compass sea and land to make one proselyte, and when he is made, ye make him twofold more the child of hell than yourselves."

Jesus (Today):
You'll cross land and sea just to convert one person, and when you do, you turn them into twice the child of hell you are.

Matthew 23:16 (KJV)
"Woe unto you, ye blind guides, which say, Whosoever shall swear by the temple, it is nothing; but whosoever shall swear by the gold of the temple, he is a debtor!"

Jesus (Today):
You're in serious trouble, you blind guides. You say if someone swears by the temple, it means nothing. But if they swear by the gold in the temple, they're on the hook.

Matthew 23:17 (KJV)
"Ye fools and blind: for whether is greater, the gold, or the temple that sanctifieth the gold?"

Jesus (Today):
You're blind and foolish. What's more sacred: the gold, or the temple that makes the gold holy?

Matthew 23:18 (KJV)
"And, Whosoever shall swear by the altar, it is nothing; but whosoever sweareth by the gift that is upon it, he is guilty."

Jesus (Today):
You say if someone swears by the altar, it doesn't count, but if they swear by the offering on the altar, then it matters. You've completely missed the point.

Matthew 23:19 (KJV)
"Ye fools and blind: for whether is greater, the gift, or the altar that sanctifieth the gift?"

Jesus (Today):
You're blind and foolish. What's more important: the offering, or the altar that makes the offering holy?

Matthew 23:20 (KJV)
"Whoso therefore shall swear by the altar, sweareth by it, and by all things thereon."

Jesus (Today):
If you swear by the altar, you're swearing by everything on it too.

Matthew 23:21 (KJV)
"And whoso shall swear by the temple, sweareth by it, and by him that dwelleth therein."
Jesus (Today):
And whoever swears by the temple swears by it and by the One who dwells in it.

Matthew 23:22 (KJV)
"And he that shall swear by heaven, sweareth by the throne of God, and by him that sitteth thereon."
Jesus (Today):
If you swear by heaven, you're swearing by God's throne and by God who sits there.

Matthew 23:23 (KJV)
"Woe unto you, scribes and Pharisees, hypocrites! for ye pay tithe of mint and anise and cummin, and have omitted the weightier matters of the law, judgment, mercy, and faith: these ought ye to have done, and not to leave the other undone."
Jesus (Today):
Warning to you religious experts, hypocrites! You carefully give a tenth of your spices like mint, dill, and cumin, but you ignore the bigger things God cares about: justice, mercy, and faith. You should do both, not skip either.

Matthew 23:24 (KJV)
"Ye blind guides, which strain at a gnat, and swallow a camel."
Jesus (Today):

You're careful to strain out a tiny gnat, but then you gulp down a whole camel.

Matthew 23:25 (KJV)
"Woe unto you... for ye make clean the outside of the cup and of the platter, but within they are full of extortion and excess."

Jesus (Today):
You clean the outside of the cup and plate, but inside they're full of greed and self-indulgence.

Matthew 23:26 (KJV)
"Thou blind Pharisee, cleanse first that which is within the cup and platter, that the outside of them may be clean also."

Jesus (Today):
You're blind. First clean the inside of the cup and dish, and then the outside will also be clean.

Matthew 23:27 (KJV)
"Woe unto you, scribes and Pharisees, hypocrites! for ye are like unto whited sepulchres, which indeed appear beautiful outward, but are within full of dead men's bones, and of all uncleanness."

Jesus (Today):
You look polished on the outside, like clean white tombs, but inside you're full of dead bones and everything rotten.

Matthew 23:28 (KJV)
"Even so ye also outwardly appear righteous unto men, but within ye are full of hypocrisy and iniquity."

Jesus (Today):
You look righteous on the outside, but underneath you're full of hypocrisy and rebellion.

Matthew 23:29 (KJV)
"Woe unto you, scribes and Pharisees, hypocrites! because ye build the tombs of the prophets, and garnish the sepulchres of the righteous,"

Jesus (Today):
How terrible it will be for you, teachers of the law and Pharisees, you hypocrites. You build tombs for the prophets and decorate the graves of the righteous.

Matthew 23:30 (KJV)
"And say, If we had been in the days of our fathers, we would not have been partakers with them in the blood of the prophets."

Jesus (Today):
And you say, If we had lived back then, we wouldn't have joined our ancestors in killing the prophets.

Matthew 23:31 (KJV)
"Wherefore ye be witnesses unto yourselves, that ye are the children of them which killed the prophets."

Jesus (Today):
But you testify against yourselves that you're the descendants of those who murdered the prophets.

Matthew 23:32 (KJV)
"Fill ye up then the measure of your fathers."

Jesus (Today):
Go ahead then and finish what your ancestors started.

Matthew 23:33 (KJV)
"Ye serpents, ye generation of vipers, how can ye escape the damnation of hell?"

Jesus (2025):

You snakes. You generation of vipers. How will you escape being condemned to hell?

Matthew 23:34 (KJV)
"Wherefore, behold, I send unto you prophets, and wise men, and scribes: and some of them ye shall kill and crucify; and some of them shall ye scourge in your synagogues, and persecute them from city to city:"

Jesus (2025):
That's why I'm sending you prophets, wise men, and teachers. Some of them you'll kill and crucify. Others you'll beat in your synagogues and chase from town to town.

Matthew 23:35 (KJV)
"That upon you may come all the righteous blood shed upon the earth, from the blood of righteous Abel unto the blood of Zacharias son of Barachias, whom ye slew between the temple and the altar."

Jesus (2025):
And so you will be held responsible for all the righteous blood that has been shed on earth, from the blood of Abel to the blood of Zechariah, son of Berekiah, whom you murdered between the temple and the altar.

Matthew 23:36 (KJV)
"Verily I say unto you, All these things shall come upon this generation."

Jesus (2025):
I tell you the truth. All of this will come on this generation.

Matthew 23:37 (KJV)
"O Jerusalem, Jerusalem, thou that killest the prophets, and stonest them which are sent unto thee, how often would I have gathered thy children together, even as a hen gathereth her chickens under her wings, and ye would not!"

Jesus (Today):

Jerusalem, Jerusalem. you who kill the prophets and stone those sent to you, how often I wanted to gather your children together like a hen gathers her chicks under her wings, but you were not willing.

Matthew 23:38 (KJV)
"Behold, your house is left unto you desolate."
Jesus (Today):
Look, your house is left to you desolate.

Matthew 23:39 (KJV)
"For I say unto you, Ye shall not see me henceforth, till ye shall say, Blessed is he that cometh in the name of the Lord."
Jesus (Today):
I tell you this. You won't see Me again until you say, Blessed is He who comes in the name of the Lord.

Matthew 24

Matthew 24:2 (KJV)
"See ye not all these things? verily I say unto you, There shall not be left here one stone upon another, that shall not be thrown down."
Jesus (Today):
Do you see all this? I'm telling you, not one stone will be left standing. Every last one will be torn down.

Matthew 24:4–5 (KJV)
"Take heed that no man deceive you. For many shall come in my name, saying, I am Christ; and

shall deceive many."
Jesus (Today):
Be careful. Don't let anyone mislead you. A lot of people will show up using My name, claiming to be Me, and they'll lead many people off course.

Matthew 24:6-7 (KJV)
"And ye shall hear of wars and rumours of wars: see that ye be not troubled: for all these things must come to pass, but the end is not yet. For nation shall rise against nation, and kingdom against kingdom: and there shall be famines, and pestilences, and earthquakes, in divers places."
Jesus (Today):
You'll hear about wars and threats of war, don't panic. These things must happen, but that doesn't mean it's the end yet. Nations will turn on each other. Kingdoms will collide. There will be famines, outbreaks, and earthquakes in all kinds of places.

Matthew 24:8 (KJV)
"All these are the beginning of sorrows."
Jesus (Today):
What you're seeing now? It's just the beginning of the sorrows to come.

Matthew 24:9 (KJV)
"Then shall they deliver you up to be afflicted, and shall kill you: and ye shall be hated of all nations for my name's sake."
Jesus (Today):
They're going to hand you over to be hurt and killed. You'll be hated by every nation, just because of Me.

Matthew 24:10 (KJV)
"And then shall many be offended, and shall betray one another, and shall hate one another."

Jesus (Today):
At that time, a lot of people will fall away. Betrayals, bitterness. People will turn on each other. And hate will run wild.

Matthew 24:11 (KJV)
"And many false prophets shall rise, and shall deceive many."
Jesus (Today):
Fake prophets will rise, and they'll lead so many off track.

Matthew 24:12 (KJV)
"And because iniquity shall abound, the love of many shall wax cold."
Jesus (Today):
With so much evil flooding the world, love will grow cold in a lot of hearts.

Matthew 24:13 (KJV)
"But he that shall endure unto the end, the same shall be saved."
Jesus (Today):
But the one who hangs on and stays faithful to the end, that's the one who'll be saved.

Matthew 24:14 (KJV)
"And this gospel of the kingdom shall be preached in all the world... and then shall the end come."
Jesus (Today):
This message about the Kingdom will be preached all over the world as a witness to every nation. Then the end will come.

Matthew 24:15 (KJV)
"When ye therefore shall see the abomination of desolation, spoken of by Daniel the prophet, stand in the holy place, (whoso readeth, let him understand)"

Jesus (Today):
When you see the defiling thing that brings destruction, the one Daniel the prophet warned about, standing in the sacred place, don't miss what that means. If you're reading this, take it seriously.

Matthew 24:16 (KJV)
"Then let them which be in Judaea flee into the mountains."
Jesus (Today):
If you're in Judea when this happens, run to the mountains. Don't wait.

Matthew 24:18 (KJV)
"Neither let him which is in the field return back to take his clothes."
Jesus (Today):
If you're out in the field, don't turn back to grab your things. Just go.

Matthew 24:19 (KJV)
"And woe unto them that are with child, and to them that give suck in those days!"
Jesus (Today):
It's going to be especially hard for pregnant women and nursing mothers in those days.

Matthew 24:20 (KJV)
"But pray ye that your flight be not in the winter, neither on the sabbath day."
Jesus (Today):
Pray that you won't have to run in the dead of winter or on a Sabbath day.

Matthew 24:21 (KJV)
"For then shall be great tribulation, such as was not since the beginning of the world to this time, no, nor ever shall be."
Jesus (Today):
Because what's coming will be the worst suffering the world has ever seen. Worse than anything since the beginning, and nothing will ever compare again.

Matthew 24:22 (KJV)
"And except those days should be shortened, there should no flesh be saved: but for the elect's sake those days shall be shortened."
Jesus (Today):
If those days weren't cut short, no one would survive. But for the sake of the ones God has chosen, they will be.

Matthew 24:23 (KJV)
"Then if any man shall say unto you, Lo, here is Christ, or there; believe it not."
Jesus (Today):
If anyone tells you, "Look, here's the Messiah" or "There He is" don't believe it.

Matthew 24:24 (KJV)
"For there shall arise false Christs, and false prophets... insomuch that, if it were possible, they shall deceive the very elect."
Jesus (Today):
Fake messiahs and false prophets will rise up and perform impressive signs and miracles so convincing they could fool even God's chosen ones, if that were possible.

Matthew 24:25 (KJV)
"Behold, I have told you before."
Jesus (Today):
Look, I'm telling you this ahead of time.

Matthew 24:26 (KJV)
"Wherefore if they shall say unto you, Behold, he is in the desert; go not forth: behold, he is in the secret chambers; believe it not."
Jesus (Today):
So if they say, "Look, He's out in the wilderness" don't go. Or "He's hiding in a secret room" don't believe it.

Matthew 24:27 (KJV)
"For as the lightning cometh out of the east, and shineth even unto the west; so shall also the coming of the Son of man be."
Jesus (Today):
When the Son of Man returns? It'll be like lightning flashing across the entire sky. From east to west. You won't miss it.

Matthew 24:28 (KJV)
"For wheresoever the carcase is, there will the eagles be gathered together."
Jesus (Today):
Wherever there's a dead body, that's where the vultures will show up.

Matthew 24:29 (KJV)
"Immediately after the tribulation of those days shall the sun be darkened, and the moon shall not give her light, and the stars shall fall from heaven, and the powers of the heavens shall be shaken."
Jesus (Today):
Right after those days of trouble, the sun will go dark, the moon

won't shine, the stars will fall from the sky, and the powers of the heavens will be shaken.

Matthew 24:30 (KJV)
"...and then shall all the tribes of the earth mourn, and they shall see the Son of man coming in the clouds of heaven with power and great glory."
Jesus (Today):
Then the sign of My return will appear in the sky. The whole world will mourn when they see the Son of Man coming in the clouds with power and overwhelming glory.

Matthew 24:31 (KJV)
"And he shall send his angels with a great sound of a trumpet, and they shall gather together his elect from the four winds, from one end of heaven to the other."
Jesus (Today):
He will send out His angels with a loud trumpet blast, and they'll gather His chosen people from every direction, from one end of heaven to the other.

Matthew 24:32 (KJV)
"Now learn a parable of the fig tree; When his branch is yet tender, and putteth forth leaves, ye know that summer is nigh."
Jesus (Today):
Learn this from the fig tree, when its branches get soft and start sprouting leaves, you know summer is close.

Matthew 24:33 (KJV)
"So likewise ye, when ye shall see all these things, know that it is near, even at the doors."
Jesus (Today):
In the same way, when you see all these things happening, know this, it's right at the door.

Matthew 24:34 (KJV)
"Verily I say unto you, This generation shall not pass, till all these things be fulfilled."

Jesus (Today):

I'm telling you the truth, this generation won't pass away until all of this takes place.

Matthew 24:35 (KJV)
"Heaven and earth shall pass away, but my words shall not pass away."

Jesus (Today):

Heaven and earth will disappear, but My words will never fade.

Matthew 24:36 (KJV)
"But of that day and hour knoweth no man… but my Father only."

Jesus (Today):

No one knows the day or the hour. Not even the angels in heaven. Only My Father knows.

Matthew 24:37 (KJV)
"But as the days of Noe were, so shall also the coming of the Son of man be."

Jesus (Today):

Just like it was in the days of Noah, that's how it will be when the Son of Man returns.

Matthew 24:38 (KJV)
"For as in the days that were before the flood they were eating and drinking, marrying and giving in marriage, until the day that Noe entered into the ark."

Jesus (Today):

Before the flood, people were eating and drinking, getting

married and planning weddings, right up until the day Noah went into the ark.

Matthew 24:39 (KJV)
"And knew not until the flood came, and took them all away; so shall also the coming of the Son of man be."
Jesus (Today):
They had no idea what was coming until the flood hit and swept them all away. That's exactly how it'll be when the Son of Man returns.

Matthew 24:40 (KJV)
"Then shall two be in the field; the one shall be taken, and the other left."
Jesus (Today):
Two people will be working in a field; one will be taken, the other left behind.

Matthew 24:41 (KJV)
"Two women shall be grinding at the mill; the one shall be taken, and the other left."
Jesus (Today):
Two women will be grinding together at the mill; one will be taken, and the other left.

Matthew 24:42 (KJV)
"Watch therefore: for ye know not what hour your Lord doth come."
Jesus (Today):
Stay alert. You don't know the exact hour your Lord is coming.

Matthew 24:43 (KJV)

"But know this, that if the goodman of the house had known in what watch the thief would come, he would have watched, and would not have suffered his house to be broken up."

Jesus (Today):
But understand this; if the homeowner knew when the thief was coming, he would've stayed awake and stopped his house from being broken into.

Matthew 24:44 (KJV)

"Therefore be ye also ready: for in such an hour as ye think not the Son of man cometh."

Jesus (Today):
Be ready. The Son of Man will come at a time you're not expecting.

Matthew 24:45 (KJV)

"Who then is a faithful and wise servant, whom his lord hath made ruler over his household, to give them meat in due season?"

Jesus (Today):
So who is the faithful and wise servant, the one the master puts in charge of the house to give everyone what they need at the right time?

Matthew 24:46 (KJV)

"Blessed is that servant, whom his lord when he cometh shall find so doing."

Jesus (Today):
Blessed is the servant the master finds doing his job when he comes back.

Matthew 24:47 (KJV)

"Verily I say unto you, That he shall make him ruler over all his goods."

Jesus (Today):

That servant will be put in charge of everything the master owns.

Matthew 24:48–51 (KJV)
"But and if that evil servant shall say in his heart, My lord delayeth his coming and shall begin to smite his fellowservants, and to eat and drink with the drunken; the lord of that servant shall come in a day when he looketh not for him, and in an hour that he is not aware of,"

Jesus (Today):
But if that wicked servant thinks to himself, My master isn't coming back anytime soon, and he starts beating his fellow servants and spending his days eating and drinking with drunkards, then that servant's master will return on a day he doesn't expect and at an hour he isn't ready for. The master will cut him off and give him his place among the hypocrites, where there will be weeping and grinding of teeth.

Matthew 25

Matthew 25: 1-13 (KJV)
"Then shall the kingdom of heaven be likened unto ten virgins, which took their lamps, and went forth to meet the bridegroom. And five of them were wise, and five were foolish.
They that were foolish took their lamps, and took no oil with them: But the wise took oil in their vessels with their lamps. While the bridegroom tarried, they all slumbered and slept.
And at midnight there was a cry made, Behold, the bridegroom cometh; go ye out to meet him. Then all those virgins arose, and trimmed their lamps. And the foolish said unto the wise, Give us of your oil; for our lamps are gone out. But the wise answered, saying, Not so; lest there be not enough for us and you: but go ye rather to them that sell, and buy for yourselves. Afterward came also the other virgins, saying, Lord, Lord, open to us. But he answered and said, Verily I say unto you, I know you not. Watch therefore, for ye know neither the day nor the hour wherein the Son of man cometh."

Jesus (Today):
At that time the kingdom of heaven will be like ten young women who took their lamps and went out to meet the groom.

Five of them were wise, and five were foolish. The foolish ones took their lamps but didn't take any oil with them. The wise ones, however, brought oil in jars along with their lamps. The groom was delayed a long time, and they all became drowsy and fell asleep. At midnight the cry rang out: Look, the groom is coming! Come out to meet him! Then all the young women woke up and trimmed their lamps. The foolish ones said to the wise, give us some of your oil; our lamps are going out. The wise replied, no, there might not be enough for both us and you. Go instead to those who sell oil and buy some for yourselves. But while they were on their way to buy the oil, the groom arrived. The young women who were ready went in with him to the wedding banquet. Then the door was shut. Later the others also came. They said, Lord, Lord, open the door for us! But he replied, "Truly I tell you, I don't know you. So stay alert, because you don't know the day or the hour."

Matthew 25:14–28 (KJV)

"For the kingdom of heaven is as a man travelling into a far country, who called his own servants, and delivered unto them his goods. And unto one he gave five talents, to another two, and to another one; to every man according to his several ability; and straightway took his journey. Then he that had received the five talents went and traded with the same, and made them other five talents. And likewise he that had received two, he also gained other two. But he that had received one went and digged in the earth, and hid his lord's money.
After a long time the lord of those servants cometh, and reckoneth with them.
And so he that had received five talents came and brought other five talents, saying, Lord, thou deliveredst unto me five talents: behold, I have gained beside them five talents more.
His lord said unto him, Well done, thou good and faithful servant: thou hast been faithful over a few things, I will make thee ruler over many things: enter thou into the joy of thy lord.
He also that had received two talents came and said, Lord, thou deliveredst unto me two talents: behold, I have gained two other talents beside them. His lord said unto him, Well done, good and faithful servant; thou hast been faithful over a few things, I will make thee ruler over many things: enter thou into the joy of thy lord. Then he which had received the one talent came and said, Lord, I knew thee that thou art an hard man, reaping where thou hast not sown, and gathering where thou hast not strawed:
And I was afraid, and went and hid thy talent in the earth: lo, there thou hast that is thine.
His lord answered and said unto him, Thou wicked and slothful servant, thou knewest that I reap where I sowed not, and gather where I have not strawed: Thou oughtest therefore to have put my money to the exchangers, and then at my coming I should have received mine own with usury. Take therefore the talent from him, and give it unto him which hath ten talents."

Jesus (Today):
The kingdom of heaven is like a man who went on a journey. He called his servants and entrusted them with what belonged to him. To one he gave five talents, to another two, and to another one, each according to their ability. Then he left. The one who received five talents went at once and put them to work and earned five more. The one with two talents did the same and earned two more. But the one who had received just one talent went away, dug a hole in the ground, and hid his master's money. After a long time, the master of those servants returned and settled accounts with them. The one who had received five talents came and said, Master, you entrusted me with five talents. Look, I've gained five more. His master said to him, well done, good and faithful servant. You have been faithful with a few things. I will put you in charge of many things. Enter into the joy of your master. The one with two talents also came and said, Master, you entrusted me with two talents. Look, I've gained two more. His master said to him, well done, good and faithful servant. You have been faithful with a few things. I will put you in charge of many things. Enter into the joy of your master. Then the one who had received one talent came and said, Master, I knew you to be a hard man, harvesting where you did not sow and gathering where you did not scatter. I was afraid, and I went and hid your talent in the ground. See, here is what belongs to you. But his master replied, "You wicked and lazy servant. You knew that I harvest where I did not sow and gather where I did not scatter? Then you should have at least put my money with the bankers so that when I returned, I would have received it back with interest. So take the talent from him and give it to the one who has ten."

Matthew 25:29 (KJV)

"For unto every one that hath shall be given... but from him that hath not shall be taken away even that which he hath."

Jesus (Today):
If you're faithful with what you have, more will be given, until it overflows. But if you've done nothing with it, even the little you had will be taken away.

Matthew 25:30 (KJV)
"And cast ye the unprofitable servant into outer darkness: there shall be weeping and gnashing of teeth."

Jesus (Today):
Now remove that servant who wasted what he was given, and send him into the darkness, where there's only deep sorrow and anguish.

Matthew 25:31 (KJV)
"When the Son of man shall come in his glory, and all the holy angels with him, then shall he sit upon the throne of his glory:"

Jesus (Today):
When the Son of Man comes in his glory, and all the holy angels with him, then he will sit on his glorious throne.

Matthew 25:32 (KJV)
"And before him shall be gathered all nations: and he shall separate them one from another, as a shepherd divideth his sheep from the goats:"

Jesus (Today):
All the nations will be gathered before him, and he will separate the people one from another as a shepherd separates the sheep from the goats.

Matthew 25:33 (KJV)
"And he shall set the sheep on his right hand, but the goats on the left."

Jesus (Today):
He will put the sheep on his right hand and the goats on his left.

Matthew 25:34 (KJV)
"Then shall the King say unto them on his right hand, Come, ye blessed of my Father, inherit the kingdom prepared for you from the foundation of the world:"
Jesus (Today):
Then the King will say to those on His right, Come, you who are blessed by My Father. Step into the Kingdom that's been waiting for you since the beginning of the world.

Matthew 25:35 (KJV)
"For I was an hungred, and ye gave me meat: I was thirsty, and ye gave me drink: I was a stranger, and ye took me in:"
Jesus (Today):
I was hungry and you gave me something to eat. I was thirsty and you gave me something to drink. I was a stranger and you welcomed me in.

Matthew 25:36 (KJV)
"Naked, and ye clothed me: I was sick, and ye visited me: I was in prison, and ye came unto me."
Jesus (Today):
I had nothing to wear, and you gave Me clothes. I was sick, and you showed up. I was in prison, and you came to see Me.

Matthew 25:37 (KJV)
"Then shall the righteous answer him, saying, Lord, when saw we thee an hungred, and fed thee? or thirsty, and gave thee drink?"
Jesus (Today):
Then the righteous will say, Lord, when did we see You hungry

and feed You? Or thirsty and give You something to drink?

Matthew 25:38 (KJV)
"When saw we thee a stranger, and took thee in? or naked, and clothed thee?"
Jesus (Today):
When did we see You as a stranger and welcome You? Or without clothes and give You something to wear?

Matthew 25:39 (KJV)
"Or when saw we thee sick, or in prison, and came unto thee?"
Jesus (Today):
Or when did we see You sick or in prison and come to visit You?

Matthew 25:40 (KJV)
"And the King shall answer and say unto them, Verily I say unto you, Inasmuch as ye have done it unto one of the least of these my brethren, ye have done it unto me."
Jesus (Today):
Every time you showed love to someone overlooked, forgotten, or struggling, you were showing it to Me. What you did for those who seem like they matter least, you did for Me.

Matthew 25:42 (KJV)
"For I was an hungred, and ye gave me no meat: I was thirsty, and ye gave me no drink:"
Jesus (Today):
Because I was hungry, and you didn't feed Me. I was thirsty, and you didn't give Me anything to drink.

Matthew 25:43 (KJV)

"I was a stranger, and ye took me not in: naked, and ye clothed me not: sick, and in prison, and ye visited me not."

Jesus (Today):
I was a stranger, and you didn't welcome Me. I didn't have clothes, and you didn't offer any. I was sick. I was in prison. And you never showed up.

Matthew 25:45 (KJV)
"Then shall he answer them... Inasmuch as ye did it not to one of the least of these, ye did it not to me."

Jesus (Today):
And I'll tell them...every time you turned your back on one of the forgotten ones, you were turning your back on Me.

Matthew 26

Matthew 26:2 (KJV)
"Ye know that after two days is the feast of the passover, and the Son of man is betrayed to be crucified."

Jesus (Today):
You know the Passover is two days away. And the Son of Man? He's about to be betrayed and handed over to be crucified.

Matthew 26:10 (KJV)
"Why trouble ye the woman? for she hath wrought a good work upon me."

Jesus (Today):
Why are you giving her a hard time? What she just did was beautiful to Me.

Matthew 26:11 (KJV)
"For ye have the poor always with you; but me ye have not always."

Jesus (Today):
You'll always have the poor. You won't always have Me.

Matthew 26:18 (KJV)
"Go into the city to such a man, and say unto him, The Master saith, My time is at hand; I will keep the passover at thy house with my disciples."

Jesus (Today):
Go into the city. Tell them, the Teacher says, "My time is almost here. I'm celebrating Passover at your house with My disciples."

Matthew 26:21 (KJV)
"Verily I say unto you, that one of you shall betray me."

Jesus (Today):
I'm telling you right now, one of you is about to betray Me.

Matthew 26:23 (KJV)
"He that dippeth his hand with me in the dish, the same shall betray me."

Jesus (Today):
The one who dipped his hand in the bowl with Me, that's the one who will betray Me.

Matthew 26:24 (KJV)
"The Son of man goeth as it is written of him: but woe unto that man by whom the Son of man is betrayed! it had been good for that man if he had not been born."

Jesus (Today):
The Son of Man will go just as it's been written. The consequences will be severe for the one who betrays Him. It would've been better for that man if he had never been born.

Matthew 26:25 (KJV)
"Thou hast said."
Jesus (Today):
You said it yourself.

Matthew 26:26 (KJV)
"Take, eat; this is my body."
Jesus (Today):
Take this and eat. This is My body, given for you.

Matthew 26:27-28 (KJV)
"Drink ye all of it; For this is my blood of the new testament, which is shed for many for the remission of sins."
Jesus (Today):
Drink from it, all of you. This is my blood, poured out for many, sealing the new covenant and forgiving sins.

Matthew 26:29 (KJV)
"But I say unto you, I will not drink henceforth of this fruit of the vine, until that day when I drink it new with you in my Father's kingdom."
Jesus (Today):
I'm not drinking from this cup again until the day I drink it fresh with you in My Father's Kingdom.

Matthew 26:31 (KJV)
"All ye shall be offended because of me this night: for it is written, I will smite the shepherd, and the sheep of the flock shall be scattered abroad."
Jesus (Today):
Tonight, all of you will fall away because of Me. It's already written; "I will strike the Shepherd, and the sheep will scatter."

Matthew 26:32 (KJV)
"But after I am risen again, I will go before you into Galilee."

Jesus (Today):
But after I rise, I'll go ahead of you to Galilee.

Matthew 26:34 (KJV)
"Verily I say unto thee, That That this night, before the cock crow, thou shalt deny me thrice."

Jesus (Today):
Tonight, before the rooster crows, you're going to deny Me three times.

Matthew 26:36 (KJV)
" Sit ye here, while I go and pray yonder."

Jesus (Today):
Sit here while I go over there and pray.

Matthew 26:38 (KJV)
"Then saith he unto them, My soul is exceeding sorrowful, even unto death: tarry ye here, and watch with me."

Jesus (Today):
My soul is overwhelmed with sorrow, so deep it could kill Me. Stay here and keep watch with Me.

Matthew 26:39 (KJV)
"O my Father, if it be possible, let this cup pass from me: nevertheless not as I will, but as thou wilt."

Jesus (Today):
My Father, if it is possible, let this cup pass from me. Yet not as I will, but as you will.

Matthew 26:40 (KJV)
"What, could ye not watch with me one hour?"
Jesus (Today):
You couldn't stay awake and watch with Me for even one hour?

Matthew 26:41 (KJV)
"Watch and pray, that ye enter not into temptation: the spirit indeed is willing, but the flesh is weak."
Jesus (Today):
Stay alert and pray so you don't fall into temptation. Your spirit wants to do right, but your body is weak.

Matthew 26:42 (KJV)
"O my Father, if this cup may not pass away from me, except I drink it, thy will be done."
Jesus (Today):
My Father, if this cup cannot be taken away unless I drink it, then let Your will be done.

Matthew 26:45 (KJV)
"Sleep on now, and take your rest: behold, the hour is at hand, and the Son of man is betrayed into the hands of sinners."
Jesus (Today):
Go ahead and sleep. Get your rest. But the time has come, the Son of Man is being handed over into the hands of sinners.

Matthew 26:46 (KJV)
"Rise, let us be going: behold, he is at hand that doth betray me."
Jesus (Today):
Get up, let's go. My betrayer is here.

Matthew 26:50 (KJV)
"Friend, wherefore art thou come?"

Jesus (Today):
Friend, why are you here?

Matthew 26:52 (KJV)
"Put up again thy sword into his place: for all they that take the sword shall perish with the sword."

Jesus (Today):
Put your sword away. If you live by it, you'll die by it.

Matthew 26:53 (KJV)
"Thinkest thou that I cannot now pray to my Father, and he shall presently give me more than twelve legions of angels?"

Jesus (Today):
Don't you think I could call on My Father right now and He'd send more than twelve armies of angels to rescue Me?

Matthew 26:54 (KJV)
"But how then shall the scriptures be fulfilled, that thus it must be?"

Jesus (Today):
But if I did that, how would the Scriptures be fulfilled? This has to happen.

Matthew 26:55 (KJV)
"Are ye come out as against a thief with swords and staves for to take me? I sat daily with you teaching in the temple, and ye laid no hold on me."

Jesus (Today):
Really? You came at Me like I'm a criminal, with swords and

clubs? I was in the temple everyday teaching, and you didn't lay a finger on Me.

Matthew 26:64 (KJV)
"Hereafter shall ye see the Son of man sitting on the right hand of power, and coming in the clouds of heaven."
Jesus (Today):
You said it. But hear Me now, soon you'll see the Son of Man seated in power at the right hand of God, coming in the clouds of heaven.

Matthew 27

Matthew 27:11 (KJV)
"Thou sayest."
Jesus (Today):
That's what you're saying.

Matthew 27:46 (KJV)
"Eli, Eli, lama sabachthani? that is to say, My God, my God, why hast thou forsaken me?"
Jesus (Today):
My God, My God, why have You abandoned Me?

Matthew 28

Matthew 28:9 (KJV)
"All hail."
Jesus (Today):
Rejoice, it's Me.

Matthew 28:10 (KJV)
"Be not afraid: go tell my brethren that they go into Galilee, and there shall they see me."
Jesus (Today):
Don't be afraid. Go tell My brothers to meet Me in Galilee, I'll be waiting for them there.

Matthew 28:18 (KJV)
"All power is given unto me in heaven and in earth."
Jesus (Today):
All power in Heaven and on Earth has been given to Me.

Matthew 28:19-20 (KJV)
"Go ye therefore, and teach all nations, baptizing them in the name of the Father, and of the Son, and of the Holy Ghost: Teaching them to observe all things whatsoever I have commanded you: and, lo, I am with you alway, even unto the end of the world. Amen."
Jesus (Today):
Go. Reach every nation. Invite them to follow Me.
Teach them everything I've shown you. Every word, every truth.
And don't forget this, I am with you. Always.
You'll never walk alone. Not now. Not ever.
Not even at the end of the world. Amen.

Mark

Mark 9:23 (KJV)
"If thou canst believe, all things are possible to him that believeth."
Jesus (Today):
If you believe, even a little, nothing is off limits.
Everything becomes possible.

"Power in Motion"
Jesus moves fast. Every word hits with purpose. This is the gospel of action, authority, and undeniable presence.

Mark 1

Mark 1:15 (KJV)
"The time is fulfilled, and the kingdom of God is at hand: repent ye, and believe the gospel."
Jesus (Today):
This is it. The time is now. God's kingdom is right here, right now. Turn your life around and believe the gospel.

Mark 1:17 (KJV)
"Come ye after me, and I will make you to become fishers of men."
Jesus (Today):
Follow Me, and I'll show you how to reach people like never before.

Mark 1:25 (KJV)
"Hold thy peace, and come out of him."
Jesus (Today):
Be quiet. Come out of him. Now.

Mark 1:38 (KJV)
"Let us go into the next towns, that I may preach there also: for therefore came I forth."
Jesus (Today):
Let's head to the next towns. I have to share this message there too. That's why I came.

Mark 1:41 (KJV)
"I will; be thou clean."

Jesus (Today):
I want to heal you. Be clean.

Mark 1:44 (KJV)
"See thou say nothing to any man: but go thy way, shew thyself to the priest, and offer for thy cleansing those things which Moses commanded, for a testimony unto them."
Jesus (Today):
Don't tell anyone. Just go. Show the priest, and give the offering Moses taught, for proof you're healed.

Mark 2

Mark 2:5 (KJV)
"Son, thy sins be forgiven thee."
Jesus (Today):
Son, your sins are forgiven.

Mark 2:8–9 (KJV)
"Why reason ye these things in your hearts? Whether is it easier to say to the sick of the palsy, Thy sins be forgiven thee; or to say, Arise, and take up thy bed, and walk?"
Jesus (Today):
Why are you arguing about this inside your hearts? What's easier to say: "Your sins are forgiven," or "Get up, grab your mat, and walk"?

Mark 2:10–11 (KJV)
"But that ye may know that the Son of man hath power on earth to forgive sins, (he saith to the sick of the palsy,) I say unto thee, Arise, and take up thy bed, and go thy way into thine house."
Jesus (Today):

But just so you know the Son of Man has authority here on earth to forgive sins, I say to you, get up.
Pick up your mat and go home.

Mark 2:14 (KJV)
"Follow me."
Jesus (Today):
Follow Me.

Mark 2:17 (KJV)
"They that are whole have no need of the physician... I came not to call the righteous, but sinners to repentance."
Jesus (Today):
Healthy people don't need a doctor. Sick people do. I didn't come to call the righteous. I came for sinners.

Mark 2:19 (KJV)
"Can the children of the bridechamber fast, while the bridegroom is with them? as long as they have the bridegroom with them, they cannot fast.
Jesus (Today):
Do wedding guests fast while the groom is still with them? Of course not. As long as the groom's here, they celebrate.

Mark 2:20 (KJV)
"But the days will come, when the bridegroom shall be taken away from them, and then shall they fast in those days."
Jesus (Today):
But the time will come when the groom is taken from them. That's when they'll fast.

Mark 2:21 (KJV)
"No man also seweth a piece of new cloth on an old garment: else the new piece that filled it up taketh away from the old, and the rent is made worse."

Jesus (Today):
You don't patch old clothes with new fabric. The tear just gets worse.

Mark 2:22 (KJV)
"And no man putteth new wine into old bottles: else the new wine doth burst the bottles, and the wine is spilled, and the bottles will be marred: but new wine must be put into new bottles."

Jesus (Today):
You don't pour fresh wine into old bottles. If you do, the bottles will break, the wine will spill, and everything will be ruined. New wine needs a new bottle.

Mark 2:25-26 (KJV)
"Have ye never read what David did, when he had need, and was an hungred, he, and they that were with him? How he went into the house of God in the days of Abiathar the high priest, and did eat the shewbread, which is not lawful to eat but for the priests, and gave also to them which were with him?"

Jesus (Today):
Haven't you ever read what David did when he and his companions were hungry and in need? He went into the house of God during the time of Abiathar the high priest and ate the bread of the Presence, which is lawful only for priests to eat. He even gave some to his companions.

Mark 2:27 (KJV)
"The sabbath was made for man, and not man for the sabbath:"

Jesus (Today):
The Sabbath was made for people, not the other way around.

Mark 2:28 (KJV)
"Therefore the Son of man is Lord also of the sabbath."
Jesus (Today):
That's why I, the Son of Man, am Lord also over the Sabbath.

Mark 3

Mark 3:3 (KJV)
"Stand forth."
Step forward.

Mark 3:4 (KJV)
"Is it lawful to do good on the sabbath days, or to do evil? to save life, or to kill?"
Jesus (Today):
Let Me ask you, on the Sabbath, should we do good or evil? To save a life or to take one?

Mark 3:5 (KJV)
"Stretch forth thine hand."
Jesus (Today):
Stretch out your hand.

Mark 3:23 (KJV)
"How can Satan cast out Satan?"
Jesus (Today):
Come here and listen. How can Satan fight against himself and win?

Mark 3:24-25 (KJV)
"And if a kingdom be divided against itself, that kingdom cannot stand. And if a house be divided against itself, that house cannot stand."

Jesus (Today):
A nation tearing itself apart will collapse.
And if a family turns on each other, it's already falling. Division doesn't win. It destroys.

Mark 3:26-27 (KJV)
"And if Satan rise up against himself, and be divided, he cannot stand, but hath an end. "No man can enter into a strong man's house, and spoil his goods, except he will first bind the strong man; and then he will spoil his house."

Jesus (Today):
If Satan's turning on himself, his kingdom's finished.
You can't just walk into a strong man's house and take what's his, unless you tie him up first. Then you can clear him out.

Mark 3:28-29 (KJV)
"Verily I say unto you, All sins shall be forgiven unto the sons of men, and blasphemies wherewith soever they shall blaspheme: But he that shall blaspheme against the Holy Ghost hath never forgiveness, but is in danger of eternal damnation."

Jesus (Today):
I'm telling you, every sin people commit can be forgiven, even all kinds of blasphemy. But if you mock the Holy Spirit, there's no forgiveness. That sin puts you right in the path of eternal danger.

Mark 3:33-35 (KJV)
"Who is my mother, or my brethren? Behold my mother and my brethren! For whosoever shall do the will of God, the same is my brother, and my sister, and mother."

Jesus (Today):
Who's My family? You want to know who My real people are?

Anyone who does what God asks, that's My brother. My sister. My mother. That's family.

Mark 4

Mark 4:3–9 (KJV)
"Hearken; Behold, there went out a sower to sow: And it came to pass, as he sowed, some fell by the way side, and the fowls of the air came and devoured it up. And some fell on stony ground, where it had not much earth; and immediately it sprang up, because it had no depth of earth: But when the sun was up, it was scorched; and because it had no root, it withered away. And some fell among thorns, and the thorns grew up, and choked it, and it yielded no fruit. And other fell on good ground, and did yield fruit that sprang up and increased; and brought forth, some thirty, and some sixty, and some an hundred. He that hath ears to hear, let him hear."

Jesus (Today):
Listen. A farmer went out to sow his seed. As he scattered it, some fell along the path, and the birds came and ate it up. Some fell on rocky ground, where it didn't have much soil. It sprang up quickly because the soil was shallow. But when the sun came up, the plants were scorched, and since they had no root, they withered away. Other seed fell among thorns, which grew up and choked the plants, so they didn't bear grain. Still other seed fell on good soil. It came up, grew, and produced a crop. Some thirty, some sixty, some a hundred times what was sown. If you have ears to hear, then listen.

Mark 4:11 (KJV)
"Unto you it is given to know the mystery of the kingdom of God: but unto them that are without, all these things are done in parables:

Jesus (Today):
You've been given the gift to understand the secrets of God's Kingdom. But for the others on the outside, I use parables, so they'll have to look deeper.

Mark 4:12 (KJV)
That seeing they may see, and not perceive; and hearing they may hear, and not understand; lest at any time they should be converted, and their sins should be forgiven them."

Jesus (Today)
They look, but they don't really see. They hear, but they don't get it. Because if they truly understood, they'd turn around, and they'd be forgiven.

Mark 4:13 (KJV)
"Know ye not this parable? and how then will ye know all parables?"

Jesus (Today):
You don't understand this story? How are you going to understand any of them?

Mark 4:14 (KJV)
"The sower soweth the word."

Jesus (Today):
The farmer is planting the Word of God.

Mark 4:15 (KJV)
"And these are they by the way side, where the word is sown; but when they have heard, Satan cometh immediately, and taketh away the word that was sown in their hearts."

Jesus (Today):
These are the ones along the path, they hear the Word, but right away, Satan comes and snatches it out of their hearts.

Mark 4:16-17 (KJV)
"And these are they likewise which are sown on stony ground; who, when they have heard the

word, immediately receive it with gladness; And have no root in themselves, and so endure but for a time: afterward, when affliction or persecution ariseth for the word's sake, immediately they are offended."

Jesus (Today):
Others? They're like rocky soil. They get excited at first, fired up, emotional. But the roots never go deep. The moment life punches back, when trials hit, when faith costs something, they fall away. They were in, until it got difficult.

Mark 4:18-19 (KJV)
"And these are they which are sown among thorns; such as hear the word, And the cares of this world, and the deceitfulness of riches, and the lusts of other things entering in, choke the word, and it becometh unfruitful."

Jesus (Today):
Others hear it, but they're surrounded by distractions. Money lies, constant craving, and stress from trying to keep up with the world. That noise chokes out the truth. So nothing grows.

Mark 4:20 (KJV)
"And these are they which are sown on good ground; such as hear the word, and receive it, and bring forth fruit, some thirtyfold, some sixty, and some an hundred."

Jesus (Today):
But the ones with good soil? They hear it, they take it seriously, and they live it out. And the return? It multiplies thirty, sixty, a hundred times over.

Mark 4:21 (KJV)
"And he said unto them, Is a candle brought to be put under a bushel, or under a bed? and not to be set on a candlestick?"

Jesus (Today):
You don't light a lamp to hide it under a basket or a bed.
You put it up high, where it can shine.

Mark 4:22 (KJV)
"For there is nothing hid, which shall not be manifested; neither was any thing kept secret, but that it should come abroad."

Jesus (Today):
Anything hidden will come to light. Secrets won't stay secret. It's all going to be revealed.

Mark 4:23 (KJV)
"If any man have ears to hear, let him hear."

Jesus (Today):
If you've got ears, use them. Really listen.

Mark 4:24 (KJV)
"And he said unto them, Take heed what ye hear: with what measure ye mete, it shall be measured to you: and unto you that hear shall more be given."

Jesus (Today):
Pay attention to what you're listening to. The measure you use for others is the one that'll be used for you. If you truly listen, you'll be given even more.

Mark 4:25 (KJV)
"For he that hath, to him shall be given: and he that hath not... shall be taken even that which he hath."

Jesus (Today):
If you're holding on to truth, more will be given. But if you're careless with what you've got, even that will be taken away.

Mark 4:26–29 (KJV)
"So is the kingdom of God, as if a man should cast seed into the ground; And should sleep, and rise night and day, and the seed should spring and grow up, he knoweth not

how. For the earth bringeth forth fruit of herself; first the blade, then the ear, after that the full corn in the ear. But when the fruit is brought forth, immediately he putteth in the sickle, because the harvest is come."

Jesus (Today)

This is what the kingdom of God is like. A man scatters seed on the ground. Night and day, whether he sleeps or gets up, the seed sprouts and grows, though he does not know how. The soil produces grain by itself: first the stalk, then the head, then the full kernel in the head. As soon as the grain is ripe, he puts in the sickle because the harvest has come.

Mark 4:30–32 (KJV)

"Whereunto shall we liken the kingdom of God? or with what comparison shall we compare it? It is like a grain of mustard seed, which, when it is sown in the earth, is less than all the seeds that be in the earth: But when it is sown, it groweth up, and becometh greater than all herbs, and shooteth out great branches; so that the fowls of the air may lodge under the shadow of it."

Jesus (Today)

What can I compare the Kingdom of God to? What picture will help you understand? It's like a mustard seed. One of the tiniest seeds you can plant. But when it hits the soil, it grows. And not just a little. It becomes bigger than every other plant in the garden. It stretches out its branches so wide that birds come and make their home in its shade.

Mark 4:35 (KJV)

"Let us pass over unto the other side."

Jesus (Today):

Let's cross to the other side.

Mark 4:39 (KJV)

"Peace, be still."

Jesus (Today):

Peace. Be still.

Mark 4:40 (KJV)
"Why are ye so fearful? how is it that ye have no faith?"
Jesus (Today):
Why are you so afraid? Do you still have no faith?

Mark 5

Mark 5:8 (KJV)
"Come out of the man, thou unclean spirit."
Jesus (Today):
Come out of him. Now. You unclean spirit.

Mark 5:9 (KJV)
"What is thy name?"
Jesus (Today):
What's your name?

Mark 5:19 (KJV)
"Go home to thy friends, and tell them how great things the Lord hath done for thee, and hath had compassion on thee."
Jesus (Today):
Go home. Tell your people what God did for you, how He showed up with mercy.

Mark 5:30 (KJV)
"Who touched my clothes?"
Jesus (Today):
Who just touched Me?

Mark 5:34 (KJV)
"Daughter, thy faith hath made thee whole; go in peace, and be whole of thy plague."
Jesus (Today):
Daughter, your faith healed you. Go in peace. You're free from your suffering.

Mark 5:36 (KJV)
"Be not afraid, only believe."
Jesus (Today):
Don't be afraid. Just believe.

Mark 5:39 (KJV)
"Why make ye this ado, and weep? the damsel is not dead, but sleepeth."
Jesus (Today):
Why all the crying and chaos? She's not dead. She's just sleeping.

Mark 5:41 (KJV)
"Damsel, I say unto thee, arise."
Jesus (Today):
Little girl, get up.

Mark 6

Mark 6:4 (KJV)
"A prophet is not without honour, but in his own country, and among his own kin, and in his own house."
Jesus (Today):

A prophet gets respect, just not in his hometown, around his own family, or in his own house.

Mark 6:10 (KJV)
"In what place soever ye enter into an house, there abide till ye depart from that place."
Jesus (Today):
When you're welcomed into a home, stay there until you leave that town.

Mark 6:11 (KJV)
"And whosoever shall not receive you, nor hear you, when ye depart thence, shake off the dust under your feet for a testimony against them. Verily I say unto you, It shall be more tolerable for Sodom and Gomorrha in the day of judgment, than for that city."
Jesus (Today):
If people won't welcome you or listen, shake the dust off your feet when you leave. Let that be your message to them.

Mark 6:31 (KJV)
"Come ye yourselves apart into a desert place, and rest a while."
Jesus (Today):
Come with Me to a quiet place. You need to rest.

Mark 6:37 (KJV)
"Give ye them to eat."
Jesus (Today):
You give them something to eat.

Mark 6:38 (KJV)
"How many loaves have ye? go and see."

Jesus (Today):
How many loaves do we have? Go check.

Mark 6:50 (KJV)
"Be of good cheer: it is I; be not afraid."
Jesus (Today):
Take heart. It's Me. Don't be afraid.

Mark 7

Mark 7:6–7 (KJV)
"Well hath Esaias prophesied of you hypocrites, as it is written, This people honoureth me with their lips, but their heart is far from me. Howbeit in vain do they worship me, teaching for doctrines the commandments of men."
Jesus (Today):
You talk like you honor Me, but your heart is nowhere near Me. Your worship is pointless when all you teach are man-made rules and call them divine.

Mark 7:8 (KJV)
"For laying aside the commandment of God, ye hold the tradition of men, as the washing of pots and cups: and many other such like things ye do."
Jesus (Today):
You throw out God's commands just to hang on to your own traditions.

Mark 7:9 (KJV)
"Full well ye reject the commandment of God, that ye may keep your own tradition."
Jesus (Today):
You've flat-out rejected God's command so you can hold on to

your own traditions.

Mark 7:10 (KJV)
"For Moses said, Honour thy father and thy mother; and, Whoso curseth father or mother, let him die the death:"

Jesus (Today):
Moses said, "Honor your father and mother," and, "Anyone who curses them should be put to death."

Mark 7:11 (KJV)
"But ye say, If a man shall say to his father or mother, It is Corban, that is to say, a gift, by whatsoever thou mightest be profited by me; he shall be free."

Jesus (Today):
But you say, "If I tell my parents, What I would've given you is now a gift to God," then I don't owe them anything.

Mark 7:12 (KJV)
"And ye suffer him no more to do ought for his father or his mother;"

Jesus (Today):
You won't let people help their own parents after that.

Mark 7:13 (KJV)
"Making the word of God of none effect through your tradition, which ye have delivered: and many such like things do ye."

Jesus (Today):
You cancel out God's word just to protect your traditions. And that's just one of many things you twist.

Mark 7:14 (KJV)
"Hearken unto me every one of you, and understand:"

Jesus (Today):
Everybody, listen to Me and try to understand what I'm saying.

Mark 7:15 (KJV)
There is nothing from without a man, that entering into him can defile him: but the things which come out of him, those are they that defile the man."

Jesus (Today):
It's not what goes into a person that makes them unclean. It's what comes out of them that does.

Mark 7:16 (KJV)
"If any man have ears to hear, let him hear."

Jesus (Today):
If you've got ears, use them. Really listen.

Mark 7:18 (KJV)
"Are ye so without understanding also? Do ye not perceive, that whatsoever thing from without entereth into the man, it cannot defile him;"

Jesus (Today):
Are you still not getting it? Don't you see? What goes into your body from outside doesn't make you unclean.

Mark 7:19 (KJV)
Because it entereth not into his heart, but into the belly, and goeth out into the draught, purging all meats?"

Jesus (Today):
It doesn't touch your heart, it goes into your stomach, then out of your body. That's just food.

Mark 7:20-23 (KJV)
"That which cometh out of the man, that defileth the man .For from within, out of the heart of men, proceed evil thoughts, adulteries, fornications, murders, Thefts, covetousness, wickedness, deceit, lasciviousness, an evil eye, blasphemy, pride, foolishness:
All these evil things come from within, and defile the man."

Jesus (Today):
What comes out of a person is what makes them unclean. From within, out of the human heart, come evil thoughts, sexual immorality, theft, murder, adultery, greed, wickedness, deceit, lust, envy, slander, pride, and foolishness. All these evils come from within, and they make a person unclean.

Mark 7:27 (KJV)
"Let the children first be filled: for it is not meet to take the children's bread, and to cast it unto the dogs."

Jesus (Today):
Let the kids at the table eat first. It wouldn't be right to take their food and throw it to the dogs.

Mark 7:29 (KJV)
"For this saying go thy way; the devil is gone out of thy daughter."

Jesus (Today):
Because you answered like that?
Go, your daughter is free.

Mark 8

Mark 8:2 (KJV)
"I have compassion on the multitude, because they have now been with me three days, and have nothing to eat:"
Jesus (Today):
My heart breaks for these people. They've stuck with Me for three days, and now they've got nothing left to eat.

Mark 8:3 (KJV)
And if I send them away fasting to their own houses, they will faint by the way: for divers of them came from far."
Jesus (Today):
If I send them home hungry, some of them will collapse before they make it. A lot of them came a long way just to be here.

Mark 8:5 (KJV)
"How many loaves have ye?"
Jesus (Today):
How many loaves of bread do we have?

Mark 8:12 (KJV)
"Why doth this generation seek after a sign? verily I say unto you, There shall no sign be given unto this generation."
Jesus (Today):
Why is this generation always asking for a sign? I'm telling you, no sign will be given to them.

Mark 8:15 (KJV)
"Take heed, beware of the leaven of the Pharisees, and of the leaven of Herod."
Jesus (Today):
Listen carefully, watch out for the influence of the Pharisees.

That mindset spreads like yeast and poisons everything. Their influence is dangerous.

Mark 8:17 (KJV)
"Why reason ye, because ye have no bread? perceive ye not yet, neither understand? have ye your heart yet hardened?"

Jesus (Today):
Why are you talking about bread?
Do you still not get it?
Is your heart still shut down?

Mark 8:18 (KJV)
"Having eyes, see ye not? and having ears, hear ye not? and do ye not remember?"

Jesus (Today):
You've got eyes, can't you see?
You've got ears, can't you hear?
And you still don't remember?

Mark 8:19 (KJV)
"When I brake the five loaves among five thousand, how many baskets full of fragments took ye up?"

Jesus (Today):
When I broke the five loaves for the five thousand, how many baskets of leftovers did you collect?

Mark 8:20 (KJV)
"And when the seven among four thousand, how many baskets full of fragments took ye up? And they said, Seven."

Jesus (Today):
And when I broke the seven loaves for the four thousand, how many baskets were left over then?

Mark 8:21 (KJV)
"How is it that ye do not understand?"
Jesus (Today):
How do you still not get it?

Mark 8:26 (KJV)
"Neither go into the town, nor tell it to any in the town."
Jesus (Today):
Go straight home. Don't go into the village or talk to anyone there about this.

Mark 8:27 (KJV)
"Whom do men say that I am?"
Jesus (Today):
Who do people say I am?

Mark 8:29 (KJV)
"But whom say ye that I am?"
Jesus (Today):
But what about you? Who do *you* say I am?

Mark 8:30 (KJV)
"And he charged them that they should tell no man of him."
Jesus (Today):
Don't tell anyone about Me yet.

Mark 8:31 (KJV)
"The Son of man must suffer many things, and be rejected of the elders, and of the chief priests, and scribes, and be killed, and after three days rise again."

Jesus (Today):
The Son of Man is going to suffer. The elders, chief priests, and religious experts of the law will reject Him. He'll be killed. But after three days, He'll rise again.

Mark 8:33 (KJV)
"Get thee behind me, Satan: for thou savourest not the things that be of God, but the things that be of men."

Jesus (Today):
Get behind Me, Satan. You're focused on human stuff, not God's purpose.

Mark 8:34 (KJV)
"Whosoever will come after me, let him deny himself, and take up his cross, and follow me."

Jesus (Today):
If you want to follow Me, let go of yourself, pick up your cross, and come with Me.

Mark 8:35 (KJV)
"For whosoever will save his life shall lose it; but whosoever shall lose his life for my sake... shall save it."

Jesus (Today):
If you're trying to save your own life, you'll lose it. But if you give up your life for Me and the message I bring, that's how you'll find true life.

Mark 8:36 (KJV)
"For what shall it profit a man, if he shall gain the whole world, and lose his own soul?"

Jesus (Today):

What good is it to win the whole world, if you lose your soul doing it?

Mark 8:37 (KJV)
"Or what shall a man give in exchange for his soul?"
Jesus (Today):
What could you possibly trade that's worth your soul?

Mark 8:38 (KJV)
"Whosoever therefore shall be ashamed of me and of my words in this adulterous and sinful generation; of him also shall the Son of man be ashamed, when he cometh in the glory of his Father with the holy angels."
Jesus (Today):
If you're ashamed of Me and what I say in this corrupt, unfaithful generation, then I'll be ashamed of you when I return with the glory of My Father and the angels with Me.

Mark 9

Mark 9:1 (KJV)
"Verily I say unto you, That there be some of them that stand here, which shall not taste of death, till they have seen the kingdom of God come with power."
Jesus (Today):
Listen to Me. Some of you standing here right now won't die before you see the Kingdom of God show up in full power.

Mark 9:12 (KJV)
"Elias verily cometh first, and restoreth all things; and how it is written of the Son of man, that he must suffer many things, and be set at nought.

Jesus (Today):
Elijah does come first to set everything right. And just like it's written, the Son of Man has to suffer deeply and be rejected.

Mark 9:13 (KJV)
But I say unto you, That Elias is indeed come, and they have done unto him whatsoever they listed, as it is written of him."

Jesus (Today):
But I'm telling you the truth, Elijah already came, and they did whatever they wanted to him, just like the scriptures said they would.

Mark 9:19 (KJV)
"O faithless generation, how long shall I be with you? how long shall I suffer you? bring him unto me."

Jesus (Today):
You faithless generation, how much longer do I have to be with you? How long do I have to put up with this? Bring the boy to Me.

Mark 9:21 (KJV)
"How long is it ago since this came unto him?"

Jesus (Today):
How long has he been like this?

Mark 9:23 (KJV)
"If thou canst believe, all things are possible to him that believeth."

Jesus (Today):
If you believe, even a little, nothing is off limits. Everything becomes possible.

Mark 9:25 (KJV)
"Thou dumb and deaf spirit, I charge thee, come out of him, and enter no more into him."
Jesus (Today):
You spirit that makes him deaf and mute, I'm commanding you: get out of him and never come back.

Mark 9:29 (KJV)
"This kind can come forth by nothing, but by prayer and fasting."
Jesus (Today):
This kind only comes out through prayer and fasting.

Mark 9:31 (KJV)
"The Son of man is delivered into the hands of men, and they shall kill him; and after that he is killed, he shall rise the third day."
Jesus (Today):
The Son of Man is going to be handed over and killed. But after He's killed, He'll rise again on the third day.

Mark 9:33 (KJV)
"What was it that ye disputed among yourselves by the way?"
Jesus (Today):
What were you all arguing about on the way here?

Mark 9:35 (KJV)
"If any man desire to be first, the same shall be last of all, and servant of all."
Jesus (Today):

You want to be first?
Then be last. Be the one who serves everybody else.

Mark 9:37 (KJV)
"Whosoever shall receive one of such children in my name, receiveth me: and whosoever shall receive me, receiveth not me, but him that sent me."
Jesus (Today):
If you welcome a child in My name, you're welcoming *Me*. And when you welcome Me? You're really welcoming the One who sent Me.

Mark 9:39–40 (KJV)
"Forbid him not: for there is no man which shall do a miracle in my name, that can lightly speak evil of me. For he that is not against us is on our part."
Jesus (Today):
If someone does a miracle in My name, they're not about to speak evil of Me. If they're not against us, they're *for* us.

Mark 9:41 (KJV)
"For whosoever shall give you a cup of water to drink in my name, because ye belong to Christ, verily I say unto you, he shall not lose his reward."
Jesus (Today):
Even if someone just gives you a cup of water because you belong to Me, I promise you this; they won't miss their reward.

Mark 9:42 (KJV)
"And whosoever shall offend one of these little ones that believe in me, it is better for him that a millstone were hanged about his neck, and he were cast into the sea."
Jesus (Today):
If you lead even one child who trusts in Me down the wrong path, you'd be better off tied to a block of concrete and thrown into the sea.

Mark 9:43 (KJV)
"And if thy hand offend thee, cut it off: it is better for thee to enter into life maimed, than having two hands to go into hell, into the fire that never shall be quenched:"
Jesus (Today):
If your hand is causing you to sin, cut it out of your life. It's better to step into eternal life missing something than to be fully whole and thrown into the fire that never ends.

Mark 9:45 (KJV)
"And if thy foot offend thee, cut it off: it is better for thee to enter halt into life, than having two feet to be cast into hell, into the fire that never shall be quenched:"
Jesus (Today):
If your feet are taking you places you shouldn't go, stop. Whatever it costs you, it's worth it to walk into life with God than to run straight into hell.

Mark 9:47 (KJV)
"And if thine eye offend thee, pluck it out: it is better for thee to enter into the kingdom of God with one eye, than having two eyes to be cast into hell fire:"
Jesus (Today):
If your eye is pulling you into sin, get rid of what's feeding it. It's better to step into the Kingdom of God with blurred vision than to have perfect sight and end up in hell.

Mark 9:48 (KJV)
"Where their worm dieth not, and the fire is not quenched."
Jesus (Today):
Because there, the torment never stops, and the fire never dies.

Mark 9:49 (KJV):
"For every one shall be salted with fire, and every sacrifice shall be salted with salt."
Jesus (Today):
Everyone's going to be tested by fire. Every sacrifice must be purified.

Mark 9:50 (KJV)
"Salt is good: but if the salt have lost his saltness, wherewith will ye season it? Have salt in yourselves, and have peace one with another."
Jesus (Today):
Keep salt in your life. But if it stops tasting like salt, what good is it? Let your life still carry flavor, truth, and purpose. Have peace with another.

Mark 10

Mark 10:3-5 (KJV)
"What did Moses command you? For the hardness of your heart he wrote you this precept."
Jesus (Today):
What did Moses actually tell you to do?
Yes, he let you write divorce papers and send your wives away, but that was only because your hearts were hard.

Mark 10:6-9 (KJV):
"But from the beginning of the creation God made them male and female. For this cause shall a man leave his father and mother, and cleave to his wife; And they twain shall be one flesh: so then they are no more twain, but one flesh. What therefore God hath joined together, let not man put asunder."
Jesus (Today):
From the very beginning, God made humans male and female. That's why a man leaves his parents and becomes one with his

wife. They're no longer two, but one.
So if God brought them together, no one should tear them apart.

Mark 10:11-12 (KJV):

"Whosoever shall put away his wife, and marry another, committeth adultery against her. And if a woman shall put away her husband, and be married to another, she committeth adultery."

Jesus (2025):

If a man divorces his wife and marries someone else, he's committing adultery against her. Same goes for a woman who divorces her husband and remarries.

Mark 10:14-15 (KJV):

"Suffer the little children to come unto me, and forbid them not: for of such is the kingdom of God. Verily I say unto you, Whosoever shall not receive the kingdom of God as a little child, he shall not enter therein."

Jesus (2025):

Let the children come to Me. Don't block them. The kingdom of God belongs to hearts like theirs. I'm telling you the truth, if you don't receive God's kingdom like a child, you won't enter it at all.

Mark 10:18 (KJV)

"Why callest thou me good? there is none good but one, that is, God."

Jesus (Today):

Why do you call Me good?
Only One is truly good, and that's God.

Mark 10:19 (KJV)

Thou knowest the commandments, Do not commit adultery, Do not kill, Do not steal, Do not bear false witness, Defraud not, Honour thy father and mother."

Jesus (Today):

You know the commandments: don't cheat, don't kill,

don't steal, don't lie, don't take advantage of others, and honor your parents.

Mark 10:21 (KJV)
"One thing thou lackest: go thy way, sell whatsoever thou hast, and give to the poor, and thou shalt have treasure in heaven: and come, take up the cross, and follow me."

Jesus (Today):
You're close, but one thing's holding you back.
Go. Sell what you've got. Give it to the poor.
You'll have treasure waiting in Heaven. Then come, carry your cross, and follow Me.

Mark 10:23 (KJV)
"How hardly shall they that have riches enter into the kingdom of God!"

Jesus (Today):
How hard it is for those who have riches to enter the kingdom of God.

Mark 10:24–25 (KJV)
"Children, how hard is it for them that trust in riches to enter into the kingdom of God! It is easier for a camel to go through the eye of a needle, than for a rich man to enter into the kingdom of God."

Jesus (Today):
Children, it's nearly impossible for those who trust in wealth to enter God's kingdom. It's easier for a camel to squeeze through the eye of a needle than for a rich man to walk into the kingdom of heaven.

Mark 10:27 (KJV)
"With men it is impossible, but not with God: for with God all things are possible."

Jesus (Today):

On your own, it's impossible. But not with God. With God, anything is possible.

Mark 10:29-30 (KJV)
"Verily I say unto you, There is no man that hath left house, or brethren, or sisters, or father, or mother, or wife, or children, or lands, for my sake, and the gospel's, But he shall receive an hundredfold now in this time, houses, and brethren, and sisters, and mothers, and children, and lands, with persecutions; and in the world to come eternal life."

Jesus (Today):
Anyone who's left behind home, family, or land for Me and this message will be given a hundred times more in this life, homes, family, land, plus persecution.
And in the life to come, eternal life.

Mark 10:31 (KJV)
"But many that are first shall be last; and the last first."

Jesus (Today):
The ones who are first now? They'll be last.
And the ones who are last? They're going to the front.

Mark 10:33-34 (KJV)
"Behold, we go up to Jerusalem; and the Son of man shall be delivered unto the chief priests, and unto the scribes; and they shall condemn him to death, and shall deliver him to the Gentiles: And they shall mock him, and shall scourge him, and shall spit upon him, and shall kill him: and the third day he shall rise again."

Jesus (Today):
We're heading to Jerusalem.
The Son of Man will be handed over to the chief priests and scholars. They'll sentence Him to death, hand Him to outsiders, mock Him, beat Him, spit on Him, and kill Him.
But on the third day, He will rise.

Mark 10:36 (KJV):
"What would ye that I should do for you?"

Jesus (Today):
What do you want Me to do for you?

Mark 10:38-39 (KJV)
"Ye know not what ye ask: can ye drink of the cup that I drink of? and be baptized with the baptism that I am baptized with? Ye shall indeed drink of the cup that I drink of; and with the baptism that I am baptized withal shall ye be baptized:"

Jesus (Today):
You have no idea what you're asking. Can you handle the cup I'm about to drink? Can you go through what I'm about to go through? You will drink from My cup. You'll go through what I go through.

Mark 10:40 (KJV):
"But to sit on my right hand and on my left hand is not mine to give; but it shall be given to them for whom it is prepared."

Jesus (2025):
But sitting at My right or left hand isn't Mine to give.
That spot is reserved for those it's been prepared for.

Mark 10:42-44 (KJV):
"Ye know that they which are accounted to rule over the Gentiles exercise lordship over them; and their great ones exercise authority upon them. But so shall it not be among you: but whosoever will be great among you, shall be your minister: And whosoever of you will be the chiefest, shall be servant of all."

Jesus (2025):
You know that those who are considered rulers among the nations use their power to dominate, and their high officials make their authority felt. But it must not be that way among you. Whoever wants to become great among you must be your servant, and whoever wants to be first must be the servant of everyone else.

Mark 10:45 (KJV):
"For even the Son of man came not to be ministered unto, but to minister, and to give his life a ransom for many."
Jesus (2025):
Even the Son of Man didn't come to be served. He came to serve and give His life to save many.

Mark 10:51 (KJV):
"What wilt thou that I should do unto thee?"
Jesus (2025):
What do you want Me to do for you?

Mark 10:52 (KJV):
"Go thy way; thy faith hath made thee whole."
Jesus (2025):
Go. Your faith has healed you.

Mark 11

Mark 11:2–3 (KJV)
"Go your way into the village over against you: and as soon as ye be entered into it, ye shall find a colt tied, whereon never man sat; loose him, and bring him.
And if any man say unto you, Why do ye this? say ye that the Lord hath need of him; and straightway he will send him hither."
Jesus (Today):
Go into the village ahead of you. As soon as you get there, you'll find a young donkey tied up that no one's ever ridden.

Untie it and bring it here. If anyone asks why, just say, "The Lord needs it," and they'll let it go.

Mark 11:14 (KJV):
"No man eat fruit of thee hereafter for ever."
Jesus (Today):
No one will ever eat fruit from you again.

Mark 11:17 (KJV)
"Is it not written, My house shall be called of all nations the house of prayer? but ye have made it a den of thieves."
Jesus (Today):
Doesn't scripture say, "My house will be called a house of prayer for all nations"? But you've turned it into a den of thieves.

Mark 11:22-23 (KJV):
"Have faith in God. For verily I say unto you, That whosoever shall say unto this mountain, Be thou removed, and be thou cast into the sea; and shall not doubt in his heart, but shall believe that those things which he saith shall come to pass; he shall have whatsoever he saith."

Have faith in God. If anyone says to this mountain, "Move and throw yourself into the sea," and doesn't doubt but truly believes it will happen, it will be done.

Mark 11:24 (KJV)
"Therefore I say unto you, What things soever ye desire, when ye pray, believe that ye receive them, and ye shall have them."
Jesus (Today):
When you pray, believe you've already received it, and it's yours.

Mark 11:25–26 (KJV):

"And when ye stand praying, forgive, if ye have ought against any: that your Father also which is in heaven may forgive you your trespasses. But if ye do not forgive, neither will your Father which is in heaven forgive your trespasses."

Jesus (Today):

And when you're praying, forgive anyone you're holding something against, so your Father in heaven will forgive you too. But if you won't forgive others, your Father won't forgive you either.

Mark 11:29–30 (KJV)

"I will also ask of you one question, and answer me, and I will tell you by what authority I do these things. The baptism of John, was it from heaven, or of men? answer me."

Jesus (Today):

I'll ask you one question. Answer me, and I'll tell you by what authority I do these things. John's baptism; was it from heaven or from people? Tell me.

Mark 12

Mark 12:1–9 (KJV)

*"A certain man planted a vineyard, and set an hedge about it, and digged a place for the winefat, and built a tower, and let it out to husbandmen, and went into a far country.
And at the season he sent to the husbandmen a servant, that he might receive from the husbandmen of the fruit of the vineyard. And they caught him, and beat him, and sent him away empty. And again he sent unto them another servant; and at him they cast stones, and wounded him in the head, and sent him away shamefully handled. And again he sent another; and him they killed, and many others; beating some, and killing some. Having yet therefore one son, his wellbeloved, he sent him also last unto them, saying, They will reverence my son. But those husbandmen said among themselves, This is the heir; come, let us kill him, and the inheritance shall be ours. And they took him, and killed him, and cast him out of the vineyard. What shall therefore the lord of the vineyard do? he will come and destroy the husbandmen, and will give the vineyard unto others."*

Jesus (Today):

A man planted a vineyard. He put a wall around it, dug a pit for the winepress, and built a watchtower. Then he rented it to some farmers and went on a journey. At harvest time he sent a servant to the tenants to collect from them some of the fruit of the vineyard. But they seized him, beat him, and sent him away empty-handed. Then he sent another servant to them. They struck this man on the head and treated him shamefully. He sent another, and that one they killed. He sent many others, some they beat, and others they killed.

He still had one left to send, his beloved son. Last of all he sent him, saying, They will respect my son. But the tenants said to each other, This is the heir. Come, let's kill him, and the inheritance will be ours. So they took him and killed him, and threw him out of the vineyard.

What then will the owner of the vineyard do? He will come and kill those tenants and give the vineyard to others.

Mark 12:10-11 (KJV):
"And have ye not read this scripture; The stone which the builders rejected is become the head of the corner: This was the Lord's doing, and it is marvellous in our eyes?"

Jesus (Today):
Haven't you read this?
The stone the builders rejected became the cornerstone.
God did it and it's powerful and undeniable.

Mark 12:15 (KJV)
"Why tempt ye me? bring me a penny, that I may see it."

Jesus (Today):
Why are you trying to trap me? Bring me a coin so I can look at it.

Mark 12:16 (KJV)
"Whose is this image and superscription?"
Jesus (Today):
Whose image and name are on this?

Mark 12:17 (KJV)
"Render to Caesar the things that are Caesar's, and to God the things that are God's."
Jesus (Today):
Give Caesar what belongs to him.
But give God what's His.

Mark 12:24 (KJV)
"Do ye not therefore err, because ye know not the scriptures, neither the power of God?"
Jesus (Today):
You're wrong, because you don't know the scriptures,
and you don't know God's power.

Mark 12:25 (KJV)
"For when they shall rise from the dead, they neither marry, nor are given in marriage; but are as the angels which are in heaven."
Jesus (Today):
When people rise from the dead, they won't marry or be given in marriage. They will be like the angels in heaven.

Mark 12:26-27 (KJV)
"And as touching the dead, that they rise: have ye not read in the book of Moses, how in the bush God spake unto him, saying, I am the God of Abraham, and the God of Isaac, and the God of Jacob? He is not the God of the dead, but the God of the living: ye therefore do greatly err."
Jesus (Today):
As for the dead being raised, haven't you read in the book of Moses, in the account of the burning bush, how God said to him,

I am the God of Abraham, the God of Isaac, and the God of Jacob? He is not the God of the dead but of the living. You are badly mistaken.

Mark 12:29-31 (KJV)
"The first of all the commandments is, Hear, O Israel; The Lord our God is one Lord: And thou shalt love the Lord thy God with all thy heart, and with all thy soul, and with all thy mind, and with all thy strength: this is the first commandment. And the second is like, namely this, Thou shalt love thy neighbour as thyself. There is none other commandment greater than these."

Jesus (Today):
Here's the greatest command: Love God with all your heart, all your soul, all your mind, and all your strength.
And the second one? Love your neighbor like you love yourself. Nothing matters more than these.

Mark 12:34 (KJV):
"Thou art not far from the kingdom of God."

Jesus (Today):
You're closer to God's kingdom than you think.

Mark 12:35-37 (KJV):
"How say the scribes that Christ is the Son of David? For David himself said by the Holy Ghost, The Lord said to my Lord, Sit thou on my right hand, till I make thine enemies thy footstool. David therefore himself calleth him Lord; and whence is he then his son?"

Jesus (Today):
Why do the teachers say the Messiah is just David's son? David himself, led by the Spirit, said: "The Lord said to my Lord, sit at My right hand until I put Your enemies under Your feet." So if David calls Him "Lord," how can He just be his son?

Mark 12:38–40 (KJV):
"Beware of the scribes, which love to go in long clothing, and love salutations in the marketplaces, And the chief seats in the synagogues, and the uppermost rooms at feasts:
Which devour widows' houses, and for a pretence make long prayers: these shall receive greater damnation."

Jesus (Today):
Watch out for the religious show-offs. They love wearing fancy clothes, getting praised in public, sitting in the best seats at church, and being treated like royalty at events.
But behind the scenes, they exploit widows and hide it with long-winded prayers. They'll be judged more severely for it.

Mark 12:43–44 (KJV):
"Verily I say unto you, That this poor widow hath cast more in, than all they which have cast into the treasury: For all they did cast in of their abundance; but she of her want did cast in all that she had, even all her living."

Did you see that? This poor widow gave more than all the others combined. They gave from their leftovers. She gave everything she had. Her whole life.

Mark 13

Mark 13:2 (KJV)
"Seest thou these great buildings? there shall not be left one stone upon another, that shall not be thrown down."

Jesus (Today):
You see all these great buildings? Not one stone will be left standing. Every single one will be torn down.

Mark 13:5-6 (KJV)
"Take heed lest any man deceive you: For many shall come in my name, saying, I am Christ; and shall deceive many."

Jesus (Today):
Stay alert so no one misleads you. Plenty will come using My name, claiming to represent Me, or even be Me, and they'll fool a lot of people.

Mark 13:7-8 (KJV)
"And when ye shall hear of wars and rumours of wars, be ye not troubled: for such things must needs be; but the end shall not be yet. For nation shall rise against nation, and kingdom against kingdom: and there shall be earthquakes in divers places, and there shall be famines and troubles: these are the beginnings of sorrows."

Jesus (Today):
When you hear about wars and rumors of war, don't panic. This has to happen first. Nations will rise against nations, disasters will strike, and hunger will spread. There'll be earthquakes and disasters everywhere. Famines. Chaos. But this is just the beginning.

Mark 13:9-11 (KJV):
"But take heed to yourselves: for they shall deliver you up to councils; and in the synagogues ye shall be beaten: and ye shall be brought before rulers and kings for my sake, for a testimony against them. But when they shall lead you, and deliver you up, take no thought beforehand what ye shall speak, neither do ye premeditate: but whatsoever shall be given you in that hour, that speak ye: for it is not ye that speak, but the Holy Ghost."

Jesus (Today):
Be ready. They'll arrest you, drag you into court, beat you in places of worship, and put you in front of powerful people because of Me. That's your moment to speak truth.
But this message has to reach every nation first.
And when they take you in, don't panic about what to say. Say whatever God gives you in that moment, it won't even be you talking. It'll be the Holy Spirit speaking through you.

Mark 13:12-13 (KJV):
"Now the brother shall betray the brother to death, and the father the son; and children shall rise

up against their parents, and shall cause them to be put to death.
And ye shall be hated of all men for my name's sake: but he that shall endure unto the end, the same shall be saved. But when ye shall see the abomination of desolation, spoken of by Daniel the prophet, standing where it ought not, (let him that readeth understand,) then let them that be in Judaea flee to the mountains: And let him that is on the housetop not go down into the house, neither enter therein, to take any thing out of his house:
And let him that is in the field not turn back again for to take up his garment."

Jesus (Today):
Family will turn on family; brothers, sons, even kids will betray their parents to death.
And you'll be hated by everyone because you follow Me.
But if you hold on till the end, you'll be saved.

Mark 13:14–16 (KJV):
"But when ye shall see the abomination of desolation, spoken of by Daniel the prophet, standing where it ought not, (let him that readeth understand,) then let them that be in Judaea flee to the mountains. And let him that is on the housetop not go down into the house, neither enter therein, to take any thing out of his house. And let him that is in the field not turn back again for to take up his garment."

Jesus (Today):
When you see the desecration Daniel warned about standing where it has no business being, pay attention:
if you're in Judea, run for the mountains.
If you're on the roof, don't go back inside for anything.
If you're in the field, don't turn around to grab your coat. Just go.

Mark 13:17–18 (KJV):
"But woe to them that are with child, and to them that give suck in those days! And pray ye that your flight be not in the winter."

Jesus (Today):
It's going to be especially hard for pregnant women and nursing mothers in those days. Pray it doesn't happen in winter.

Mark 13:19–20 (KJV):
"For in those days shall be affliction, such as was not from the beginning of the creation which

God created unto this time, neither shall be. And except that the Lord had shortened those days, no flesh should be saved: but for the elect's sake, whom he hath chosen, he hath shortened the days."

Jesus (Today):
Those days will be filled with suffering worse than anything the world has ever seen. Nothing like it since creation.
If God didn't shorten it, no one would survive.
But for the sake of the ones He's chosen, He cut the time short.

Mark 13:21–23 (KJV):
"And then if any man shall say to you, Lo, here is Christ; or, lo, he is there; believe him not: For false Christs and false prophets shall rise, and shall shew signs and wonders, to seduce, if it were possible, even the elect. But take ye heed: behold, I have foretold you all things."

Jesus (Today):
So if someone tells you, "Look! There's the Messiah!" or "There He is!" don't believe them.
Fake messiahs and false prophets will show up doing signs and wonders trying to fool even God's chosen.
Stay sharp. I've told you everything ahead of time.

Mark 13:24–25 (KJV):
"But in those days, after that tribulation, the sun shall be darkened, and the moon shall not give her light, And the stars of heaven shall fall, and the powers that are in heaven shall be shaken."

Jesus (Today):
But after all that chaos, the sun will go dark. The moon won't shine. Stars will fall, and the heavens themselves will tremble.

Mark 13:26-27 (KJV)
"And then shall they see the Son of man coming in the clouds with great power and glory. And then shall he send his angels, and shall gather together his elect from the four winds, from the uttermost part of the earth to the uttermost part of heaven."

Jesus (Today):
Then the whole world will see *Me*.

Coming through the clouds, radiant with unstoppable power and glory that shakes heaven and earth.
And I will send My angels to gather My chosen ones from every corner. From the farthest edge of the earth to the highest place in heaven.

Mark 13:28–29 (KJV):
"Now learn a parable of the fig tree; When her branch is yet tender, and putteth forth leaves, ye know that summer is near: So ye in like manner, when ye shall see these things come to pass, know that it is nigh, even at the doors."

Jesus (Today):
Here's a lesson from the fig tree;
When its branches start to soften and the leaves come in, you know summer's almost here.
In the same way, when you see all these things happen, know the end is right at the door.

Mark 13:30-31 (KJV)
"Verily I say unto you, that this generation shall not pass, till all these things be done. Heaven and earth shall pass away: but my words shall not pass away."

Jesus (Today):
Listen closely, this generation won't pass away until all this happens. Heaven and earth will fade, but My words will never fade.

Mark 13:32–33 (KJV):
"But of that day and that hour knoweth no man, no, not the angels which are in heaven, neither the Son, but the Father."

Jesus (Today):
No one knows the day or the hour. Not the angels, not even the Son. Only the Father. So stay awake. Stay ready. Keep praying.

Mark 13:34–36 (KJV):
"For the Son of man is as a man taking a far journey, who left..."
Jesus (Today):
It's like a man going on a long trip. He leaves his house, gives each servant a job, and tells the doorkeeper to keep watch. So you keep watch too. You don't know when the Master will come. Evening, midnight, before dawn, or morning.
Don't let Him show up and find you asleep.

Mark 13:37 (KJV)
"And what I say unto you I say unto all, Watch."
Jesus (Today):
And this isn't just for you,
It's for *everyone*: Stay awake.

Mark 14

Mark 14:6-9 (KJV)
"Let her alone; why trouble ye her? she hath wrought a good work on me. For ye have the poor with you always, and whensoever ye will ye may do them good: but me ye have not always. She hath done what she could: she is come aforehand to anoint my body to the burying. Verily I say unto you, Wheresoever this gospel shall be preached throughout the whole world, this also that she hath done shall be spoken of for a memorial of her."
Jesus (Today):
Leave her alone. Why are you giving her a hard time? What she did for Me is beautiful. You'll always have the poor, and you can help them whenever you choose. But you won't always have Me here. She did what she could. She poured this on Me ahead of time to prepare Me for burial. Mark My words: wherever this message is preached in the world, what she just did will be remembered.

Mark 14:14 (KJV):
"Say ye to the goodman of the house, The Master saith, where"
Jesus (Today):
Tell the owner of the house, The Teacher says, where's the room where I can eat the Passover with My disciples?"

Mark 14:18 (KJV)
"Verily I say unto you, One of you which eateth with me shall betray me."
Jesus (Today):
I'm telling you, one of you eating with Me right now is going to betray Me.

Mark 14:20 (KJV):
"It is one of the twelve, that dippeth with me in the dish."
Jesus (Today):
It's one of the Twelve. Someone sharing this very dish with Me.

Mark 14:21 (KJV):
"The Son of man indeed goeth, as it is written of him: but woe to that man by whom the Son of man is betrayed! good were it for that man if he had never been born."
Jesus (Today):
The Son of Man will go, just like the Scriptures said.
But the one who betrays Him; what a tragedy. It would've been better if he had never been born.

Mark 14:22 (KJV)
"Take, eat: this is my body."
Jesus (Today):
Take it. Eat. This is My body.

Mark 14:24 (KJV)
"This is my blood of the new testament, which is shed for many."
Jesus (Today):
This is My blood, poured out for many.
It seals the new covenant.

Mark 14:25 (KJV):
"Verily I say unto you, I will drink no more of the fruit of the vine, until that day that I drink it new in the kingdom of God."
Jesus (Today):
Know this for sure: I won't drink wine again until I drink it fresh with you in God's kingdom.

Mark 14:27 (KJV)
"All ye shall be offended because of me this night: for it is written, I will smite the shepherd, and the sheep shall be scattered."
Jesus (Today):
Tonight, all of you will fall away because of Me.
It's written, "Strike the shepherd, and the sheep will scatter."

Mark 14:28 (KJV)
"But after that I am risen, I will go before you into Galilee."
Jesus (Today):
But after I have risen, I will go ahead of you into Galilee.

Mark 14:30 (KJV)
"Verily I say unto thee, That this day, even in this night, before the cock crow twice, thou shalt deny me thrice."
Jesus (Today):

Peter, I'm telling you now, before the rooster crows twice, you'll deny three times that you even know Me.

Mark 14:32 (KJV):
"Sit ye here, while I shall pray."
Jesus (Today):
Stay here while I go pray.

Mark 14:34 (KJV):
"My soul is exceeding sorrowful unto death: tarry ye here, and watch."
Jesus (Today):
My soul is crushed with grief. It feels like death. Stay here and keep watch.

Mark 14:36 (KJV)
"Abba, Father, all things are possible unto thee... nevertheless not what I will, but what thou wilt."
Jesus (Today):
Father, You can do anything.
If there's another way, take this cup away from Me.
But not what I want, what You want.
Your will be done.

Mark 14:37-38 (KJV)
"Simon, sleepest thou? couldest not thou watch one hour? Watch ye and pray, lest ye enter into temptation. The spirit truly is ready, but the flesh is weak."
Jesus (Today):
Simon, are you sleeping? You couldn't stay awake with Me for one hour? Pray so you don't fall into temptation.
The spirit is willing, but the body gives out.

Mark 14:41-42 (KJV)
"Sleep on now, and take your rest: it is enough, the hour is come; behold, the Son of man is betrayed into the hands of sinners. Rise up, let us go; lo, he that betrayeth me is at hand."

Jesus (Today):
Go ahead, sleep and rest...The hour has come.
I'm about to be handed over to sinners.
Get up. Let's go. The one betraying Me is here.

Mark 14:48–49 (KJV)
"Are ye come out, as against a thief, with swords and with staves to take me? I was daily with you in the temple teaching, and ye took me not: but the scriptures must be fulfilled."

Jesus (Today):
Am I some kind of criminal that you needed swords and clubs to arrest Me? I was in the temple every day teaching, and you didn't lay a hand on Me. But the Scriptures had to be fulfilled.

Mark 14:62 (KJV):
"I am: and ye shall see the Son of man sitting on the right hand of power, and coming in the clouds of heaven."

Jesus (Today):
I am. And you will see the Son of Man seated in power at God's right hand, coming on the clouds of heaven.

Mark 15

Mark 15:2 (KJV)
"Thou sayest it."

Jesus (Today):
You said it.

Mark 15:34 (KJV)
"My God, my God, why hast thou forsaken me?"
Jesus (Today):
My God... My God...
Why have you left me?

Mark 16

Mark 16:15 (KJV)
"Go ye into all the world, and preach the gospel to every creature."
Jesus (Today):
Go. Take this to the ends of the earth.
Tell everyone, every single soul, everywhere; about the gospel.

Mark 16:16 (KJV):
"He that believeth and is baptized shall be saved; but he that believeth not shall be damned."
Jesus (Today):
Whoever believes and is baptized will be saved. But anyone who refuses to believe will be lost.

Mark 16:17-18 (KJV)
"And these signs shall follow them that believe; In my name shall they cast out devils; they shall speak with new tongues; They shall take up serpents; and if they drink any deadly thing, it shall not hurt them; they shall lay hands on the sick, and they shall recover."
Jesus (Today):
And these are the signs that will follow those who believe:

In My name they'll drive out demons. They'll speak in new languages. They'll handle snakes and won't be harmed by poison. They'll lay their hands on the sick, and the sick will be healed.

Luke

Luke 19:10 (KJV)
"For the Son of man is come to seek and to save that which was lost."
Jesus (Today):
I came to find the ones who are lost, and to save them. That's why I'm here.

"Mercy for the Misunderstood"
Jesus speaks with compassion to the outsiders, the overlooked, and the hurting. Every word reaches the heart.

Luke 2

Luke 2:49 (KJV):
"How is it that ye sought me? wist ye not that I must be about my Father's business?"
Jesus (Today):
Why were you looking for Me? Didn't you know I had to be in My Father's house, doing His work?

Luke 4

Luke 4:4 (KJV)
"It is written, That man shall not live by bread alone, but by every word of God."
Jesus (Today):
Scripture says, people don't live by bread alone, but by every word that comes from God.

Luke 4:8 (KJV)
"Get thee behind me, Satan: for it is written, Thou shalt worship the Lord thy God, and him only shalt thou serve."
Jesus (Today):
Back off, Satan. The Word is clear, you worship only the Lord your God. He's the only One you serve.

Luke 4:12 (KJV)
"It is said, Thou shalt not tempt the Lord thy God."

Jesus (Today):
It also says, don't you dare test the Lord your God.

Luke 4:18-19 (KJV)
"The Spirit of the Lord is upon me, because he hath anointed me to preach the gospel to the poor; he hath sent me to heal the brokenhearted, to preach deliverance to the captives, and recovering of sight to the blind, to set at liberty them that are bruised,
To preach the acceptable year of the Lord."

Jesus (Today):
The Spirit of the Lord is on Me. He chose Me to bring the gospel to the poor. He sent Me to heal broken hearts, break chains off prisoners, open blind eyes, set the wounded free,
to lift the weight off the oppressed, and declare, this is the year God's showing up.

Luke 4:21 (KJV)
"This day is this scripture fulfilled in your ears."

Jesus (Today):
What you just heard? It's happening. Right now.

Luke 4:23 (KJV)
"Ye will surely say unto me this proverb, Physician, heal thyself: whatsoever we have heard done in Capernaum, do also here in thy country."

Jesus (Today):
You're probably thinking, "Physician, heal Yourself."
You want me to do the same miracles here that you heard about.

Luke 4:24 (KJV)
"Verily I say unto you, No prophet is accepted in his own country."

Jesus (Today):
Believe me, no prophet is welcomed in their own hometown.

Luke 4:25–27 (KJV):
"But I tell you of a truth, many widows were in Israel in the days of Elias, when the heaven was shut up three years and six months, when great famine was throughout all the land;
But unto none of them was Elias sent, save unto Sarepta, a city of Sidon, unto a woman that was a widow. And many lepers were in Israel in the time of Eliseus the prophet; and none of them was cleansed, saving Naaman the Syrian."

Let's be honest; there were a lot of struggling widows in Israel when Elijah was around, during that three-and-a-half-year drought where the whole country was starving.
But God didn't send him to any of them. He sent him to help a widow *outside* of Israel, up in Zarephath.
And when it came to lepers in Elisha's time? Israel had plenty. But the only one God healed was Naaman. A Syrian outsider.

Luke 5

Luke 5:4 (KJV)
"Launch out into the deep, and let down your nets for a draught."
Jesus (Today):
Push out deeper. Drop your nets for a catch.

Luke 5:10 (KJV)
"Fear not; from henceforth thou shalt catch men".
Jesus (Today):
Don't be afraid. From now on, you're going to fish for people.

Luke 5:13 (KJV)
"I will: be thou clean."
Jesus (Today):
I want to, be healed.

Luke 5:14 (KJV)
"Go, and shew thyself to the priest, and offer for thy cleansing, according,"

Jesus (Today):
Now go show yourself to the priest and offer the sacrifice Moses commanded as proof you've been made clean.

Luke 5:20 (KJV)
"Man, thy sins are forgiven thee."

Jesus (Today):
My friend, your sins are forgiven.

Luke 5:22–23 (KJV)
"What reason ye in your hearts? Whether is easier, to say, Thy sins be forgiven thee; or to say, Rise up and walk?"

Jesus (Today):
Why are you questioning this in your hearts?
What's easier to say, "Your sins are forgiven" or "Get up and walk"?

Luke 5:24 (KJV)
"But that ye may know that the Son of man hath power upon earth to forgive sins... I say unto thee, Arise, and take up thy couch, and go into thine house."

Jesus (Today):
But just so you know the Son of Man has real power on earth to forgive sins, I'm saying this to you: Get up. Grab your mat. Go home healed.

Luke 5:27 (KJV)
"Follow me."

Jesus (Today):
Come follow Me.

Luke 5:31–32 (KJV)
*"They that are whole need not a physician; but they that are sick.
I came not to call the righteous, but sinners to repentance."*

Jesus (Today):
Healthy people don't need a doctor, sick ones do.
I didn't come to call those who think they're righteous. I came for the ones who know they're not and are ready to change.

Luke 5:34–35 (KJV)
"Can ye make the children of the bridechamber fast, while the bridegroom is with them? But the days will come, when the bridegroom shall be taken away from them, and then shall they fast in those days."

Jesus (Today):
Do you expect the wedding guests to fast while the groom is still with them? The time will come when the groom is taken away, and *then* they'll fast.

Luke 6

Luke 6:3 (KJV)
"Have ye not read so much as this, what David did, when himself was an hungred, and they which were with him; How he went into the house of God, and did take and eat the shewbread, and gave also to them that were with him; which it is not lawful to eat but for the priests alone?"

Jesus (Today):
Haven't you even read what David did when he and his companions were hungry? He went into the house of God, took the bread of the Presence, and ate what is lawful only for priests. He even gave some to his companions.

Luke 6:5 (KJV)
"The Son of man is Lord also of the sabbath."

Jesus (Today):
The Son of Man is Lord. Even over the Sabbath.

Luke 6:8 (KJV)
"Rise up and stand forth in the midst."

Jesus (Today):
Get up. Come stand right here in front of everyone.

Luke 6:9 (KJV)
"I will ask you one thing; Is it lawful on the sabbath days to do good, or to do evil? to save life, or to destroy it?"

Jesus (Today):
Let Me ask you, on the Sabbath, is it right to do good or evil? To save life, or to destroy it?

Luke 6:10 (KJV)
"Stretch forth thy hand."

Jesus (Today):
Reach out your hand.

Luke 6:20–23 (KJV)
"Blessed be ye poor: for yours is the kingdom of God. Blessed are ye that hunger now: for ye shall be filled. Blessed are ye that weep now: for ye shall laugh. Blessed are ye, when men shall hate you, and when they shall separate you from their company, and shall reproach you, and cast out your name as evil, for the Son of man's sake. Rejoice ye in that day, and leap for joy: for, behold, your reward is great in heaven: for in the like manner did their fathers unto the prophets."

Jesus (Today):
If you're broke and barely hanging on, listen to Me. You're blessed. Heaven belongs to you. If your stomach's been empty and your soul's been starving; just wait. You're about to be filled. If you've been crying behind closed doors, if the grief

won't let up; your laughter's coming. Joy is on its way. And if people hate you, block you, leave you out, drag your name, or twist your reputation because you stand with Me, you are overflowing with favor. When that happens, don't shrink back. Jump. For. Joy. Because heaven has got something for you so big, so eternal, so unstoppable, it'll make all this pain look small. You're not the first. This is how they treated every prophet God ever sent.

Luke 6:24–26 (KJV)
"But woe unto you that are rich! for ye have received your consolation. Woe unto you that are full! for ye shall hunger. Woe unto you that laugh now! for ye shall mourn and weep. Woe unto you, when all men shall speak well of you! for so did their fathers to the false prophets."

Jesus (Today):
But how tragic for you who are rich now, because you've already gotten all the comfort you're going to have.
How tragic for you who are full now, because you're going to be hungry. How tragic for you who laugh now, because you're going to grieve and cry. And how tragic when everyone speaks highly of you, because that's exactly how their ancestors treated the false prophets.

Luke 6:27–28 (KJV)
"But I say unto you which hear, Love your enemies, do good to them which hate you, Bless them that curse you, and pray for them which despitefully use you."

Jesus (Today):
Love your enemies. Do good to the ones who hate you.
Speak blessings over the people cursing your name.
And pray. Pray for the ones who use you and talk about you behind your back.

Luke 6:29 (KJV)

"And unto him that smiteth thee on the one cheek offer also the other; and him that taketh away thy cloke forbid not to take thy coat also."

Jesus (Today):

If someone slaps you across the face, don't swing back. Offer the other cheek. If they take what's on your back, offer them your coat too.

Luke 6:30 (KJV)

"Give to every man that asketh of thee...Give to every man that asketh of thee; and of him that taketh away thy goods ask them not again."

Jesus (Today):

If someone asks you for help; give it.
And if they take something from you, don't chase it down. Let it go.

Luke 6:31 (KJV)

"And as ye would that men should do to you, do ye also to them likewise."

Jesus (Today):

Treat people the way you'd want them to treat you.

Luke 6:32–34 (KJV):

"For if ye love them which love you, what thank have ye? for sinners also love those that love them. And if ye do good to them which do good to you, what thank have ye? for sinners also do even the same. And if ye lend to them of whom ye hope to receive, what thank have ye? for sinners also lend to sinners, to receive as much again."

Jesus (Today):

If you only love the people who love you back, that's nothing special. Everybody does that. If you're only kind to the ones who treat you right, that's nothing new. And if you only give to people who can pay you back, what's so special about that? Even the worst of people do that much.

Luke 6:35-36 (KJV)

"But love ye your enemies, and do good, and lend, hoping for nothing again; and your reward shall be great, and ye shall be the children of the Highest: for he is kind unto the unthankful and to the evil. Be ye therefore merciful, as your Father also is merciful."

Jesus (Today):
Love your enemies. Be generous without expecting anything back, and you'll be like your Father. Show mercy. That's who your Father is, mercy in motion.

Luke 6:37 (KJV)

"Judge not, and ye shall not be judged: condemn not, and ye shall not be condemned: forgive, and ye shall be forgiven:"

Jesus (Today):
Don't judge, and you won't be judged.
Don't condemn, and you won't be condemned.
Forgive, and you'll be forgiven.

Luke 6:38 (KJV)

"Give, and it shall be given unto you; good measure, pressed down, and shaken together, and running over, shall men give into your bosom. For with the same measure that ye mete withal it shall be measured to you again."

Jesus (Today):
Give, and it'll be given back to you.
Pressed down, shaken together, overflowing.
The way you give is the way it'll be given back to you.

Luke 6:39 (KJV)

"Can the blind lead the blind? Shall they not both fall into the ditch?"

Jesus (Today):
Can a blind person lead another blind person? Won't they both fall into the ditch?

Luke 6:40 (KJV):
"The disciple is not above his master: but every one that is perfect shall be as his master."
Jesus (Today):
Students aren't greater than their teacher.
But when they've been fully trained; they'll become like their teacher.

Luke 6:41–42 (KJV)
"And why beholdest thou the mote that is in thy brother's eye, but perceivest not the beam that is in thine own eye? Either how canst thou say to thy brother, Brother, let me pull out the mote that is in thine eye, when thou thyself beholdest not the beam that is in thine own eye? Thou hypocrite, cast out first the beam out of thine own eye, and then shalt thou see clearly to pull out the mote that is in thy brother's eye."
Jesus (Today):
Why do you look at the speck in your brother's eye but fail to notice the beam in your own eye? How can you say, "Brother, let me take out the speck in your eye," when you do not see the beam in your own? You hypocrite, first take the beam out of your own eye, and then you will see clearly to remove the speck from your brother's eye.

Luke 6:43–44 (KJV):
"For a good tree bringeth not forth corrupt fruit; neither doth a corrupt tree bring forth good fruit. For every tree is known by his own fruit. For of thorns men do not gather figs, nor of a bramble bush gather they grapes."
Jesus (Today):
A good tree doesn't grow rotten fruit. And a bad tree can't produce what's good. You know what kind of tree it is by what grows from it.
Nobody picks figs from thornbushes, or grapes from a weed patch.

Luke 6:45 (KJV)

"A good man out of the good treasure of his heart bringeth forth that which is good; and an evil man out of the evil treasure of his heart bringeth forth that which is evil: for of the abundance of the heart his mouth speaketh."

Jesus (Today):
A good person brings good out of the goodness stored in their heart. An evil person brings out what's corrupt from what's inside them. Because whatever your heart is full of; that's what's going to come out of your mouth.

Luke 6:46 (KJV)
"And why call ye me, Lord, Lord, and do not the things which I say?"
Jesus (Today):
Why do you keep calling Me, "Lord, Lord," but ignore what I say?

Luke 6:47–49 (KJV)
"Whosoever cometh to me, and heareth my sayings, and doeth them, I will shew you to whom he is like: He is like a man which built an house, and digged deep, and laid the foundation on a rock: and when the flood arose, the stream beat vehemently upon that house, and could not shake it: for it was founded upon a rock. But he that heareth, and doeth not, is like a man that without a foundation built an house upon the earth; against which the stream did beat vehemently, and immediately it fell; and the ruin of that house was great."

Jesus (Today):
Everyone who comes to me, hears my words, and puts them into practice, I will show you what they are like. They are like a person building a house who dug deep and laid the foundation on solid rock. When the flood came and the river crashed against that house, it could not shake it because it was well built. But the one who hears my words and does not put them into practice is like a person who built a house on the ground without a foundation. The river struck it and immediately it collapsed, and the destruction of that house was complete.

Luke 7

Luke 7:9 (KJV)
"I say unto you, I have not found so great faith, no, not in Israel."
Jesus (Today):
I haven't seen faith like this, not anywhere in Israel.

Luke 7:13 (KJV)
"Weep not."
Jesus (Today):
Don't cry.

Luke 7:14 (KJV)
"Young man, I say unto thee, Arise."
Jesus (Today):
Young man, listen to Me, get up.

Luke 7:22-23 (KJV)
"Go your way, and tell John what things ye have seen and heard...the blind see, the lame walk, the lepers are cleansed, the deaf hear, the dead are raised, to the poor the gospel is preached. And blessed is he, whosoever shall not be offended in me."
Jesus (Today):
Go tell John what you've seen and heard:
Blind eyes are opening. Crippled legs are walking. Outcasts are clean. The deaf can hear. The dead are getting back up. And the poor are finally hearing the gospel. If you're not offended by Me, you're blessed.

Luke 7:24 (KJV)
"What went ye out into the wilderness for to see? A reed shaken with the wind?"
Jesus (Today):

What did you expect to see out in the wilderness? Just a weak reed blowing in the wind?

Luke 7:25 (KJV)
"But what went ye out for to see? A man clothed in soft raiment? Behold, they which are gorgeously apparelled, and live delicately, are in kings' courts."

Jesus (Today):
Then what were you looking for? A man in luxury clothes? People dressed like that live in palaces, not deserts.

Luke 7:26 (KJV)
"But what went ye out for to see? A prophet? Yea, I say unto you, and much more than a prophet."

Jesus (Today):
So what did you really go out there to see? A prophet? Yes. I'm telling you, he's even more than that.

Luke 7:27 (KJV)
"This is he, of whom it is written, Behold, I send my messenger before thy face, which shall prepare thy way before thee."

Jesus (Today):
This is the one the Scriptures talked about:
The messenger I'm sending ahead of You. He'll get everything ready.

Luke 7:28 (KJV)
"For I say unto you, Among those that are born of women there is not a greater prophet than John the Baptist: but he that is least in the kingdom of God is greater than he."

Jesus (Today):
No one born has been greater than John, the Baptist. But even the least in God's kingdom? Still greater than him.

Luke 7:31-32 (KJV)
"Whereunto then shall I liken the men of this generation? and to what are they like? They are like unto children sitting in the marketplace, and calling one to another, and saying, We have piped unto you, and ye have not danced; we have mourned to you, and ye have not wept."

Jesus (Today):
What is this generation even like?
You are like kids in the street yelling at each other,
We played music, you didn't dance.
We cried but you didn't cry with us.

Luke 7:33-34 (KJV)
"For John the Baptist came neither eating bread nor drinking wine; and ye say, He hath a devil. The Son of man is come eating and drinking; and ye say, Behold a gluttonous man, and a winebibber, a friend of publicans and sinners!"

Jesus (Today):
John came fasting, and you said he was possessed.
I came eating and drinking, and you call me a glutton and drunk? Because I am a friend of tax collectors and sinners?

Luke 7:40 (KJV)
"Simon, I have somewhat to say unto thee."

Jesus (Today):
Simon, I have something to say to you.

Luke 7:42-43 (KJV)
"And when they had nothing to pay, he frankly forgave them both. Tell me therefore, which of them will love him most? Thou hast rightly judged."

Jesus (Today):
Neither of them could pay him back, so he forgave both debts.
Now tell Me, who do you think would love him more?
You're right. The one who was forgiven more.

Luke 7:44–46 (KJV)
"Seest thou this woman? I entered into thine house, thou gavest me no water for my feet: but she hath washed my feet with tears, and wiped them with the hairs of her head.
Thou gavest me no kiss: but this woman since the time I came in hath not ceased to kiss my feet. My head with oil thou didst not anoint: but this woman hath anointed my feet with ointment."

Jesus (Today):
You see this woman?
I walked into your house,
You didn't give Me water for My feet.
But she washed them with her tears.
You didn't greet Me with a kiss.
She hasn't stopped kissing My feet.
You didn't anoint My head with oil,
She poured perfume on Me.

Luke 7:47 (KJV)
"Wherefore I say unto thee, Her sins, which are many, are forgiven; for she loved much: but to whom little is forgiven, the same loveth little."

Jesus (Today):
So let Me tell you: her sins were many, but they've all been forgiven. And that's why her love is so deep. But the one who thinks they've only been forgiven a little, loves little.

Luke 7:48 (KJV)
"Thy sins are forgiven."

Jesus (Today):
Your sins are forgiven.

Luke 7:50 (KJV)
"Thy faith hath saved thee; go in peace."

Jesus (Today):
Your faith saved you.
Go in peace.

Luke 8

Luke 8:5–8 (KJV)
"A sower went out to sow his seed: and as he sowed, some fell by the way side; and it was trodden down, and the fowls of the air devoured it. And some fell upon a rock; and as soon as it was sprung up, it withered away, because it lacked moisture. And some fell among thorns; and the thorns sprang up with it, and choked it. And other fell on good ground, and sprang up, and bare fruit an hundredfold. He that hath ears to hear, let him hear."

Jesus (Today):
A farmer went out to plant his seed, some landed on the path and got trampled or eaten, some hit rocky ground and couldn't grow roots, some got choked out by thorns,
but some fell on good soil and grew strong.
If you've got ears, use them. Listen.

Luke 8:10 (KJV)
"Unto you it is given to know the mysteries of the kingdom of God: but to others in parables; that seeing they might not see, and hearing they might not understand."

Jesus (Today):
You've been given insight into the deep things of God's kingdom.
But for others, I speak in parables;
so they hear it, but don't really hear it; see it, but don't fully see.
Others just hear stories, but you get the real meaning.

Luke 8:11–15 (KJV)
"Now the parable is this: The seed is the word of God. Those by the way side are they that hear; then cometh the devil, and taketh away the word out of their hearts, lest they should believe and be saved. They on the rock are they, which, when they hear, receive the word with joy; and these have no root, which for a while believe, and in time of temptation fall away. And that which fell among thorns are they, which, when they have heard, go forth, and are choked with cares and riches and pleasures of this life, and bring no fruit to perfection. But that on the good ground are they, which in an honest and good heart, having heard the word, keep it, and bring forth fruit

with patience."

Jesus (Today):
Here's what the story means: the seed is God's word.
The seeds on the road? That's when someone hears the word, but before it can sink in, the devil snatches it out of their heart. The rocky ground? That's people who hear the word and love it, but it never takes root. So when things get hard, they give up. The thorny ground? That's when the word gets choked out by stress, money, and pleasure. No growth, no fruit. But the good soil? That's the one who hears the word, holds onto it with an honest and open heart,
and through perseverance produces real fruit.

Luke 8:16 (KJV)
"No man, when he hath lighted a candle, covereth it with a vessel, or putteth it under a bed; but setteth it on a candlestick, that they which enter in may see the light."

Jesus (Today):
No one lights a lamp and hides it under the bed. You put it on a stand so everyone who walks in can see the light.

Luke 8:17 (KJV)
"For nothing is secret, that shall not be made manifest..."

Jesus (Today):
Because nothing that's hidden will stay hidden.
Everything done in secret will come to light.

Luke 8:18 (KJV)
"Take heed therefore how ye hear: for whosoever hath, to him shall be given; and whosoever hath not, from him shall be taken even that which he seemeth to have."

Jesus (Today):
Pay attention to *how* you listen.
If you lean in and receive, more will be given.

But if you don't; if you take it lightly, even what you think you have will be taken away.

Luke 8:21 (KJV)
"My mother and my brethren are these which hear the word of God, and do it."
Jesus (Today):
My true family? It's the ones who *hear* God's word and *live it.*

Luke 8:22-25 (KJV)
"Let us go over unto the other side of the lake."
Jesus (Today):
Let's cross over to the other side of the lake. Where is your faith?

Luke 8:30 (KJV)
"What is thy name?"
Jesus (Today):
What's your name?

Luke 8:39 (KJV)
"Return to thine own house, and shew how great things God hath done unto thee."
Jesus (Today):
Go home.
Tell everybody what God just did for you.

Luke 9

Luke 9:3-5 (KJV)
"Take nothing for your journey, neither staves, nor scrip, neither bread, neither money; neither have two coats apiece. And whatsoever house ye enter into, there abide, and thence depart. And whosoever will not receive you, when ye go out of that city, shake off the very dust from your feet for a testimony against them."

Jesus (Today):
Don't pack anything for the trip. No bag, no food, no money, not even a change of clothes. When someone welcomes you into their home, stay there until it's time to move on.
And if a town rejects you, leave. Shake the dust off your feet as a sign that you tried.

Luke 9:13 (KJV)
"Give ye them to eat."

Jesus (Today):
You feed them.

Luke 9:14 (KJV)
"Make them sit down by fifties in a company."

Jesus (Today):
Have them sit in groups of fifty.

Luke 9:18 (KJV)
"Whom say the people that I am?"

Jesus (Today):
What are people saying about Me?
Who do they think I am?

Luke 9:20 (KJV)
"But whom say ye that I am?"

Jesus (Today):
Who do *you* say I am?

Luke 9:22 (KJV)
"'The Son of man must suffer many things... and be raised the third day."
Jesus (Today):
The Son of Man is going to suffer deeply, get rejected, killed...but on the third day? He's getting up.

Luke 9:23 (KJV)
"If any man will come after me, let him deny himself, and take up his cross daily, and follow me."
Jesus (Today):
If you want to follow Me, let go of yourself. Pick up your cross every single day, and come with Me.

Luke 9:24-25 (KJV)
"For whosoever will save his life shall lose it: but whosoever will lose his life for my sake, the same shall save it. For what is a man advantaged, if he gain the whole world, and lose himself, or be cast away?"
Jesus (Today):
If you try to save your own life, you'll lose it.
But if you lose it for Me? You'll find what life really is.
What good is it to win the whole world, if you lose *yourself* in the process?

Luke 9:26 (KJV)
"For whosoever shall be ashamed of me and of my words, of him shall the Son of man be ashamed, when he shall come in his own glory, and in his Father's, and of the holy angels."

If you're ashamed of Me and My words now, then I will be ashamed of you when I return in glory with the Father and the angels.

Luke 9:27 (KJV):

"But I tell you of a truth, there be some standing here, which shall not taste of death, till they see the kingdom of God."

Jesus (Today):
Let Me tell you the truth; some of you standing here won't die before you see the kingdom of God come in power.

Luke 9:41 (KJV)
""O faithless and perverse generation, how long shall I be with you, and suffer you? Bring thy son hither."

Jesus (Today):
You faithless, twisted generation, how long do I have to put up with this? Bring your son here.

Luke 9:44 (KJV)
"Let these sayings sink down into your ears: for the Son of man shall be delivered into the hands of men."

Jesus (Today):
Let this sink in: The Son of Man is about to be handed over.

Luke 9:48 (KJV)
"Whosoever shall receive this child in my name receiveth me: and whosoever shall receive me receiveth him that sent me: for he that is least among you all, the same shall be great."

Jesus (Today):
If you welcome this child in My name, you're welcoming *Me*. And if you welcome Me, you're welcoming the One who sent Me. The least among you, that's the one who's truly great.

Luke 9:50 (KJV)
"Forbid him not: for he that is not against us is for us."

Jesus (Today):
If they're not against us, they're *for* us.

Luke 9:55–56 (KJV)
"Ye know not what manner of spirit ye are of... For the Son of man is not come to destroy men's lives, but to save them."

Jesus (Today):
You don't even know what spirit is driving you.
I didn't come to destroy lives, I came to *save* them.

Luke 9:58 (KJV)
"Foxes have holes, and birds... have nests; but the Son of man hath not where to lay his head."

Jesus (Today):
Foxes have dens. Birds have nests. But Me? I have no place to lay My head.

Luke 9:59 (KJV)
"Follow me."

Jesus (Today):
Follow Me.

Luke 9:60 (KJV)
"Let the dead bury their dead: but go thou and preach the kingdom of God."

Jesus (Today):
Let the dead bury their dead. You? Go and spread the message of God's kingdom.

Luke 9:62 (KJV)
"No man, having put his hand to the plough, and looking back, is fit for the kingdom of God."

Jesus (Today):
If you start this journey and keep looking back, you're not ready for the kingdom.

Luke 10

Luke 10:2 (KJV)
"The harvest truly is great, but the labourers are few: pray ye therefore the Lord of the harvest, that he would send forth labourers into his harvest."

Jesus (Today):
There's a massive harvest out there, but barely any workers. Ask God to send more people into the field.

Luke 10:3 (KJV)
"Go your ways: behold, I send you forth as lambs among wolves."

Jesus (Today):
Go. I'm sending you out like lambs into a wolf pack.

Luke 10:4 (KJV):
"Carry neither purse, nor scrip, nor shoes: and salute no man by the way."

Jesus (Today):
Don't pack money, bags, or extra shoes. Stay focused. No distractions on the way.

Luke 10:5-6 (KJV)
"And into whatsoever house ye enter, first say, Peace be to this house. And if the son of peace be there, your peace shall rest upon it: if not, it shall turn to you again."

Jesus (Today):
When you walk into a house, speak peace over it.
If someone there is open to peace, it'll rest on them. If not, that peace will return to you.

Luke 10:7 (KJV)
"And in the same house remain, eating and drinking such things as they give: for the labourer is worthy of his hire. Go not from house to house."
Jesus (Today):
Stay in one place, eat what they offer. A worker deserves their pay. Don't bounce from house to house looking for better.

Luke 10:8-9 (KJV)
"And into whatsoever city ye enter, and they receive you, eat such things as are set before you: And heal the sick that are therein, and say unto them, The kingdom of God is come nigh unto you."
Jesus (Today):
If a town welcomes you, accept their food. Heal the sick and say this loud, God's kingdom just showed up at your door.

Luke 10:10-11 (KJV)
"But into whatsoever city ye enter, and they receive you not, go your ways out into the streets of the same, and say, Even the very dust of your city, which cleaveth on us, we do wipe off against you: notwithstanding be ye sure of this, that the kingdom of God is come nigh unto you."
Jesus (Today):
But if a city rejects you, step into the street and say this loud and clear: "We're shaking your dust off our feet as a warning to you. But know this, God's kingdom still came to your doorstep."

Luke 10:12 (KJV):
"But I say unto you, that it shall be more tolerable in that day for Sodom, than for that city."
Jesus (Today):
I'm telling you: on judgment day, even Sodom will be better off than that city.

Luke 10:13–15 (KJV):
"Woe unto thee, Chorazin! woe unto thee, Bethsaida! for if the mighty works had been done in Tyre and Sidon, which have been done in you, they had a great while ago repented, sitting in

sackcloth and ashes. But it shall be more tolerable for Tyre and Sidon at the judgment, than for you. And thou, Capernaum, which art exalted to heaven, shalt be thrust down to hell."

Jesus (Today):
Trouble's coming for you, Chorazin. And you too, Bethsaida. If Tyre and Sidon had seen what you've seen, they would've broken down in repentance long ago. It'll go easier for them than for you when judgment comes. And you, Capernaum? You think you're sitting high in heaven? You'll be brought down hard.

Luke 10:16 (KJV)

"He that heareth you heareth me; and he that despiseth you despiseth me; and he that despiseth me despiseth him that sent me."

Jesus (Today):
If they listen to you, they're listening to Me.
If they reject you, they're rejecting Me.
And if they reject Me, they're rejecting Him who sent Me.

Luke 10:18-19 (KJV)

"I beheld Satan as lightning fall from heaven. Behold, I give unto you power to tread on serpents and scorpions, and over all the power of the enemy: and nothing shall by any means hurt you.

Jesus (Today):
I saw Satan fall from heaven like lightning. Look, I have given you authority to trample on snakes and scorpions and to overcome all the power of the enemy. Nothing will harm you.

Luke 10:20 (KJV)

Notwithstanding in this rejoice not, that the spirits are subject unto you; but rather rejoice, because your names are written in heaven."

Jesus (Today):
Don't rejoice that the spirits submit to you. Rejoice instead that your names are written in heaven.

Luke 10:21 (KJV)

"I thank thee, O Father, Lord of heaven and earth, that thou hast hid these things from the wise and prudent, and hast revealed them unto babes: even so, Father; for so it seemed good in thy sight."

Jesus (Today):
Father, Lord of heaven and earth, I praise you.
You hid this from the proud and self-important,
and gave it to the humble, the open, the hungry.
Yes, Father, this was Your perfect plan.

Luke 10:22 (KJV)

"All things are delivered to me of my Father: and no man knoweth who the Son is, but the Father; and who the Father is, but the Son, and he to whom the Son will reveal him."

Jesus (Today):
My Father handed Me everything.
No one truly knows who I am, except the Father.
And no one truly knows the Father, unless I reveal Him.

Luke 10:23–24 (KJV)

"Blessed are the eyes which see the things that ye see: For I tell you, that many prophets and kings have desired to see those things which ye see, and have not seen them; and to hear those things which ye hear, and have not heard them."

Jesus (Today):
You don't even realize how blessed you are, to see what you're seeing right now. Prophets and kings longed for this moment. They dreamed of seeing what you see, hearing what you hear. But they never did. You just did.

Luke 10:26 (KJV)

"What is written in the law? how readest thou?"

Jesus (Today):
What's the law say? How do you read it?

Luke 10:28 (KJV)
"Thou hast answered right: this do, and thou shalt live."
Jesus (Today):
You answered right. Do that, and you'll live.

Luke 10:30-35 (KJV)
"A certain man went down from Jerusalem to Jericho, and fell among thieves, which stripped him of his raiment, and wounded him, and departed, leaving him half dead. And by chance there came down a certain priest that way: and when he saw him, he passed by on the other side. And likewise a Levite, when he was at the place, came and looked on him, and passed by on the other side. But a certain Samaritan, as he journeyed, came where he was: and when he saw him, he had compassion on him, And went to him, and bound up his wounds, pouring in oil and wine, and set him on his own beast, and brought him to an inn, and took care of him. And on the morrow when he departed, he took out two pence, and gave them to the host, and said unto him, Take care of him; and whatsoever thou spendest more, when I come again, I will repay thee."
Jesus (Today):
A man was walking from Jerusalem to Jericho when he got jumped by robbers. They beat him, stripped him, and left him half dead. A priest saw him lying there but crossed to the other side. Same with a Levite, he looked and walked on by. But then a Samaritan came by. When he saw the man, his heart broke. He went to him, cleaned up his wounds, poured on oil and wine, put him on his own ride, and brought him to an inn to care for him. The next day, he gave the innkeeper money and said, "Take care of him. Whatever it costs, I'll pay you back when I return."

Luke 10:36-37 (KJV):
"Which now of these three, thinkest thou, was neighbour unto him that fell among the thieves? Go, and do thou likewise."
Jesus (Today):
Which one of these three do you think truly acted like a neighbor? Go. Do the same.

Luke 11

Luke 11:2-4 (KJV)
"When ye pray, say, Our Father which art in heaven, Hallowed be thy name. Thy kingdom come. Thy will be done, as in heaven, so in earth. Give us day by day our daily bread. And forgive us our sins; for we also forgive every one that is indebted to us. And lead us not into temptation; but deliver us from evil."

Jesus (Today):
When you pray, say this:
Father...You're close, but still holy. Above everything, yet right here with us. Your name is sacred. It means everything.
Let Your kingdom come.
Right here. Right now.
Take over this broken world. Take over my broken heart.
Let Your will be done.
Not mine. Not theirs.
Even when it's hard. Even when I don't understand it.
Do whatever You want, because what You want is better than anything I could come up with.
Give us today what we need.
Not just food.
Peace. Strength. Mercy.
The stuff we don't even know how to ask for.
Forgive us.
For every way we've messed it up.
For everything we said, did, and thought that hurt You, and others.
Forgive us for our sins, just like we forgive the people who've wronged us.
And don't let us fall into temptation. Rescue us from evil.
And help us forgive the people who broke us.
Even if they never say sorry.
Don't let us fall again.
We know how easily we slip.

Pull us out before we get too deep.
Protect us from the things that keep pulling us back in.
You're the One in charge.
The One with power.
The One who gets the glory.
Now and always. Forever and ever. Amen.

Luke 11:5–8 (KJV)
"Which of you shall have a friend, and shall go unto him at midnight, and say unto him, Friend, lend me three loaves; For a friend of mine in his journey is come to me, and I have nothing to set before him? And he from within shall answer and say, Trouble me not: the door is now shut, and my children are with me in bed; I cannot rise and give thee. I say unto you, Though he will not rise and give him, because he is his friend, yet because of his importunity he will rise and give him as many as he needeth."

Jesus (Today):
Imagine this; you go to a friend's house at midnight and say, "Hey, can I borrow three loaves of bread? I've got a guest and nothing to feed him." And your friend shouts from inside, "Don't bother me. The door's locked, my kids are asleep. I can't help you right now." I'm telling you, even if he won't get up just because you're friends, he'll do it because you kept knocking. He'll give you whatever you need.

Luke 11:9-10 (KJV)
"And I say unto you, Ask, and it shall be given you; seek, and ye shall find; knock, and it shall be opened unto you. For every one that asketh receiveth; and he that seeketh findeth; and to him that knocketh it shall be opened."

Jesus (Today):
So I'm telling you; ask, and you'll receive.
Seek, and you'll find. Knock, and the door will open.
Everyone who asks, receives. Everyone who seeks, finds.
And if you knock, the door will open for you.

Luke 11:11-13 (KJV)

"If a son shall ask bread of any of you that is a father, will he give him a stone? or if he ask a fish, will he for a fish give him a serpent? Or if he shall ask an egg, will he offer him a scorpion? If ye then, being evil, know how to give good gifts unto your children: how much more shall your heavenly Father give the Holy Spirit to them that ask him?"

Jesus (Today):
If your child asks for bread, would you hand him a rock?
If he wants a fish, would you give him a snake?
Or if he asks for an egg, would you give him a scorpion?
Of course not. And if you, flawed as you are, know how to give good things to your kids, how much more will your Father in heaven give the Holy Spirit to anyone who asks Him?

Luke 11:17-20 (KJV)

"Every kingdom divided against itself is brought to desolation; and a house divided against a house falleth. If Satan also be divided against himself, how shall his kingdom stand? because ye say that I cast out devils through Beelzebub. And if I by Beelzebub cast out devils, by whom do your sons cast them out? therefore shall they be your judges."

Jesus (Today):
Any nation that turns on itself will collapse. A house divided falls apart. If Satan is fighting against himself, how could his kingdom survive? You say I drive out demons by the power of Satan. Well then, who gives your own people the power to cast them out? Let them be the ones to judge.
But if I'm casting out demons by the power of God;
then the kingdom of God has already come to you.

Luke 11:20 (KJV)

"But if I with the finger of God cast out devils, no doubt the kingdom of God is come upon you."

Jesus (Today)
But if I drive out demons by the finger of God, then you can be sure that the kingdom of God has come upon you.

Luke 11:21-22 (KJV)
"When a strong man armed keepeth his palace, his goods are in peace: But when a stronger than he shall come upon him, and overcome him, he taketh from him all his armour wherein he trusted, and divideth his spoils."

Jesus (Today):
When a strong man guards his house with weapons, everything inside feels secure. But if someone stronger shows up and beats him, he strips away that armor and divides up the prize.

Luke 11:23 (KJV)
"He that is not with me is against me: and he that gathereth not with me scattereth."

Jesus (Today):
If you're not with Me, you're against Me.
And if you're not gathering with Me, you're tearing it all apart.

Luke 11:24 (KJV)
"When the unclean spirit is gone out of a man, he walketh through dry places, seeking rest; and finding none, he saith, I will return unto my house whence I came out.

Jesus (Today):
When a demon leaves someone, it wanders through empty places looking for rest. When it doesn't find any, it says, "I'll go back to the house I came from."

Luke 11:25 (KJV)
"And when he cometh, he findeth it swept and garnished."

Jesus (Today):
When it returns, it finds that place cleaned up and ready.

Luke 11:26 (KJV)
Then goeth he, and taketh to him seven other spirits more wicked than himself; and they enter in, and dwell there: and the last state of that man is worse than the first."

Jesus (Today):
Then it brings back seven spirits worse than itself. They move

in, and that person ends up worse than before.

Luke 11:28 (KJV)
"But he said, Yea rather, blessed are they that hear the word of God, and keep it."
Jesus (Today):
You want to talk about blessing?
The real blessing is on those who hear God's word, and live it out.

Luke 11:29-30 (KJV):
"This is an evil generation: they seek a sign; and there shall no sign be given it, but the sign of Jonas the prophet. For as Jonas was a sign unto the Ninevites, so shall also the Son of man be to this generation."
Jesus (Today):
This generation is chasing after signs.
But the only sign they'll get is Jonah.
Just like Jonah was a sign to Nineveh,
the Son of Man will be a sign to this generation.

Luke 11:31-32 (KJV):
"The queen of the south shall rise up in the judgment with the men of this generation, and condemn them: for she came from the utmost parts of the earth to hear the wisdom of Solomon; and, behold, a greater than Solomon is here. The men of Nineve shall rise up in the judgment with this generation, and shall condemn it: for they repented at the preaching of Jonas; and, behold, a greater than Jonas is here."
The Queen of the South will rise on judgment day and call this generation out: because she traveled across the earth just to hear Solomon's wisdom. And now, someone greater than Solomon is standing right here. The people of Nineveh will rise up too, because they repented when Jonah spoke.
And now, someone greater than Jonah is here.

Luke 11:33 (KJV):
"No man, when he hath lighted a candle, putteth it in a secret place, neither under a bushel, but on a candlestick, that they which come in may see the light."

Jesus (Today):
No one lights a lamp and hides it.
You put it up high so everyone who walks in can see the light.

Luke 11:34–36 (KJV)
*"The light of the body is the eye: therefore when thine eye is single, thy whole body also is full of light; but when thine eye is evil, thy body also is full of darkness.
Take heed therefore that the light which is in thee be not darkness.
If thy whole body therefore be full of light, having no part dark, the whole shall be full of light, as when the bright shining of a candle doth give thee light."*

Jesus (Today):
Your eyes are like lamps for your body.
If your eyes are clear, your whole body lights up.
But if your eyes are clouded or dark, your whole body stays in the dark. So be careful. Don't let your light turn into darkness. If your whole being is full of light, with no darkness left, you'll shine like a lamp lighting up the entire room.

Luke 11:39-40 (KJV)
"Now do ye Pharisees make clean the outside of the cup and the platter; but your inward part is full of ravening and wickedness. Ye fools, did not he that made that which is without make that which is within also?"

Jesus (Today):
You Pharisees are all about appearances. You scrub the outside of the cup, but inside, you're full of greed and filth.
Fools. Don't you get it? The One who made the outside also made your heart.

Luke 11:41 (KJV)
"Give alms of such things as ye have; and, behold, all things are clean unto you."

Jesus (Today):
If you really want to be clean, start by giving generously from your heart. That's what makes everything clean.

Luke 11:42 (KJV)
"But woe unto you, Pharisees! for ye tithe mint and rue and all manner of herbs, and pass over judgment and the love of God: these ought ye to have done, and not to leave the other undone."

Jesus (Today):
Watch out, religious experts! Uou tithe your herbs and spices down to the smallest leaf, but ignore justice and the love for God. You should've done both, and never left the deeper things undone.

Luke 11:43 (KJV)
"Woe unto you, Pharisees! for ye love the uppermost seats in the synagogues, and greetings in the markets."

Jesus (Today):
You love front-row seats in church and hearing your name in public. That's what drives you.

Luke 11:44 (KJV)
"Woe unto you, scribes and Pharisees, hypocrites! for ye are as graves which appear not, and the men that walk over them are not aware of them."

Jesus (Today):
Watch out, hypocrites!, You're like hidden graves. People walk right over you and don't even realize they're stepping into death.

Luke 11:46 (KJV)
"Woe unto you also, ye lawyers! for ye lade men with burdens grievous to be borne, and ye yourselves touch not the burdens with one of your fingers."

Jesus (Today):
And you lawyers, you're no better.
You pile heavy burdens on people's backs and don't lift a single finger to help.

Luke 11:47-48 (KJV)
"Woe unto you! for ye build the sepulchres of the prophets, and your fathers killed them. Truly ye bear witness that ye allow the deeds of your fathers: for they indeed killed them, and ye build their sepulchres."

Jesus (Today):
You build tombs to honor the prophets, but it was your ancestors who killed them. And by doing this, you're admitting that you approve of what they did.

Luke 11:49-51 (KJV)
"Therefore also said the wisdom of God, I will send them prophets and apostles, and some of them they shall slay and persecute: That the blood of all the prophets, which was shed from the foundation of the world, may be required of this generation; From the blood of Abel unto the blood of Zacharias, which perished between the altar and the temple: verily I say unto you, It shall be required of this generation."

Jesus (Today):
That's why God's wisdom speaks this truth. I keep sending you prophets and messengers, but you keep killing them and driving them out. And now all the blood of every prophet murdered since the beginning of the world is about to fall on this generation. From Abel's blood to the blood of Zechariah who was slaughtered right there between the altar and the temple I promise you this generation will answer for it all.

Luke 11:52 (KJV)
"Woe unto you, lawyers! for ye have taken away the key of knowledge: ye entered not in yourselves, and them that were entering in ye hindered."

Jesus (Today):
You're in serious trouble, scholars. You've stolen the key to true

knowledge. You won't enter it yourselves and you block everyone else who's trying to get in.

Luke 12

Luke 12:1 (KJV)
"Beware ye of the leaven of the Pharisees, which is hypocrisy."
Jesus (Today):
Watch out for the influence of the Pharisees because their lives are full of hypocrisy.

Luke 12:2-3 (KJV)
"For there is nothing covered, that shall not be revealed; neither hid, that shall not be known. Therefore whatsoever ye have spoken in darkness shall be heard in the light; and that which ye have spoken in the ear in closets shall be proclaimed upon the housetops."
Jesus (Today):
Nothing you try to cover up will stay hidden. Every secret will be exposed. Everything you've whispered in the dark will be shouted in the light. Every quiet word you thought was private will be broadcast for everyone to hear.

Luke 12:4-5 (KJV)
"And I say unto you my friends, Be not afraid of them that kill the body, and after that have no more that they can do. But I will forewarn you whom ye shall fear: Fear him, which after he hath killed hath power to cast into hell; yea, I say unto you, Fear him."
Jesus (Today):
Listen to Me, My friends. Don't be afraid of people who can kill your body but can't touch your soul. I'll tell you who you should fear. Fear the One who has the power not just to take your life but to throw you into hell afterward. Yes, I'm telling you; fear

Him.

Luke 12:6-7 (KJV)
"Are not five sparrows sold for two farthings, and not one of them is forgotten before God? But even the very hairs of your head are all numbered. Fear not therefore: ye are of more value than many sparrows."

Jesus (Today):
Aren't five sparrows sold for just a couple of coins? Yet not a single one of them is forgotten by God. Every single hair on your head is counted. So don't be afraid. You are worth far more than a whole flock of sparrows.

Luke 12:8-9 (KJV)
"Also I say unto you, Whosoever shall confess me before men, him shall the Son of man also confess before the angels of God: But he that denieth me before men shall be denied before the angels of God."

Jesus (Today):
If you stand up for Me in front of people, I'll stand for you in front of heaven. But if you deny Me here, I'll deny you there.

Luke 12:10 (KJV)
"And whosoever shall speak a word against the Son of man, it shall be forgiven him: but unto him that blasphemeth against the Holy Ghost it shall not be forgiven."

Jesus (Today):
You can talk bad about Me and still be forgiven, but if you blaspheme the Holy Spirit, there is no forgiveness.

Luke 12:11-12 (KJV)
"And when they bring you unto the synagogues, and unto magistrates, and powers, take ye no thought how or what thing ye shall answer, or what ye shall say: For the Holy Ghost shall teach you in the same hour what ye ought to say."

Jesus (Today):
When they drag you into the synagogues, courts, and before powerful people, don't worry about how you'll defend yourself

or what to say. Because in that very moment, the Holy Spirit will teach you exactly what you need to say.

Luke 12:14 (KJV)
"Man, who made me a judge or a divider over you?"

Jesus (Today):
Man, who put Me in charge of dividing up your inheritance or settling your disputes?

Luke 12:15 (KJV)
"Take heed, and beware of covetousness: for a man's life consisteth not in the abundance of the things which he possesseth."

Jesus (Today)
Pay attention and guard yourselves against greed, because your life is not defined by how much stuff you own.

Luke 12:16-20 (KJV)
"The ground of a certain rich man brought forth plentifully: And he thought within himself, saying, What shall I do, because I have no room where to bestow my fruits? And he said, This will I do: I will pull down my barns, and build greater; and there will I bestow all my fruits and my goods. And I will say to my soul, Soul, thou hast much goods laid up for many years; take thine ease, eat, drink, and be merry. But God said unto him, Thou fool, this night thy soul shall be required of thee: then whose shall those things be, which thou hast provided?"

Jesus (Today):
There was a rich man whose land produced a huge harvest. He thought to himself, "What should I do? I don't even have room to store all this." Then he decided, "I know what I'll do. I'll tear down my barns and build bigger ones. Then I can store all my grain and goods there. And I'll tell myself, "You've got plenty saved up for years. Relax. Eat. Drink. Celebrate." But God said to him, "You fool. Tonight your life will be demanded from you. Then who's going to get everything you piled up?"

Luke 12:21 (KJV)
"So is he that layeth up treasure for himself, and is not rich toward God."
Jesus (Today):
That's how it ends for anyone who stores up riches for themselves but stays empty toward God.

Luke 12:22-23 (KJV)
"Therefore I say unto you, Take no thought for your life, what ye shall eat; neither for the body, what ye shall put on. The life is more than meat, and the body is more than raiment."
Jesus (Today):
Stop stressing about what you're going to eat or wear. Your life is worth more than food, and your body is worth more than clothes.

Luke 12:24 (KJV)
"Consider the ravens: for they neither sow nor reap; which neither have storehouse nor barn; and God feedeth them: how much more are ye better than the fowls?"
Jesus (Today):
Look at the ravens, they don't plant, harvest, or store food, yet God feeds them. Aren't you worth way more than a bird?

Luke 12:25-26 (KJV)
"And which of you with taking thought can add to his stature one cubit? If ye then be not able to do that thing which is least, why take ye thought for the rest?"
Jesus (Today):
And tell Me, Can worrying make you taller? Or add a single hour to your life? If you can't control the little stuff, why worry about everything else?

Luke 12:27-28 (KJV)
"Consider the lilies how they grow: they toil not, they spin not; and yet I say unto you, that Solomon in all his glory was not arrayed like one of these. If then God so clothe the grass, which is to day in the field, and to morrow is cast into the oven; how much more will he clothe you, O ye of

little faith?"

Jesus (Today):
Look at the lilies. They don't work or sew.
But even Solomon in all his glory never looked that good.
If God takes care of flowers that are here today and gone
tomorrow, don't you think He'll take care of you?
Where's your faith?

Luke 12:29-30 (KJV)
"And seek not ye what ye shall eat, or what ye shall drink, neither be ye of doubtful mind. For all these things do the nations of the world seek after: and your Father knoweth that ye have need of these things."

Jesus (Today):
So don't chase after what you're going to eat or drink, and don't live in fear or worry. That's what everyone else in the world is running after, but your Father already knows you need these things.

Luke 12:31 (KJV):
"But rather seek ye the kingdom of God; and all these things"

Jesus (Today):
Instead, make God's kingdom your first priority, and all these other things will be given to you as well.

Luke 12:32 (KJV)
"Fear not, little flock; for it is your Father's good pleasure to give you the kingdom."

Jesus (Today):
Don't be scared, my few faithful ones,
your Father *wants* to give you the kingdom.

Luke 12:33-34 (KJV)
"Sell that ye have, and give alms; provide yourselves bags which wax not old, a treasure in the

heavens that faileth not, where no thief approacheth, neither moth corrupteth. For where your treasure is, there will your heart be also."

Jesus (Today):
Let go of the things that weigh you down.
Give generously. Build up treasure that never rots, never fades, and can't be stolen; heaven's treasure. Because wherever your treasure is, that's where your heart will be.

Luke 12:35-36 (KJV)
"Let your loins be girded about, and your lights burning; And ye yourselves like unto men that wait for their lord, when he will return from the wedding; that when he cometh and knocketh, they may open unto him immediately."

Jesus (Today):
Stay dressed. Stay ready. Keep your light on.
Be like servants waiting for their master to come home from a wedding, ready to open the door and welcome Him the moment He knocks.

Luke 12:37 (KJV)
"Blessed are those servants, whom the lord when he cometh shall find watching: verily I say unto you, that he shall gird himself, and make them to sit down to meat, and will come forth and serve them."

Jesus (Today):
Blessed are the ones I find wide awake and ready when I come back. I promise you this, I'll roll up My sleeves, seat you at My table, and serve *you* Myself.

Luke 12:38 (KJV)
"And if he shall come in the second watch, or come in the third watch, and find them so, blessed are those servants."

Jesus (Today):
Even if I show up late in the night or early before dawn,
if you're still ready? Still watching? They're still blessed.

Luke 12:39-40 (KJV)

"And this know, that if the goodman of the house had known what hour the thief would come, he would have watched, and not have suffered his house to be broken through.
Be ye therefore ready also: for the Son of man cometh at an hour when ye think not."

Jesus (Today):

Understand this; if the homeowner knew when the thief was coming, he would've stayed awake and kept his house from being broken into. Stay alert and you must be ready too, because I will come at a time you don't expect.

Luke 12:42–44 (KJV)

"Who then is that faithful and wise steward, whom his lord shall make ruler over his household, to give them their portion of meat in due season? Blessed is that servant, whom his lord when he cometh shall find so doing. Of a truth I say unto you, that he will make him ruler over all that he hath."

Jesus (Today):

So who's the wise and faithful one, the one the Master trusts to manage things right? It's the one He finds doing the job when He returns. That one will be given even more; put in charge of everything.

Luke 12:45–46 (KJV)

"But and if that servant say in his heart, My lord delayeth his coming; and shall begin to beat the menservants and maidens, and to eat and drink, and to be drunken; The lord of that servant will come in a day when he looketh not for him, and at an hour when he is not aware, and will cut him in sunder, and will appoint him his portion with the unbelievers."

Jesus (Today):

But if that servant says to himself, "He's not coming back anytime soon," and starts mistreating people, getting drunk, and living reckless; the Master will show up when he least expects it. And He'll cut him off completely, like he was never part of the house.

Luke 12:47–48 (KJV)

"And that servant, which knew his lord's will, and prepared not himself, neither did according to his will, shall be beaten with many stripes. But he that knew not, and did commit things worthy of stripes, shall be beaten with few stripes. For unto whomsoever much is given, of him shall be much required: and to whom men have committed much, of him they will ask the more."

Jesus (Today):
If you knew exactly what He asked and chose not to do it, you'll be held fully responsible. But if you didn't know, and still messed up, the consequences will be lighter. The more you've been given, the more that's expected.
The more responsibility you hold, the more accountability you carry.

Luke 12:49 (KJV)

"I am come to send fire on the earth; and what will I, if it be already kindled?"

Jesus (Today):
I came to set the world on fire, and I'm ready to watch it burn with purpose.

Luke 12:50 (KJV)

"But I have a baptism to be baptized with; and how am I straitened till it be accomplished!"

Jesus (Today):
But first I have a baptism I must undergo, and how burdened I am until it is finished.

Luke 12:51-53 (KJV)

"Suppose ye that I am come to give peace on earth? I tell you, Nay; but rather division: For from henceforth there shall be five in one house divided, three against two, and two against three. The father shall be divided against the son, and the son against the father; the mother against the daughter, and the daughter against the mother; the mother in law against her daughter in law, and the daughter in law against her mother in law."

Jesus (Today):

Do you think I came to bring peace to the earth?
No. I came to divide. From now on, families will split; three against two, two against three. Fathers and sons. Mothers and daughters. In-laws and outlaws. This message will shake every household.

Luke 12:54-56 (KJV)

"When ye see a cloud rise out of the west, straightway ye say, There cometh a shower; and so it is. And when ye see the south wind blow, ye say, There will be heat; and it cometh to pass. Ye hypocrites, ye can discern the face of the sky and of the earth; but how is it that ye do not discern this time?"

Jesus (Today):

When you see a cloud in the west, you say, "Rain's coming," and you're right. When the south wind blows, you say, "It's gonna be hot," and you're right. So how can you read the sky but miss what time it really is?

Luke 12:57 (KJV):

"Yea, and why even of yourselves judge ye not what is right?"

Jesus (Today):

Why can't you judge for yourselves what is right?

Luke 12:58–59 (KJV)

"When thou goest with thine adversary to the magistrate, as thou art in the way, give diligence that thou mayest be delivered from him; lest he hale thee to the judge, and the judge deliver thee to the officer, and the officer cast thee into prison. I tell thee, thou shalt not depart thence, till thou hast paid the very last mite."

When you're on your way to court with your accuser, do everything you can to settle with him before you get there. Otherwise, he might drag you to the judge, the judge hands you over to the officer, and the officer throws you in prison. I'm telling you; you won't get out until you've paid every last penny.

Luke 13

Luke 13:2-3 (KJV):
"Suppose ye that these Galilaeans were sinners above all the Galilaeans, because they suffered such things? I tell you, Nay: but, except ye repent, ye shall all likewise perish."
Jesus (Today):
Do you really think those Galileans were worse sinners just because they suffered like that? No. I'm telling you; unless you turn your life around, you'll be headed the same way.

Luke 13:4-5 (KJV):
"Or those eighteen, upon whom the tower in Siloam fell, and slew them, think ye that they were sinners above all men that dwelt in Jerusalem? I tell you, Nay: but, except ye repent, ye shall all likewise perish."
Jesus (Today):
And what about the eighteen who were crushed when that tower fell? You think they were guiltier than everyone else in Jerusalem? No. Unless you wake up and repent, you'll end up the same.

Luke 13:6-9 (KJV)
"A certain man had a fig tree planted in his vineyard; and he came and sought fruit thereon, and found none. Then said he unto the dresser of his vineyard, Behold, these three years I come seeking fruit on this fig tree, and find none: cut it down; why cumbereth it the ground?
And he answering said unto him, Lord, let it alone this year also, till I shall dig about it, and dung it: And if it bear fruit, well: and if not, then after that thou shalt cut it down."
Jesus (Today):
A man planted a fig tree in his vineyard.
Year after year, he came looking for fruit. Nothing.
He told the gardener, "I've been patient for three years, and still nothing. Cut it down. Why let it waste the soil?"
But the gardener said, "Give it one more year.

Let me dig around it, fertilize it, pour into it.
If it bears fruit, great. If not, then go ahead and cut it down."

Luke 13:12 (KJV):
"And when Jesus saw her, he called her to him, and said unto her,"
Jesus (Today):
Woman, you are completely set free from your pain.

Luke 13:15-16 (KJV):
"Thou hypocrite, doth not each one of you on the sabbath loose his ox or his ass from the stall, and lead him away to watering? And ought not this woman, being a daughter of Abraham, whom Satan hath bound, lo, these eighteen years, be loosed from this bond on the sabbath day?"
Jesus (Today):
You hypocrites. Don't every one of you untie your ox or donkey on the Sabbath to get it water? Then why shouldn't this woman, a daughter of Abraham, who's been chained by Satan for eighteen years, be set free, especially on the Sabbath?

Luke 13:18-19 (KJV)
"Unto what is the kingdom of God like? and whereunto shall I resemble it? It is like a grain of mustard seed, which a man took, and cast into his garden; and it grew, and waxed a great tree; and the fowls of the air lodged in the branches of it."
Jesus (Today):
What's the Kingdom of God like?
It's like a tiny mustard seed someone plants in their garden. It grows into a massive tree, and the birds come and rest in its branches.

Luke 13:20-21 (KJV)
"Whereunto shall I liken the kingdom of God? It is like leaven, which a woman took and hid in three measures of meal, till the whole was leavened."
Jesus (Today):
What else can I compare the kingdom of God to? It's like yeast

that a woman mixed into a large batch of dough until it worked through the whole thing.

Luke 13:24 (KJV):
"Strive to enter in at the strait gate: for many, I say unto you, will seek to enter in, and shall not be able."

Jesus (Today):
Fight to get through the narrow door.
Because many will try, and won't make it in.

Luke 13:25-27 (KJV):
"When once the master of the house is risen up, and hath shut to the door, and ye begin to stand without, and to knock at the door, saying, Lord, Lord, open unto us; and he shall answer and say unto you, I know you not whence ye are: Then shall ye begin to say, We have eaten and drunk in thy presence, and thou hast taught in our streets. But he shall say, I tell you, I know you not whence ye are; depart from me, all ye workers of iniquity."

Jesus (Today):
Once the door is shut, it's shut.
You'll be outside knocking, begging, "Lord, open up!"
And He'll say, "I don't know you. Where are you even from?"
You'll argue, "But we ate with You! You taught in our streets!"
And He'll answer, "I don't know you. Leave Me, you lived like I didn't matter."

Luke 13:28-29 (KJV):
"There shall be weeping and gnashing of teeth, when ye shall see Abraham, and Isaac, and Jacob, and all the prophets, in the kingdom of God, and you yourselves thrust out. And they shall come from the east, and from the west, and from the north, and from the south, and shall sit down in the kingdom of God."

Jesus (Today):
You'll cry and grind your teeth when you see Abraham, Isaac, Jacob, and all the prophets in God's kingdom, but you're left out. People will come from every direction; east, west, north, and south, and take their seats at God's table.

Luke 13:30 (KJV):
"And, behold, there are last which shall be first, and there are first which shall be last."
Jesus (Today):
Get ready, some who were last will be first.
And some who were first will end up last.

Luke 13:32–33 (KJV):
"Go ye, and tell that fox, Behold, I cast out devils, and I do cures to day and to morrow, and the third day I shall be perfected. Nevertheless I must walk to day, and to morrow, and the day following: for it cannot be that a prophet perish out of Jerusalem."
Jesus (Today):
Go and tell that fox, "I drive out demons and heal people today and tomorrow, and on the third day I will finish my work. But I must keep going today, tomorrow, and the next day, for surely no prophet can die outside Jerusalem."

Luke 13:34–35 (KJV):
"O Jerusalem, Jerusalem, which killest the prophets, and stonest them that are sent unto thee; how often would I have gathered thy children together, as a hen doth gather her brood under her wings, and ye would not! Behold, your house is left unto you desolate: and verily I say unto you, Ye shall not see me, until the time come when ye shall say, Blessed is he that cometh in the name of the Lord."
Jesus (Today):
Jerusalem, Jerusalem, you kill the prophets and stone the ones sent to you. How many times I wanted to pull you close, like a mother hen gathering her chicks, but you wouldn't let Me. So now your house is abandoned. And I'm telling you,
you won't see Me again until you finally say, "Blessed is the He who comes in the name of the Lord."

Luke 14

Luke 14:3 (KJV):
"Is it lawful to heal on the sabbath day?"
Jesus (Today):
Tell Me this, is it legal to heal someone on the Sabbath or not?

Luke 14:5 (KJV):
"Which of you shall have an ass or an ox fallen into a pit, and will not straightway pull him out on the sabbath day?"
Jesus (Today):
If your donkey or ox falls into a ditch on the Sabbath, which one of you wouldn't pull it out right away?

Luke 14:8-10 (KJV):
"When thou art bidden of any man to a wedding, sit not down in the highest room; lest a more honourable man than thou be bidden of him; And he that bade thee and him come and say to thee, Give this man place; and thou begin with shame to take the lowest room. But when thou art bidden, go and sit down in the lowest room; that when he that bade thee cometh, he may say unto thee, Friend, go up higher: then shalt thou have worship in the presence of them that sit at meat with thee."
Jesus (Today):
When you're invited to a wedding, don't grab the best seat like you're the guest of honor. Someone more important might show up, and the host will ask you to move, and you'll end up embarrassed. Instead, when you're invited, take the lowest seat. Then when the host sees you, he'll say, "Friend, move up closer." And that kind of honor will mean something, because you didn't chase it.

Luke 14:11 (KJV):
"For whosoever exalteth himself shall be abased; and he that humbleth himself shall be exalted."
Jesus (Today):

If you lift yourself up, you'll be brought down.
But if you humble yourself, you'll be lifted higher.

Luke 14:12-14 (KJV):
"When thou makest a dinner or a supper, call not thy friends, nor thy brethren, neither thy kinsmen, nor thy rich neighbours; lest they also bid thee again, and a recompence be made thee. But when thou makest a feast, call the poor, the maimed, the lame, the blind: And thou shalt be blessed; for they cannot recompense thee: for thou shalt be recompensed at the resurrection of the just."

Jesus (Today):
When you throw a party, don't just invite your friends, your brothers, or rich neighbors. They'll just invite you back and that's your only reward. Invite the poor, the disabled, the outcasts, the blind. That's when you'll be truly blessed, because they can't pay you back. But trust Me. God will repay you at the resurrection of the righteous.

Luke 14:16-24 (KJV)
"A certain man made a great supper, and bade many: And sent his servant at supper time to say to them that were bidden, Come; for all things are now ready. And they all with one consent began to make excuse. The first said unto him, I have bought a piece of ground, and I must needs go and see it: I pray thee have me excused. And another said, I have bought five yoke of oxen, and I go to prove them: I pray thee have me excused. And another said, I have married a wife, and therefore I cannot come. So that servant came, and shewed his lord these things. Then the master of the house being angry said to his servant, Go out quickly into the streets and lanes of the city, and bring in hither the poor, and the maimed, and the halt, and the blind. And the servant said, Lord, it is done as thou hast commanded, and yet there is room. And the lord said unto the servant, Go out into the highways and hedges, and compel them to come in, that my house may be filled. For I say unto you, That none of those men which were bidden shall taste of my supper."

Jesus (Today):
A man prepared a huge banquet and invited many. When it was time, he sent his servant to tell them, "Come, everything is ready." But one by one, everyone started making excuses:
"I just bought land."
"I just got new work equipment."
"I just got married."
The servant came back and told the master everything. The

master got angry and said, "Go out quickly into the streets and alleys of the city and bring in the poor, the crippled, the blind, and the lame." The servant said, "We did what you said and there's still room." Then the master said, "Go out to the roads and the country lanes and make them come so my house will be full. I'm telling you, not one of those originally invited will taste my banquet."

Luke 14:26-27 (KJV):
"If any man come to me, and hate not his father, and mother, and wife, and children, and brethren, and sisters, yea, and his own life also, he cannot be my disciple. And whosoever doth not bear his cross, and come after me, cannot be my disciple."

Jesus (Today):
If you want to follow Me, but your love for Me doesn't outshine your love for your family, or even your own life, you're not ready to be My disciple. If you won't carry your cross and come after Me, you're not ready for this path.

Luke 14:28-30 (KJV):
"For which of you, intending to build a tower, sitteth not down first, and counteth the cost, whether he have sufficient to finish it? Lest haply, after he hath laid the foundation, and is not able to finish it, all that behold it begin to mock him, Saying, This man began to build, and was not able to finish."

Jesus (Today):
Think about it, if you were building a tower, wouldn't you sit down first and figure out the cost? Otherwise, you lay the foundation and run out halfway. People will laugh and say, "This person started something they couldn't finish."

Luke 14:31-33 (KJV):
"Or what king, going to make war against another king, sitteth not down first, and consulteth whether he be able with ten thousand to meet him that cometh against him with twenty thousand? Or else, while the other is yet a great way off, he sendeth an ambassage, and desireth conditions of peace. So likewise, whosoever he be of you that forsaketh not all that he hath, he cannot be my disciple."

Jesus (Today):
Same with a king, if he's going to war, he'll count his troops and see if he can win. If not, he'll make peace before the battle starts. So hear Me: if you're not willing to let go of everything, you're not ready to be My disciple.

Luke 14:34–35 (KJV):
"Salt is good: but if the salt have lost his savour, wherewith shall it be seasoned? It is neither fit for the land, nor yet for the dunghill; but men cast it out. He that hath ears to hear, let him hear."
Jesus (Today):
Salt is good. But if it loses its flavor, how can it be made salty again? You can't use it for soil. You can't even throw it on the compost pile. It's useless. If you can hear Me, really hear Me.

Luke 15

Luke 15:4–6 (KJV):
"What man of you, having an hundred sheep, if he lose one of them, doth not leave the ninety and nine in the wilderness, and go after that which is lost, until he find it? And when he hath found it, he layeth it on his shoulders, rejoicing. And when he cometh home, he calleth together his friends and neighbours, saying unto them, Rejoice with me; for I have found my sheep which was lost."
Jesus (Today):
If you had a hundred sheep and lost one, wouldn't you leave the ninety-nine behind and go after the one that's missing?
And when you find it, you don't just drag it back.
You pick it up, throw it over your shoulders, and celebrate.
Then you call up your friends and neighbors and say,
"Come celebrate with me, I found the one that was lost."

Luke 15:7 (KJV):
"I say unto you, that likewise joy shall be in heaven over one sinner that repenteth, more than over ninety and nine just persons, which need no repentance."

Jesus (Today):
That's exactly what heaven is like, a full-on celebration over one lost soul who turns back, even more than ninety-nine who didn't need saving.

Luke 15:8–9 (KJV):
"Either what woman having ten pieces of silver, if she lose one piece, doth not light a candle, and sweep the house, and seek diligently till she find it? And when she hath found it, she calleth her friends and her neighbours together, saying, Rejoice with me; for I have found the piece which I had lost."

Jesus (Today):
Or picture a woman with ten silver coins.
If she loses one, won't she turn on every light,
tear the house apart, sweep every corner until she finds it?
And when she does, she calls up her girls and says,
"Celebrate with me! I found what I lost!"

Luke 15:10 (KJV):
"Likewise, I say unto you, there is joy in the presence of the angels of God over one sinner that repenteth."

Jesus (Today):
That's how it is in heaven, the angels break into celebration when even one person turns back to God.

Luke 15:11–32 (KJV):
"A certain man had two sons. And the younger of them said to his father, Father, give me the portion of goods that falleth to me. And he divided unto them his living. And not many days after the younger son gathered all together, and took his journey into a far country, and there wasted his substance with riotous living. And when he had spent all, there arose a mighty famine in that land; and he began to be in want. And he went and joined himself to a citizen of that country; and he sent him into his fields to feed swine. And he would fain have filled his belly with the husks that the swine did eat: and no man gave unto him. And when he came to himself, he said, How many hired servants of my father's have bread enough and to spare, and I perish with hunger! I will

arise and go to my father, and will say unto him, Father, I have sinned against heaven, and before thee, And am no more worthy to be called thy son: make me as one of thy hired servants. And he arose, and came to his father. But when he was yet a great way off, his father saw him, and had compassion, and ran, and fell on his neck, and kissed him. And the son said unto him, Father, I have sinned against heaven, and in thy sight, and am no more worthy to be called thy son. But the father said to his servants, Bring forth the best robe, and put it on him; and put a ring on his hand, and shoes on his feet: And bring hither the fatted calf, and kill it; and let us eat, and be merry: For this my son was dead, and is alive again; he was lost, and is found. And they began to be merry. Now his elder son was in the field: and as he came and drew nigh to the house, he heard musick and dancing. And he called one of the servants, and asked what these things meant. And he said unto him, Thy brother is come; and thy father hath killed the fatted calf, because he hath received him safe and sound. And he was angry, and would not go in: therefore came his father out, and intreated him. And he answering said to his father, Lo, these many years do I serve thee, neither transgressed I at any time thy commandment: and yet thou never gavest me a kid, that I might make merry with my friends: But as soon as this thy son was come, which hath devoured thy living with harlots, thou hast killed for him the fatted calf. And he said unto him, Son, thou art ever with me, and all that I have is thine. It was meet that we should make merry, and be glad: for this thy brother was dead, and is alive again; and was lost, and is found."

Jesus (Today):
A man had two sons. The younger one said, "Father, give me my share of the inheritance now." So the father divided his wealth. A few days later, the younger son packed everything and left for a far country where he blew all his money on wild living. When he ran out, a severe famine hit, and he became desperate. He took a job feeding pigs, and he was so hungry he wanted to eat the pig slop. Then he came to his senses and said, "My father's servants have more than enough to eat, and here I am starving. I'll go back and say, 'Father, I've sinned against heaven and you. I'm not worthy to be your son. Make me like one of your servants.'" So he went home.

While he was still far off, his father saw him, was filled with compassion, ran to him, hugged him, and kissed him. The son said, "Father, I've sinned against heaven and you. I'm not worthy to be called your son." But the father told his servants, "Bring the best robe and put it on him. Put a ring on his finger and sandals on his feet. Kill the fattened calf. We're going to celebrate, because my son was dead and is alive again. He was lost and now he's found."

Meanwhile the older son was in the field. When he came near the house and heard music and dancing, he asked a servant what was going on. The servant said, "Your brother is home, and your father has killed the fattened calf to celebrate his safe return." The older son got angry and refused to go in. His father came out and pleaded with him, but he said, "Look, all these years I've served you and never disobeyed, yet you never gave me a young goat to celebrate with my friends. But when this son of yours who wasted everything comes home, you kill the fattened calf for him!"

The father said, "Son, you're always with me, and everything I have is yours. But we had to celebrate and be glad because your brother was dead and is alive again. He was lost and now he's found."

Luke 16

Luke 16:1-9 (KJV):
"There was a certain rich man, which had a steward; and the same was accused unto him that he had wasted his goods. How is it that I hear this of thee? give an account of thy stewardship; for thou mayest be no longer steward. What shall I do? for my lord taketh away from me the stewardship: I cannot dig; to beg I am ashamed. I am resolved what to do, that, when I am put out of the stewardship, they may receive me into their houses. How much owest thou unto my lord? An hundred measures of oil. Take thy bill, and sit down quickly, and write fifty. And how much owest thou? An hundred measures of wheat. Take thy bill, and write fourscore. And I say unto you, Make to yourselves friends of the mammon of unrighteousness; that, when ye fail, they may receive you into everlasting habitations."

Jesus (Today):
There was a rich man who had a manager accused of wasting his property. What's this I hear about you? Bring me a report of your work because you can't be my manager anymore. What am I going to do? My boss is taking my job away. I'm not strong enough to dig and I'm too ashamed to beg. I know what I'll do so

that when I'm fired people will welcome me into their homes. How much do you owe my master? A hundred measures of oil. Take your bill, sit down quickly, and make it fifty. And how much do you owe? A hundred measures of wheat. Take your bill and make it eighty. And I tell you, use worldly wealth to make friends for yourselves so that when it's gone you'll be welcomed into eternal homes.

Luke 16:10-12 (KJV)
"He that is faithful in that which is least is faithful also in much: and he that is unjust in the least is unjust also in much. If therefore ye have not been faithful in the unrighteous mammon, who will commit to your trust the true riches? And if ye have not been faithful in that which is another man's, who shall give you that which is your own?"

Jesus (Today):
If you're trustworthy with little, you'll be trustworthy with a lot.
But if you cheat on the small stuff, you'll cheat on the big stuff too. So, if you can't handle money with integrity,
why would God trust you with true spiritual riches?
And if you're careless with what belongs to someone else,
why would anyone give you what's yours?

Luke 16:13 (KJV)
"No servant can serve two masters: for either he will hate the one, and love the other; or else he will hold to the one, and despise the other. Ye cannot serve God and mammon."

Jesus (Today):
You can't serve two masters.
You'll end up loving one and resenting the other.
You can't serve both God *and* money.

Luke 16:15 (KJV)
"Ye are they which justify yourselves before men; but God knoweth your hearts: for that which is highly esteemed among men is abomination in the sight of God."

Jesus (Today):

You're trying to prove yourselves in front of people,
but God sees what's really in your heart.
The stuff that impresses the world?
It doesn't impress Him.

Luke 16:16-17 (KJV)
"The law and the prophets were until John: since that time the kingdom of God is preached, and every man presseth into it. And it is easier for heaven and earth to pass, than one tittle of the law to fail."

Jesus (Today):
The Law and Prophets were your guide until John. Now the Kingdom of God is being preached, and people are breaking down the doors to get in. Heaven and earth could collapse, but not a single detail of God's word will ever fail.

Luke 16:18 (KJV)
"Whosoever putteth away his wife, and marrieth another, committeth adultery: and whosoever marrieth her that is put away from her husband committeth adultery."

Jesus (Today):
If you divorce your wife and marry someone else, you're committing adultery. And if you marry someone who's divorced from her husband, you're stepping into adultery too.

Luke 17

Luke 17:1-2 (KJV)
"It is impossible but that offences will come: but woe unto him, through whom they come! It were better for him that a millstone were hanged about his neck, and he cast into the sea, than that he should offend one of these little ones."

Jesus (Today):
Temptation's always going to exist,

but if you're the one causing it? Watch out.
It would be better to have a concrete block tied around your neck and be thrown into the ocean than to mess up one of these kids trying to follow God.

Luke 17:3-4 (KJV)
"Take heed to yourselves: If thy brother trespass against thee, rebuke him; and if he repent, forgive him. And if he trespass against thee seven times in a day, and seven times in a day turn again to thee, saying, I repent; thou shalt forgive him."

Jesus (Today):
Pay attention to yourselves.
If someone wrongs you; call it out.
But if they're truly sorry, forgive them.
Even if they mess up seven times in one day,
and each time come back saying, "I was wrong"
forgive them. Every time.

Luke 17:6 (KJV)
"If ye had faith as a grain of mustard seed, ye might say unto this sycamine tree, Be thou plucked up by the root, and be thou planted in the sea; and it should obey you."

Jesus (Today):
If your faith was even the size of a mustard seed,
you could tell a tree to uproot and plant itself in the ocean, *and it would.*

Luke 17:7 (KJV)
"Which of you, having a servant plowing or feeding cattle, will say unto him by and by, when he is come from the field, Go and sit down to meat?"

Jesus (Today):
If one of you has a servant out plowing or watching the sheep,
do you tell him when he comes in, "Sit down and have dinner"?

Luke 17:8 (KJV)
"And will not rather say unto him, Make ready wherewith I may sup, and gird thyself, and serve me, till I have eaten and drunken; and afterward thou shalt eat and drink?"

Jesus (Today):
No. You tell him, "Get my meal ready, put on your apron, and serve me while I eat and drink. Then you can eat and drink."

Luke 17:9 (KJV)
"Doth he thank that servant because he did the things that were commanded him? I trow not."

Jesus (Today):
Do you thank the servant for doing what he was told? Of course not.

Luke 17:10 (KJV)
"So likewise ye, when ye shall have done all those things which are commanded you, say, We are unprofitable servants: we have done that which was our duty to do."

Jesus (Today):
And when you've done everything God asked of you, just say, "I'm just a servant. I only did what I was supposed to.

Luke 17:14 (KJV)
"Go shew yourselves unto the priests."

Jesus (Today):
Go show yourselves to the priests.

Luke 17:17–19 (KJV)
"Were there not ten cleansed? but where are the nine? There are not found that returned to give glory to God, save this stranger. Arise, go thy way: thy faith hath made thee whole."

Jesus (Today):
Weren't there ten of you who got healed? Where are the other nine? Only this one outsider came back to thank Me? Get up and go, your faith is what healed you.

Luke 17:20-21 (KJV)

"The kingdom of God cometh not with observation: Neither shall they say, Lo here! or, lo there! for, behold, the kingdom of God is within you."

Jesus (Today):
God's kingdom isn't something you'll spot with your eyes.
You won't say, "Here it is!" or "There it is!",
Because the kingdom? It's *within* you.

Luke 17:22–24 (KJV)

"The days will come, when ye shall desire to see one of the days of the Son of man, and ye shall not see it. And they shall say to you, See here; or, see there: go not after them, nor follow them. For as the lightning, that lighteneth out of the one part under heaven, shineth unto the other part under heaven; so shall also the Son of man be in his day."

Jesus (Today):
A time's coming when you'll long for one more day with Me, but you won't get it. People will say, "Look over here!" or "Look, He's there!" Don't fall for it. When I return, it'll be like lightning flashing across the sky, undeniable, unmistakable, seen by everyone at once.

Luke 17:25 (KJV):

"But first must he suffer many things, and be rejected of this generation."

Jesus (Today):
But first I have to suffer many things and be rejected by this generation.

Luke 17:26–30 (KJV)

"And as it was in the days of Noe, so shall it be also in the days of the Son of man. They did eat, they drank, they married wives, they were given in marriage, until the day that Noe entered into the ark, and the flood came, and destroyed them all. Likewise also as it was in the days of Lot; they did eat, they drank, they bought, they sold, they planted, they builded; but the same day that Lot went out of Sodom it rained fire and brimstone from heaven, and destroyed them all. Even

thus shall it be in the day when the Son of man is revealed."

Jesus (Today):
When I come back, it'll be like in Noah's day,
people eating, drinking, getting married. Living normal life;
until Noah got on that boat, and the flood hit and wiped them
out. Same with Lot's day; people were shopping, planting,
building. And in one instant, fire and sulfur rained down from
heaven and destroyed the whole city. That's how sudden My
return will be.

Luke 17:31–33 (KJV)

"In that day, he which shall be upon the housetop, and his stuff in the house, let him not come down to take it away. And he that is in the field, let him likewise not return back. Remember Lot's wife. Whosoever shall seek to save his life shall lose it, and whosoever shall lose his life shall preserve it."

Jesus (Today):
When that day hits, don't turn around for anything.
Don't go back into your house for your stuff.
***Remember Lot's wife.* If you try to save your life, you'll lose it.**
But if you're willing to let it go, you'll keep it forever.

Luke 17:34–36 (KJV)

"I tell you, in that night there shall be two men in one bed; the one shall be taken, and the other shall be left. Two women shall be grinding together; the one shall be taken, and the other left. Two men shall be in the field; the one shall be taken, and the other left."

Jesus (Today):
I'm telling you, that night there will be two men in one bed. One
will be taken, and the other left. Two women will be grinding
together. One will be taken, and the other left. Two men will be
in the field. One will be taken, and the other left.

Luke 18

Luke 18:2-5 (KJV)
"There was in a city a judge, which feared not God, neither regarded man. And there was a widow in that city; and she came unto him, saying, Avenge me of mine adversary. And he would not for a while: but afterward he said within himself, Though I fear not God, nor regard man; yet because this widow troubleth me, I will avenge her, lest by her continual coming she weary me."

Jesus (Today):
There was this judge who didn't care about God or people.
A widow kept showing up, begging him, "Help me, get justice against the one who wronged me." At first, he ignored her, but finally he said to himself, "I don't care about God or anyone else." But this woman won't let up. If I don't do something, she's going to wear me down."

Luke 18:6-8 (KJV)
"And the Lord said, Hear what the unjust judge saith. And shall not God avenge his own elect, which cry day and night unto him, though he bear long with them? I tell you that he will avenge them speedily. Nevertheless when the Son of man cometh, shall he find faith on the earth?"

Jesus (Today):
Did you catch that? If even an unjust judge gives in,
how much more will God come through for His people who cry out to Him day and night? He will act fast. But when I come back, will I find anyone still living with that kind of faith?

Luke 18:10-14 (KJV)
"Two men went up into the temple to pray; the one a Pharisee, and the other a publican. The Pharisee stood and prayed thus with himself, God, I thank thee, that I am not as other men are, extortioners, unjust, adulterers, or even as this publican. I fast twice in the week, I give tithes of all that I possess. And the publican, standing afar off, would not lift up so much as his eyes unto heaven, but smote upon his breast, saying, God be merciful to me a sinner. I tell you, this man went down to his house justified rather than the other: for every one that exalteth himself shall be abased; and he that humbleth himself shall be exalted."

Jesus (Today):
Two men went to church to pray.
One was a religious leader, the other was a tax collector.
The religious guy stood tall and prayed, "God, thank You I'm not

like these awful people: cheaters, sinners, or even this tax guy. I fast twice a week, and I give money faithfully."
But the tax collector? He wouldn't even lift his head.
He beat his chest and cried, "God, please have mercy on me. I'm a sinner." Let Me tell you, that man went home right with God, not the other. Because anyone who lifts themselves up will be brought low, but the one who humbles themselves?
God will raise them up.

Luke 18:16–17 (KJV)
"Suffer little children to come unto me, and forbid them not: for of such is the kingdom of God. Verily I say unto you, Whosoever shall not receive the kingdom of God as a little child shall in no wise enter therein."

Jesus (Today):
Let the children come to Me, don't hold them back.
God's kingdom belongs to hearts like theirs. If you don't receive it like a child; open, trusting, unguarded, you won't get in.

Luke 18:19-20 (KJV)
"Why callest thou me good? none is good, save one, that is, God. Thou knowest the commandments, Do not commit adultery, Do not kill, Do not steal, Do not bear false witness, Honour thy father and thy mother."

Why do you call Me good?
Only God is truly good.
You know the commandments:
Don't commit adultery.
Don't kill.
Don't steal.
Don't lie.
Honor your father and mother.

Luke 18:22 (KJV)
"Yet lackest thou one thing: sell all that thou hast, and distribute unto the poor, and thou shalt have treasure in heaven: and come, follow me."

Jesus (Today):
There's still one thing missing.
Sell everything you've got. Give it to the poor.
You'll have treasure waiting in heaven
then come follow Me.

Luke 18:24-25 (KJV)
"How hardly shall they that have riches enter into the kingdom of God! For it is easier for a camel to go through a needle's eye, than for a rich man to enter into the kingdom of God."
Jesus (Today):
It's hard for the rich to enter God's kingdom. It's easier to squeeze a camel through the eye of a needle than for a rich person to enter the kingdom of God.

Luke 18:27 (KJV)
"The things which are impossible with men are possible with God."
Jesus (Today):
What's impossible for people, *is totally possible with God.*

Luke 18:29-30 (KJV)
"Verily I say unto you, There is no man that hath left house, or parents, or brethren, or wife, or children, for the kingdom of God's sake, who shall not receive manifold more in this present time, and in the world to come life everlasting."
Jesus (Today):
Anyone who's left their home, family, or security for My sake, they'll get back *so much more.* Even in this life, plus eternal life in the next. And eternal life is just the beginning.

Luke 18:31-33 (KJV)
"Behold, we go up to Jerusalem, and all things that are written by the prophets concerning the Son of man shall be accomplished. For he shall be delivered unto the Gentiles, and shall be mocked, and spitefully entreated, and spitted on. And they shall scourge him, and put him to death: and the third day he shall rise again."

Jesus (Today):
We're headed to Jerusalem.
Everything the prophets wrote said about Me is about to come true. I'll be handed over.
I'll be mocked, beaten, spit on.
They'll torture Me and kill Me.
But three days later, *I'm getting up.*

Luke 18:41–42 (KJV)
"What wilt thou that I shall do unto thee? Receive thy sight: thy faith hath saved thee."
Jesus (Today):
What do you want Me to do for you?
Then receive your sight. Your faith is what healed you.

Luke 19

Luke 19:5-9 (KJV)
"Zacchaeus, make haste, and come down; for to day I must abide at thy house. This day is salvation come to this house, forsomuch as he also is a son of Abraham."
Jesus (Today):
Zacchaeus, hurry and come down. Today I must stay at your house. Today salvation has come to this house, because this man too is a son of Abraham.

Luke 19:10 (KJV)
"For the Son of man is come to seek and to save that which was lost."
Jesus (Today):
I came to find the ones who are lost, and to save them. That's why I'm here.

Luke 19:12-27 (KJV):

"A certain nobleman went into a far country to receive for himself a kingdom, and to return. And he called his ten servants, and delivered them ten pounds, and said unto them, Occupy till I come. But his citizens hated him, and sent a message after him, saying, We will not have this man to reign over us. And it came to pass, that when he was returned, having received the kingdom, then he commanded these servants to be called unto him, to whom he had given the money, that he might know how much every man had gained by trading. Then came the first, saying, Lord, thy pound hath gained ten pounds. And he said unto him, Well, thou good servant: because thou hast been faithful in a very little, have thou authority over ten cities. And the second came, saying, Lord, thy pound hath gained five pounds. And he said likewise to him, Be thou also over five cities. And another came, saying, Lord, behold, here is thy pound, which I have kept laid up in a napkin. For I feared thee, because thou art an austere man: thou takest up that thou layedst not down, and reapest that thou didst not sow. And he saith unto him, Out of thine own mouth will I judge thee, thou wicked servant. Thou knewest that I was an austere man, taking up that I laid not down, and reaping that I did not sow: wherefore then gavest not thou my money into the bank, that at my coming I might have required mine own with usury? And he said unto them that stood by, Take from him the pound, and give it to him that hath ten pounds. (And they said unto him, Lord, he hath ten pounds.) For I say unto you, That unto every one which hath shall be given; and from him that hath not, even that he hath shall be taken away from him. But those mine enemies, which would not that I should reign over them, bring hither, and slay them before me."

Jesus (Today):

A man went away to another country to be crowned king and then come back. Before he left, he called in ten of his employees and gave each one a stack of cash, about three months' pay. He told them, "Invest this for me while I'm gone."

But the people in his city hated him and sent word saying, "We don't want this guy ruling over us." When he came back as king, he called in the employees to see what they'd done with his money. The first one came and said, "Boss, your money made ten times more." The king said, "Well done, good worker. You've been faithful with a little, so now you're in charge of ten cities."

The second came and said, "Your money made five times more." The king said, "Great. You're in charge of five cities."

But another came and said, "Here's your money. I kept it in a safe because I was scared of you. You're tough. You take what you didn't earn and you reap what you didn't plant."

The king said, "I'll judge you by your own words, you wicked employee. If you really thought I was so tough, why didn't you at least put my money in the bank so I could get some interest?"

Then he told the others standing nearby, "Take his money and give it to the one who made ten times more." They said, "But he already has plenty!"

The king replied, "Listen to me, everyone who does something with what they're given will get more. But whoever does nothing with what they have, even what little they have will be taken away. And as for those enemies of mine who didn't want me to rule over them; bring them here and kill them in front of me."

Luke 19:30–31 (KJV)
"Go ye into the village over against you; in the which at your entering ye shall find a colt tied, whereon yet never man sat: loose him, and bring him hither. And if any man ask you, Why do ye loose him? thus shall ye say unto him, Because the Lord hath need of him."

Jesus (Today):
Go into the village, there's a young donkey tied up that's never been ridden. Untie it and bring it to Me. If anyone asks why you're taking it, just say, "The Lord needs it."

Luke 19:40 (KJV)
"I tell you that, if these should hold their peace, the stones would immediately cry out."

Jesus (Today):
If these voices went silent, the rocks themselves would start shouting.

Luke 19:42–44 (KJV)
"If thou hadst known, even thou, at least in this thy day, the things which belong unto thy peace! but now they are hid from thine eyes. For the days shall come upon thee, that thine enemies shall cast a trench about thee, and compass thee round, and keep thee in on every side, And shall lay

thee even with the ground, and thy children within thee; and they shall not leave in thee one stone upon another; because thou knewest not the time of thy visitation."

Jesus (Today):
A time is coming when your enemies will surround you, trap you on every side, and tear everything down, even your children inside the city. They won't leave one stone standing. And it'll all be because you didn't recognize when God came to visit you.

Luke 20

Luke 20:3-4 (KJV)
"I will also ask you one thing... The baptism of John, was it from heaven, or of men?"

Jesus (Today):
Alright, I've got a question for you. Answer Me this: John's baptism, did it come from heaven or was it just from people?

Luke 20:8 (KJV)
"Neither tell I you by what authority I do these things."

Jesus (Today):
Then I'm not telling you where My authority comes from either.

Luke 20:9-16 (KJV)
"A certain man planted a vineyard, and let it forth to husbandmen, and went into a far country for a long time. And at the season he sent a servant to the husbandmen, that they should give him of the fruit of the vineyard: but the husbandmen beat him, and sent him away empty. And again he sent another servant: and they beat him also, and entreated him shamefully, and sent him away empty. And again he sent a third: and they wounded him also, and cast him out. Then said the lord of the vineyard, What shall I do? I will send my beloved son: it may be they will reverence him when they see him. But when the husbandmen saw him, they reasoned among themselves, saying, This is the heir: come, let us kill him, that the inheritance may be ours. So they cast him

out of the vineyard, and killed him. What therefore shall the lord of the vineyard do unto them? He shall come and destroy these husbandmen, and shall give the vineyard to others."

Jesus (Today):
There was a man who planted a vineyard. He poured everything into it, fenced it, stocked it, got it ready. Then he leased it out to tenants and went out of town for a while.

When harvest season came, he sent one of his people to collect his share of the fruit. But the tenants beat the messenger down and sent him back empty-handed. So the owner tried again. Sent another servant. They beat him too; this time they piled on the insults and sent him away with nothing. Still, he gave them another chance. Sent a third.

They didn't just beat this one; they wounded him and threw him out. Then the owner of the vineyard said, "What should I do now? I'll send My son. My own beloved son. Surely... surely, they'll respect him." But when the tenants saw the son coming, they started plotting. They said, "That's the heir. If we kill him, the inheritance will be ours." So, they dragged him outside the vineyard and murdered him. Now what do you think the owner's going to do? He'll come back. Wipe those men out and hand the vineyard over to someone else.

Luke 20:17 (KJV)
"What is this then that is written, The stone which the builders rejected, the same is become the head of the corner?"

Jesus (Today):
So what do you make of this Scripture:
The stone the builders rejected, that's the one God made the cornerstone?

Luke 20:18 (KJV)
"Whosoever shall fall upon that stone shall be broken; but on whomsoever it shall fall, it will grind him to powder."

Jesus (Today):

If you trip over that stone, you'll be shattered. But if this Stone falls on you? You'll be crushed to dust.

Luke 20:24–25 (KJV)
"Shew me a penny. Whose image and superscription hath it? Render therefore unto Caesar the things which be Caesar's, and unto God the things which be God's."

Jesus (Today):
Show Me a coin, whose face is on it?
Then give Caesar what belongs to Caesar.
But give God what belongs to God.

Luke 20:34–36 (KJV)
The children of this world marry, and are given in marriage: But they which shall be accounted worthy to obtain that world, and the resurrection from the dead, neither marry, nor are given in marriage: Neither can they die any more: for they are equal unto the angels; and are the children of God, being the children of the resurrection."

Jesus (Today):
People in this life get married and start families.
But those who are raised to eternal life,
they don't marry or get married. They'll never die again.
They're like the angels now. God's children, raised in power.

Luke 20:37–38 (KJV)
"Now that the dead are raised, even Moses shewed at the bush, when he calleth the Lord the God of Abraham, and the God of Isaac, and the God of Jacob. For he is not a God of the dead, but of the living: for all live unto him."

Jesus (Today):
Even Moses proved the resurrection's real.
At the burning bush, he called the Lord,
"The God of Abraham, Isaac, and Jacob."
God isn't the God of dead people, He's the God of the living.
Everyone is alive to Him.

Luke 20:41-44 (KJV)
"How say they that Christ is David's son? And David himself saith in the book of Psalms, The Lord said unto my Lord, Sit thou on my right hand, Till I make thine enemies thy footstool. David therefore calleth him Lord, how is he then his son?

Jesus (Today):
Let Me ask you this, how can people say the Messiah is David's son? Even David said in the Psalms, "The Lord said to my Lord, sit beside Me until I crush Your enemies beneath Your feet." So if David calls Him "Lord," how is He just his son?

Luke 20:46-47 (KJV)
"Beware of the scribes, which desire to walk in long robes, and love greetings in the markets, and the highest seats in the synagogues, and the chief rooms at feasts; Which devour widows' houses, and for a shew make long prayers: the same shall receive greater damnation."

Jesus (Today):
Watch out for the religious experts they love showing off in their robes, getting attention in public, and sitting in the best seats at church and fancy dinners. But behind the scenes? They take advantage of widows and pray long, loud prayers just to be seen. They're going to be judged harder than anyone.

Luke 21

Luke 21:3-4 (KJV)
"Of a truth I say unto you, that this poor widow hath cast in more than they all: For all these have of their abundance cast in unto the offerings of God: but she of her penury hath cast in all the living that she had."

Jesus (Today):
I'm telling you, this poor widow just gave more than everyone here. They gave from their overflow. She gave everything she had.

Luke 21:6 (KJV)
"As for these things which ye behold, the days will come, in the which there shall not be left one stone upon another, that shall not be thrown down."

Jesus (Today):
You see all these buildings? The day's coming when not one stone will be left standing. It's all coming down.

Luke 21:8-9 (KJV)
"Take heed that ye be not deceived: for many shall come in my name, saying, I am Christ; and the time draweth near: go ye not therefore after them. But when ye shall hear of wars and commotions, be not terrified: for these things must first come to pass; but the end is not by and by."

Jesus (Today):
Be careful that you're not fooled. Many will come using my name saying, "I am he" and "The time is near." Don't follow them. And when you hear about wars and uprisings, don't be afraid. These things have to happen first, but the end won't come right away.

Luke 21:10-11 (KJV)
"Nation shall rise against nation, and kingdom against kingdom: And great earthquakes shall be in divers places, and famines, and pestilences; and fearful sights and great signs shall there be from heaven."

Jesus (Today):
Nations will rise up against each other, and kingdoms against kingdoms. There will be powerful earthquakes in many places, along with famines and plagues. And there will be terrifying events and great signs from heaven.

Luke 21:12-15 (KJV)
"But before all these, they shall lay their hands on you, and persecute you, delivering you up to the synagogues, and into prisons, being brought before kings and rulers for my name's sake. And it shall turn to you for a testimony. Settle it therefore in your hearts, not to meditate before what ye shall answer: For I will give you a mouth and wisdom, which all your adversaries shall not be able to gainsay nor resist."

Jesus (Today):
But before all that happens, they're going to lay hands on you and persecute you. They'll drag you into synagogues and throw you into prison. You'll stand before kings and governors because of my name. This will be your opportunity to tell your story. So decide right now not to worry about what you'll say ahead of time, because I will give you the words and the wisdom, and none of your enemies will be able to refute or resist you.

Luke 21:16–19 (KJV)
"And ye shall be betrayed both by parents, and brethren, and kinsfolks, and friends; and some of you shall they cause to be put to death. And ye shall be hated of all men for my name's sake. But there shall not an hair of your head perish. In your patience possess ye your souls."

Jesus (Today):
You will be betrayed even by your own parents, brothers, relatives, and friends. Some of you will be put to death. Everyone will hate you because of me. But not a hair on your head will be lost. Stand firm, and you will win your souls.

Luke 21:20–24 (KJV)
"And when ye shall see Jerusalem compassed with armies, then know that the desolation thereof is nigh. Then let them which are in Judaea flee to the mountains; and let them which are in the midst of it depart out; and let not them that are in the countries enter thereinto. For these be the days of vengeance, that all things which are written may be fulfilled. But woe unto them that are with child, and to them that give suck, in those days! for there shall be great distress in the land, and wrath upon this people. And they shall fall by the edge of the sword, and shall be led away captive into all nations: and Jerusalem shall be trodden down of the Gentiles, until the times of the Gentiles be fulfilled."

Jesus (Today):
When you see Jerusalem surrounded by armies, then you'll know that its destruction is close. Those who are in Judea should run to the mountains. Those inside the city must get out, and those in the countryside must not go in. These are the days of punishment, when everything written will be fulfilled. How terrible it will be for pregnant women and nursing mothers in

those days. There will be great distress in the land and anger against this people. They will fall by the sword and be taken as prisoners to all nations. Jerusalem will be trampled by the Gentiles until their time is finished.

Luke 21:25–28(KJV)
"And there shall be signs in the sun, and in the moon, and in the stars; and upon the earth distress of nations, with perplexity; the sea and the waves roaring; Men's hearts failing them for fear, and for looking after those things which are coming on the earth: for the powers of heaven shall be shaken. And then shall they see the Son of man coming in a cloud with power and great glory. And when these things begin to come to pass, then look up, and lift up your heads; for your redemption draweth nigh."

Jesus (Today):
There will be signs in the sun, moon, and stars. On earth, nations will be in anguish and confused by the roaring and tossing of the sea. People will faint from terror, afraid of what's coming on the world, because the powers of heaven will be shaken. Then they will see the Son of Man coming on a cloud with power and great glory. When all these things start to happen, stand up and lift your heads, because your redemption is getting close.

Luke 21:29–33 (KJV)
"Behold the fig tree, and all the trees; When they now shoot forth, ye see and know of your own selves that summer is now nigh at hand. So likewise ye, when ye see these things come to pass, know ye that the kingdom of God is nigh at hand. Verily I say unto you, This generation shall not pass away, till all be fulfilled. Heaven and earth shall pass away: but my words shall not pass away."

Jesus (Today):
Look at the fig tree and all the trees. When they start to sprout leaves, you can see for yourselves and know that summer is near. In the same way, when you see these things happening, know that the kingdom of God is near. I tell you the truth, this generation will not pass away until all of this happens. Heaven and earth will pass away but my words will never pass away.

Luke 21:34-36 (KJV)
"And take heed to yourselves, lest at any time your hearts be overcharged with surfeiting, and drunkenness, and cares of this life, and so that day come upon you unawares. For as a snare shall it come on all them that dwell on the face of the whole earth. Watch ye therefore, and pray always, that ye may be accounted worthy to escape all these things that shall come to pass, and to stand before the Son of man."

Jesus (Today):
Stay alert.
Don't let your heart get weighed down with indulgence, drunkenness, or the stress of daily life. If you're not careful, that day will catch you by surprise. Like a trap closing on the whole world. So stay awake and pray constantly so you'll be ready to escape all that's coming and stand before Me.

Luke 22

Luke 22:15-16 (KJV)
"With desire I have desired to eat this passover with you before I suffer. For I say unto you, I will not any more eat thereof, until it be fulfilled in the kingdom of God."

Jesus (Today):
I've been longing for this meal with you. One last time before everything happens. After this, I won't eat it again until it's fulfilled in God's Kingdom.

Luke 22:17-18 (KJV)
"For I say unto you, I will not drink of the fruit of the vine, until the kingdom of God shall come."

Jesus (Today):
Take this cup. Share it with each other.
Because I'm telling you now; this is the last time I'll drink wine until God's Kingdom shows up.

Luke 22:19-20 (KJV)

"This is my body which is given for you: this do in remembrance of me. This cup is the new testament in my blood, which is shed for you."

Jesus (Today):
This is My body, broken and given for you.
Whenever you eat it, remember Me.
And this cup? It's the new covenant, sealed in My blood, poured out for you.

Luke 22:21-22 (KJV)

"But, behold, the hand of him that betrayeth me is with me on the table. And truly the Son of man goeth, as it was determined, but woe unto that man by whom he is betrayed."

Jesus (Today):
One of you sitting here with Me at this table will betray Me.
What's about to happen has to happen, but for the one who hands Me over, it will end badly for him.

Luke 22:26-27 (KJV)

"But ye shall not be so: but he that is greatest among you, let him be as the younger; and he that is chief, as he that doth serve. For whether is greater, he that sitteth at meat, or he that serveth? is not he that sitteth at meat? but I am among you as he that serveth."

Jesus (Today):
That's not how it works with you.
If you want to be the greatest, act like the youngest.
If you want to lead, serve.
Who's usually seen as greater: the one at the table, or the one serving the food? Normally, it's the one sitting down.
But look at Me, I'm here as the One who serves.

Luke 22:28-30 (KJV)

"Ye are they which have continued with me in my temptations. And I appoint unto you a kingdom, as my Father hath appointed unto me; That ye may eat and drink at my table in my kingdom, and sit on thrones judging the twelve tribes of Israel."

Jesus (Today):

You're the ones who stuck with Me through every test.
Now I'm giving you a kingdom, just like My Father gave Me.
You'll eat and drink at My table in My kingdom.
You'll sit on thrones, judging the twelve tribes of Israel.

Luke 22:31–32 (KJV)
"Simon, Simon, behold, Satan hath desired to have you, that he may sift you as wheat. But I have prayed for thee, that thy faith fail not: and when thou art converted, strengthen thy brethren."

Jesus (Today):
Simon, Simon, listen. Satan been asking to crush you, like wheat being sifted. But I've prayed for you.
But I prayed for you, so your faith won't fall apart.
And when you come back from this, strengthen your brothers.

Luke 22:34 (KJV)
"I tell thee, Peter, the cock shall not crow this day, before that thou shalt thrice deny that thou knowest me."

Jesus (Today):
Peter, before the rooster even crows today, you'll deny three times that you even know Me.

Luke 22:36-37 (KJV)
"But now, he that hath a purse, let him take it, and likewise his scrip: and he that hath no sword, let him sell his garment, and buy one. For I say unto you, that this that is written must yet be accomplished in me, And he was reckoned among the transgressors: for the things concerning me have an end."

Jesus (Today):
Remember when I sent you out with no money, no bag, no sandals. Did you lack anything? Now it's different. If you have money, bring it. If you have a bag, take it. If you don't have a sword, sell your coat and buy one. Because what's written about Me has to happen. This is the turning point.

Luke 22:40 (KJV)
"Pray that ye enter not into temptation."
Jesus (Today):
Pray so you don't fall into temptation.

Luke 22:42 (KJV)
"Father, if thou be willing, remove this cup from me: nevertheless not my will, but thine, be done."
Jesus (Today):
Father, if there's any other way, take this from Me. But it's not about what I want. Let Your will be done.

Luke 22:46 (KJV)
"Why sleep ye? rise and pray, lest ye enter into temptation."
Jesus (Today):
Why are you sleeping?
Get up, pray, so you don't fall under temptation.

Luke 22:48 (KJV)
"Judas, betrayest thou the Son of man with a kiss?"
Jesus (Today):
Judas, are you really betraying Me with a kiss?

Luke 22:51 (KJV)
"Put up thy sword into the sheath: the cup which my Father hath given me, shall I not drink it?"
Jesus (Today):
Put your sword away. The cup my Father gave me, shouldn't I drink it?

Luke 23

Luke 23:3 (KJV)
"Art thou the King of the Jews? And he answered him and said, Thou sayest it"
Jesus (Today):
You said it.

Luke 23:28–31 (KJV)
"Daughters of Jerusalem, weep not for me, but weep for yourselves, and for your children. For, behold, the days are coming, in the which they shall say, Blessed are the barren, and the wombs that never bare, and the paps which never gave suck. Then shall they begin to say to the mountains, Fall on us; and to the hills, Cover us. For if they do these things in a green tree, what shall be done in the dry?"
Jesus (Today):
Daughters of Jerusalem, don't cry for Me.
Cry for yourselves. Cry for your children.
Because the time is coming when people will say,
"It's better to have no kids at all."
They'll beg the mountains to fall on them and cover them.
If they're doing this to Me while the wood is still green,
what do you think they'll do when it's dried up?

Luke 23:34 (KJV)
"Father, forgive them; for they know not what they do."
Jesus (Today):
Father, forgive them.
They don't realize what they're doing.

Luke 23:43-46 (KJV)
"Verily I say unto thee, To day shalt thou be with me in paradise. Father, into thy hands I commend my spirit."
Jesus (Today):

Today, you'll be with Me in paradise.
Father, I give My spirit into Your hands.

Luke 24

Luke 24:5
"Why seek ye the living among the dead?"
Jesus (Today):
Why are you looking for the living among the dead?

Luke 24:6
"He is not here, but is risen: remember how he spake unto you when he was yet in Galilee,"
Jesus (Today):
He is not here. He has risen. Remember what I told you when I was still in Galilee.

Luke 24:13
"O fools, and slow of heart to believe all that the prophets have spoken:"
Jesus (Today):
You're slow to believe everything the prophets said.

Luke 24:17 (KJV)
"And he said unto them, What manner of communications are these that ye have one to another, as ye walk, and are sad?"
Jesus (Today):
What are you talking about that's got you looking so down?

Luke 24:19
"What things?"
Jesus (Today):
What things?

Luke 24:25-26 (KJV)
"O fools, and slow of heart to believe all that the prophets have spoken: Ought not Christ to have suffered these things, and to enter into his glory?"
Jesus (Today):
You're missing it. So slow to believe what the prophets said. Didn't the Messiah have to suffer before stepping into glory?

Luke 24:29 (KJV)
"Abide with us: for it is toward evening, and the day is far spent."
Jesus (Today):
Stay with us. It's getting late, and the day is almost over.

Luke 24:36 (KJV)
"Peace be unto you."
Jesus (Today):
Peace to you.

Luke 24:38-39 (KJV)
"Why are ye troubled? and why do thoughts arise in your hearts? Behold my hands and my feet, that it is I myself: handle me, and see; for a spirit hath not flesh and bones, as ye see me have."
Jesus (Today):
Why are you scared? Why are you doubting? Look at My hands and feet. It's really Me.

Touch Me and see for yourself.
A spirit doesn't have flesh and bones like I do.

Luke 24:41 (KJV)
"Have ye here any meat?"
Jesus (Today):
Do you have anything to eat?

Luke 24:43-47 (KJV)
"This is now my body which is given for you: this do in remembrance of me. These are the words which I spake unto you, while I was yet with you, that all things must be fulfilled, which were written in the law of Moses, and in the prophets, and in the psalms, concerning me. Thus it is written, and thus it behoved Christ to suffer, and to rise from the dead the third day: And that repentance and remission of sins should be preached in his name among all nations, beginning at Jerusalem."
Jesus (Today):
This is what I told you would happen.
Everything written about in the Law, the Prophets, and the Psalms, *had* to be fulfilled. It was always written:
The Messiah would suffer and rise from the dead on the third day. And His name would bring repentance and forgiveness to every nation. Starting in Jerusalem.

Luke 24:48-49 (KJV)
"Ye are witnesses of these things. And, behold, I send the promise of my Father upon you: but tarry ye in the city of Jerusalem, until ye be endued with power from on high."
Jesus (Today):
You're the witnesses of all this.
And now I'm sending you what the Father promised.
Stay in the city until you're filled with power from Heaven

John

John 10:27-28 (KJV)
"My sheep hear my voice, and I know them, and they follow me: And I give unto them eternal life; and they shall never perish, neither shall any man pluck them out of my hand."

Jesus (Today):
My people know My voice. I know them, and they follow Me. I give them eternal life, they will never die, and nothing can ever take them out of my hands.

"The Voice of Eternity"
This is Jesus, up close. Intimate, personal, and eternal. His words reveal not just who He is, but why He came.

John 1

John 1:38 (KJV)
"What seek ye?"
Jesus (Today):
What are you looking for?

John 1:42 (KJV)
"Thou art Simon the son of Jona: thou shalt be called Cephas, which is by interpretation, A stone."
Jesus (Today):"
You're Simon, son of John.
From now on, your name is Peter, which means, a rock.

John 1:43 (KJV)
"Follow me."
Jesus (Today):
Follow Me.

John 1:47 (KJV)
"Behold an Israelite indeed, in whom is no guile!"
Jesus (Today):
Look, here's a true Israelite, honest and without deceit!

John 1:50-51 (KJV)
"Because I said unto thee, I saw thee under the fig tree, believest thou? thou shalt see greater things than these. Hereafter ye shall see heaven open, and the angels of God ascending and descending upon the Son of man."
Jesus (Today):
Because I told you I saw you under the fig tree, you believe?

You're about to see *way bigger things*. You'll see heaven open, and angels ascending and descending upon the Son of Man.

John 2

John 2:4 (KJV)
"Woman, what have I to do with thee? mine hour is not yet come."
Jesus (Today):
Woman, why are you involving Me in this?
It's not My time yet.

John 2:7 (KJV)
"Fill the waterpots with water. And they filled them up to the brim."
Jesus (Today):
Fill those jars with water.

John 2:8 (KJV)
"Draw out now, and bear unto the governor of the feast."
Jesus (Today):
Now dip some out, take it to the host of the banquet.

John 3

John 3:3 (KJV)
"Verily, verily, I say unto thee, Except a man be born again, he cannot see the kingdom of God."
Jesus (Today):
I'm telling you the absolute truth, unless you're born again, you won't even be able to see the Kingdom of God.

John 3:5-8 (KJV)

"Verily, verily, I say unto thee, Except a man be born of water and of the Spirit, he cannot enter into the kingdom of God. That which is born of the flesh is flesh; and that which is born of the Spirit is spirit. Marvel not that I said unto thee, Ye must be born again. The wind bloweth where it listeth, and thou hearest the sound thereof, but canst not tell whence it cometh, and whither it goeth: so is every one that is born of the Spirit."

Jesus (Today):

Unless you're born of water and the Spirit, you can't enter the Kingdom of God. Human life gives birth to human life. But Spirit gives birth to spirit. Don't be shocked that I said, "You must be born again." The wind blows wherever it wants. You hear it, but you can't tell where it came from or where it's going. That's what it's like when someone is born of the Spirit.

John 3:11-18 (KJV)

"Verily, verily, I say unto thee, We speak that we do know, and testify that we have seen; and ye receive not our witness. If I have told you earthly things, and ye believe not, how shall ye believe, if I tell you of heavenly things? And no man hath ascended up to heaven, but he that came down from heaven, even the Son of man which is in heaven. And as Moses lifted up the serpent in the wilderness, even so must the Son of man be lifted up: That whosoever believeth in him should not perish, but have eternal life. For God so loved the world, that he gave his only begotten Son, that whosoever believeth in him should not perish, but have everlasting life. For God sent not his Son into the world to condemn the world; but that the world through him might be saved. He that believeth on him is not condemned: but he that believeth not is condemned already, because he hath not believed in the name of the only begotten Son of God.

Jesus (Today):

I'm telling you the truth. We speak what we know and testify what we've seen but you don't accept our testimony. If you don't believe me when I talk about earthly things how will you believe when I talk about heavenly things? No one has gone up to heaven except the one who came down from heaven the Son of Man who is in heaven. Just like Moses lifted up the snake in the desert the Son of Man must be lifted up so everyone who believes in him won't perish but will have eternal life. God loved the world so much that he gave his one and only Son so that whoever believes in him will not perish but have everlasting

life. God did not send his Son to condemn the world but to save it. Anyone who believes in him is not condemned but anyone who does not believe is already condemned because they have not believed in God's only Son.

John 3:19 (KJV)
"And this is the condemnation, that light is come into the world, and men loved darkness rather than light, because their deeds were evil."

Jesus (Today):
Here's the judgment: The Light came into the world, but people loved the darkness more than the Light,
because their actions were evil.

John 3:20 (KJV)
"For every one that doeth evil hateth the light, neither cometh to the light, lest his deeds should be reproved."

Jesus (Today):
People doing evil hate the light,
they won't come near it.
They know their sin will be exposed.

John 3:21 (KJV)
"But he that doeth truth cometh to the light, that his deeds may be made manifest, that they are wrought in God."

Jesus (Today):
But the ones who walk in truth?
They come toward the light,
so it's clear their lives were built through God.

John 4

John 4:7 (KJV)
"Give me to drink."
Jesus (Today):
Will you give me a drink?

John 4:10 (KJV)
"If thou knewest the gift of God, and who it is that saith to thee, Give me to drink; thou wouldest have asked of him, and he would have given thee living water."
Jesus (Today):
If you knew what God was offering, and who you're really talking to, you wouldn't be giving Me water.
You'd be asking Me. And I'd give you living water.

John 4:13-14 (KJV)
"Whosoever drinketh of this water shall thirst again; But whosoever drinketh of the water that I shall give him shall never thirst; but the water that I shall give him shall be in him a well of water springing up into everlasting life."
Jesus (Today):
Anyone who drinks this well water?
They'll be thirsty again.
But the water I give?
It becomes a spring inside you, overflowing, alive,
overflowing into eternal life.

John 4:16-18 (KJV)
"Go, call thy husband, and come hither. Thou hast well said, I have no husband: For thou hast had five husbands; and he whom thou now hast is not thy husband: in that saidst thou truly."
Jesus (Today):
Go, call your husband, and come back.

You're right, you don't have a husband.
You've had five. And the man you're with now? He's not your husband either. You told the truth.

John 4:21-24 (KJV)
"Woman, believe me, the hour cometh, when ye shall neither in this mountain, nor yet at Jerusalem, worship the Father. Ye worship ye know not what: we know what we worship: for salvation is of the Jews. But the hour cometh, and now is, when the true worshippers shall worship the Father in spirit and in truth: for the Father seeketh such to worship him. God is a Spirit: and they that worship him must worship him in spirit and in truth"

Jesus (Today):
Believe Me, soon it won't matter if you're on this mountain or in Jerusalem. Worship isn't about a place.
You're worshiping someone you don't truly know.
We know who we worship, because salvation is of the Jews.
But the time is coming, and it's already here; when real worshipers will worship the Father in spirit and in truth.
That's who the Father is searching for. God is Spirit, and the only way to truly worship Him is with your spirit, grounded in truth.

John 4:26 (KJV)
"I that speak unto thee am he."

Jesus (Today):
I am the one speaking to you.

John 4:34 (KJV)
"My meat is to do the will of him that sent me, and to finish his work."

Jesus (Today):
My food is doing what the One who sent Me wants.
Finishing the mission He gave Me.

John 4:34-38 (KJV)
"My meat is to do the will of him that sent me, and to finish his work. Say not ye, There are yet

four months, and then cometh harvest? Behold, I say unto you, Lift up your eyes, and look on the fields; for they are white already to harvest. And he that reapeth receiveth wages, and gathereth fruit unto life eternal; that both he that soweth and he that reapeth may rejoice together. And herein is that saying true, One soweth, and another reapeth."

Jesus (Today):
You say, "There's still four months till harvest." But I'm telling you. Look up! The fields are ready right now. The harvest is ripe. The one who gathers the crop is already earning their reward bringing in a harvest that leads to eternal life. So now the one who plants and the one who gathers celebrate together. You've heard it said, "One plants, another reaps." That's real. I've sent you to gather a harvest where you didn't do the hard work. Others planted the seeds, and now you're stepping into the blessing of their labor.

John 5

John 5:6 (KJV)
"Wilt thou be made whole?"
Jesus (Today):
Do you want to be healed?

John 5:8 (KJV)
"Rise, take up thy bed, and walk."
Jesus (Today):
Get up. Get out of bed. Walk.

John 5:14 (KJV)
"Behold, thou art made whole: sin no more, lest a worse thing come unto thee."
Jesus (Today):

You're healed now. Now stop sinning, or something worse could happen to you.

John 5:17 (KJV)
"My Father worketh hitherto, and I work."
Jesus (Today):
My Father has never stopped working, and neither have I.

John 5:19-21 (KJV)
"Verily, verily, I say unto you, The Son can do nothing of himself, but what he seeth the Father do: for what things soever he doeth, these also doeth the Son likewise. For the Father loveth the Son, and sheweth him all things that himself doeth: and he will shew him greater works than these, that ye may marvel. For as the Father raiseth up the dead, and quickeneth them; even so the Son quickeneth whom he will.
Jesus (Today):
I don't do anything on My own.
I only do what I see the Father doing.
Whatever He does, I do the same.

John 5:20 (KJV)
"For the Father loveth the Son, and sheweth him all things that himself doeth: and he will shew him greater works than these, that ye may marvel."
Jesus (Today):
The Father loves Me, He shows Me everything He's doing.
And He's about to show Me even *greater* things, so you'll be left speechless.

John 5:21 (KJV)
"For as the Father raiseth up the dead, and quickeneth them; even so the Son quickeneth whom he will."
Jesus (Today):

The Father raises the dead and gives life,
and I give life to whoever I choose.

John 5:22–23 (KJV)

"For the Father judgeth no man, but hath committed all judgment unto the Son: That all men should honour the Son, even as they honour the Father. He that honoureth not the Son honoureth not the Father which hath sent him."

Jesus (Today):
The Father doesn't judge anyone directly.
He handed that authority to Me.
So everyone will honor the Me just like they honor Him.
If you reject Me, you're rejecting Him too.

John 5:24 (KJV)

"Verily, verily, I say unto you, He that heareth my word, and believeth on him that sent me, hath everlasting life, and shall not come into condemnation; but is passed from death unto life."

Jesus (Today):
Listen. If you hear what I'm saying and believe the One who sent Me, you already have eternal life. You're not facing judgment. You've already crossed over from death into life.

John 5:25 (KJV)

"Verily, verily, I say unto you, The hour is coming, and now is, when the dead shall hear the voice of the Son of God: and they that hear shall live."

Jesus (Today):
The time is coming. In fact, it's already here.
The dead will hear My voice, and the ones who truly hear Me will live.

John 5:26–27 (KJV)

"For as the Father hath life in himself; so hath he given to the Son to have life in himself; And hath given him authority to execute judgment also, because he is the Son of man."

Jesus (Today):
The Father has life in Himself,
and He's given Me that same power, to carry life within Me.
He's also given Me the authority to judge,
because I am the Son of Man.

John 5:28-29 (KJV)
"Marvel not at this: for the hour is coming, in the which all that are in the graves shall hear his voice, And shall come forth; they that have done good, unto the resurrection of life; and they that have done evil, unto the resurrection of damnation."

Jesus (Today):
Don't be shocked by this.
The time is coming when everyone in the grave
will hear My voice, and they'll rise.
Those who lived right will rise to eternal life.
Those who chose evil will rise to judgment.

John 5:30 (KJV)
"I can of mine own self do nothing: as I hear, I judge: and my judgment is just; because I seek not mine own will, but the will of the Father which hath sent me."

Jesus (Today):
I don't act on My own.
I make decisions based on what the Father shows Me,
and My judgment is right. I'm not here pushing My own plan.
I'm carrying out the will of the One who sent Me.

John 5:31-32 (KJV)
"If I bear witness of myself, my witness is not true. There is another that beareth witness of me; and I know that the witness which he witnesseth of me is true."

Jesus (Today):
If I were testifying about Myself alone, it wouldn't count.
But there's Another backing Me up, and His word is true.

John 5:33–35 (KJV)

"Ye sent unto John, and he bare witness unto the truth. But I receive not testimony from man: but these things I say, that ye might be saved. He was a burning and a shining light: and ye were willing for a season to rejoice in his light."

Jesus (Today):
You went to John, and he told you the truth.
I don't rely on human testimony,
but I'm telling you this so you can be saved.
John was a burning, shining light,
and for a while, you were drawn to his light.

John 5:36 (KJV)

"But I have greater witness than that of John: for the works which the Father hath given me to finish, the same works that I do, bear witness of me, that the Father hath sent me."

Jesus (Today):
I've got something even stronger than John's testimony,
the miracles My Father gave Me to complete.
Those works speak for themselves.
They prove the Father sent Me.

John 5:37–38 (KJV)

"And the Father himself, which hath sent me, hath borne witness of me. Ye have neither heard his voice at any time, nor seen his shape. And ye have not his word abiding in you: for whom he hath sent, him ye believe not."

Jesus (Today):
My Father sent Me, but you've never heard His voice, never seen Him, and His word isn't living in you.
If it was, you'd believe the One He sent.

John 5:39–40 (KJV)

"Search the scriptures; for in them ye think ye have eternal life: and they are they which testify of me. And ye will not come to me, that ye might have life."

Jesus (Today):
You search the Scriptures thinking they will give you eternal

life, but they point straight to Me.
And you still won't come to Me to give you life.

John 5:41-42 (KJV)
"I receive not honour from men. But I know you, that ye have not the love of God in you."
Jesus (Today):
I'm not here for applause or approval.
I know what's in you, and it's not the love of God.

John 5:43 (KJV)
"I am come in my Father's name, and ye receive me not: if another shall come in his own name, him ye will receive."
Jesus (Today):
I came in My Father's name, and you rejected Me.
But someone else could come using his own name,
and you'd welcome him with open arms.

John 5:44 (KJV)
"How can ye believe, which receive honour one of another, and seek not the honour that cometh from God only?"
Jesus (Today):
How can you even believe, when all you care about is
impressing each other and not seeking the approval that comes
from God alone?

John 5:45–47 (KJV)
"Do not think that I will accuse you to the Father: there is one that accuseth you, even Moses, in whom ye trust. For had ye believed Moses, ye would have believed me: for he wrote of me. But if ye believe not his writings, how shall ye believe my words?"
Jesus (Today):
Don't think I'll be the one accusing you to the Father.
It's Moses, the one you claim to follow, who will call you out.

If you really believed Moses, you'd believe Me,
because he wrote about Me. But if you won't believe what he wrote, how will you ever believe what I say?

John 6

John 6:12 (KJV)
"Gather up the fragments that remain, that nothing be lost."
Jesus (Today):
Collect the leftovers, I don't want anything to go to waste.

John 6:20 (KJV)
"It is I; be not afraid."
Jesus (Today):
It's Me, don't be afraid.

John 6:26 (KJV)
"Verily, verily, I say unto you, Ye seek me, not because ye saw the miracles..."
Jesus (Today):
You're not chasing Me because of the miracles,
you're here because you ate bread and got full.

John 6:27 (KJV)
"Labour not for the meat which perisheth, but for that meat which endureth unto everlasting life, which the Son of man shall give unto you: for him hath God the Father sealed."
Jesus (Today):
Don't chase after food that goes bad. Go after the food that lasts

forever, the kind I'll give you. The Father has marked Me for that very purpose.

John 6:29 (KJV)
"This is the work of God, that ye believe on him whom he hath sent."

Jesus (Today):
Here's what God wants from you;
believe in the One He sent.

John 6:32-33 (KJV)
"Verily, verily, I say unto you, Moses gave you not that bread from heaven; but my Father giveth you the true bread from heaven. For the bread of God is he which cometh down from heaven, and giveth life unto the world."

Jesus (Today):
It wasn't Moses who gave you real bread from heaven.
It's My Father. The true bread from God comes down from heaven and gives life to the entire world.

John 6:35 (KJV)
"I am the bread of life: he that cometh to me shall never hunger; and he that believeth on me shall never thirst."

Jesus (Today):
I am the Bread of Life.
If you come to Me, you'll never be hungry again.
If you believe in Me, you'll never thirst.

John 6:36 (KJV)
"But I said unto you, That ye also have seen me, and believe not."

Jesus (Today):
You've seen Me, and still don't believe.

John 6:37 (KJV)
"All that the Father giveth me shall come to me; and him that cometh to me I will in no wise cast out."
Jesus (Today):
Whoever comes to Me, I will never turn away.

John 6:38 (KJV)
"For I came down from heaven, not to do mine own will, but the will of him that sent me."
Jesus (Today):
**I didn't come down from heaven to do My own will,
I came to carry out the will of the One who sent Me.**

John 6:39-40 (KJV)
"And this is the will of him that sent me, that every one which seeth the Son, and believeth on him, may have everlasting life: and I will raise him up at the last day. And this is the will of him that sent me, that every one which seeth the Son, and believeth on him, may have everlasting life: and I will raise him up at the last day."
Jesus (Today):
His will is this: That I won't lose even *one* of those He gave Me. I'll raise them all up on the last day. His will is that everyone who sees the Son and believes in Him will have eternal life. And I will raise them up.

John 6:43 (KJV)
"Murmur not among yourselves."
Jesus (Today):
Stop whispering among yourselves.

John 6:44 (KJV)
"No man can come to me, except the Father which hath sent me draw him: and I will raise him up at the last day."
Jesus (Today):

**No one can come to Me unless the Father draws them in,
and if He does, I'll raise them up on the last day.**

John 6:45-46 (KJV)
"It is written in the prophets, And they shall be all taught of God. Every man therefore that hath heard, and hath learned of the Father, cometh unto me. Not that any man hath seen the Father, save he which is of God, he hath seen the Father."

Jesus (Today):
The prophets said it, they'll all be taught by God Himself. Everyone who listens and learns from the Father comes to Me. And no one's actually seen the Father, except the One who came from Him. I've seen Him.

John 6:47 (KJV)
"Verily, verily, I say unto you, He that believeth on me hath everlasting life."

Jesus (Today):
If you believe in Me, you already have eternal life.

John 6:48 (KJV)
"I am that bread of life."

Jesus (Today):
I *am* the bread of life.

John 6:49–50 (KJV)
"Your fathers did eat manna in the wilderness, and are dead. This is the bread which cometh down from heaven, that a man may eat thereof, and not die."

Jesus (Today):
Your ancestors ate manna in the wilderness, and they still died. But this bread, the kind that comes from heaven? You eat this, you'll not die.

John 6:51 (KJV)
"I am the living bread which came down from heaven: if any man eat of this bread, he shall live for ever: and the bread that I will give is my flesh, which I will give for the life of the world."

Jesus (Today):
I'm the living bread that came from heaven.
If you eat this bread, you'll live forever.
And the bread I give for the life of the world...
is *My flesh*.

John 6:53–54 (KJV)
"Verily, verily, I say unto you, Except ye eat the flesh of the Son of man, and drink his blood, ye have no life in you. Whoso eateth my flesh, and drinketh my blood, hath eternal life; and I will raise him up at the last day."

Jesus (Today):
Truly, truly, I tell you, unless you eat the flesh of the Son of Man and drink his blood, you have no life in you. Whoever eats my flesh and drinks my blood has eternal life, and I will raise them up on the last day.

John 6:55–56 (KJV)
"For my flesh is meat indeed, and my blood is drink indeed, He that eateth my flesh, and drinketh my blood, dwelleth in me, and I in him."

Jesus (Today):
My flesh is true food, and my blood is true drink. Whoever eats my flesh and drinks my blood lives in me, and I live in him.

John 6:57 (KJV)
"As the living Father hath sent me, and I live by the Father: so he that eateth me, even he shall live by me."

Jesus (Today):
The living Father sent Me, and I live because of Him.
If you feed on Me, you'll live because of Me.

John 6:58 (KJV)
"This is that bread which came down from heaven: not as your fathers did eat manna, and are dead: he that eateth of this bread shall live for ever."

Jesus (Today):
This is the real bread from heaven.
Not like the kind your ancestors ate, then died.
Whoever eats this bread will live forever.

John 6:62 (KJV)
"Doth this offend you?..."

Jesus (Today):
Is this offending you?

John 6:63 (KJV)
"It is the spirit that quickeneth; the flesh profiteth nothing: the words that I speak unto you, they are spirit, and they are life."

Jesus (Today):
It's the Spirit that gives life.
The flesh counts for nothing.
My words, they are Spirit.
They *are* life.

John 6:64 (KJV)
"But there are some of you that believe not. For Jesus knew from the beginning who they were that believed not, and who should betray him."

Jesus (Today):
Some of you still don't believe Me,
And I've known from the start who didn't, and who would betray Me.

John 6:65 (KJV)
"Therefore said I unto you, That no man can come unto me, except it were given unto him of my Father.

Jesus (Today):
No one can come to Me unless the Father gives them the ability to.

John 6:67 (KJV)
"Will ye also go away?"
Jesus (Today):
Are you going to leave too?

John 6:70 (KJV)
"Have not I chosen you twelve, and one of you is a devil?"
Jesus (Today):
I chose all twelve of you.
And still, one of you is a traitor.

John 7

John 7:6 (KJV)
"Jesus said unto them, My time is not yet come: but your time is alway ready."
Jesus (Today):
My time hasn't come yet.
Yours? Always ready.

John 7:7 (KJV)
"The world cannot hate you; but me it hateth, because I testify of it, that the works thereof are evil."
Jesus (Today):
The world doesn't hate you.
It hates Me, because I expose it.
I call out what is broken and evil in it.

John 7:8 (KJV)
"Go ye up unto this feast: I go not up yet unto this feast; for my time is not yet full come."
Jesus (Today):
You go ahead to the feast. I'm not going. Not yet.
My time hasn't come.

John 7:16 (KJV)
"My doctrine is not mine, but his that sent me."
Jesus (Today):
This teaching? It's not from Me.
It comes straight from the One who sent Me.

John 7:17 (KJV)
"If any man will do his will, he shall know of the doctrine, whether it be of God, or whether I speak of myself."
Jesus (Today):
If you truly desire to do God's will,
you'll recognize whether this teaching comes from Him,
or if I'm just speaking on My own.

John 7:18 (KJV)
"He that speaketh of himself seeketh his own glory: but he that seeketh his glory that sent him, the same is true, and no unrighteousness is in him."
Jesus (Today):
If someone speaks only for themselves,
They're chasing attention, not truth.
But I'm here for the glory of the One who sent Me,
and that's what makes Me true.

John 7:19 (KJV)

"Did not Moses give you the law, and yet none of you keepeth the law? Why go ye about to kill me?

Jesus (Today):
Moses gave you the law, and not one of you is keeping it.
So tell Me, why are you trying to kill Me?

John 7:21-23 (KJV)

"I have done one work, and ye all marvel Moses therefore gave unto you circumcision; (not because it is of Moses, but of the fathers;) and ye on the sabbath day circumcise a man. If a man on the sabbath day receive circumcision, that the law of Moses should not be broken; are ye angry at me, because I have made a man every whit whole on the sabbath day?"

Jesus (Today):
I did one thing, and you're all amazed. You'll break Sabbath tradition to keep Moses' command, but I restore a whole person on the Sabbath, and somehow, I'm the one you're angry with?

John 7:24 (KJV)

"Judge not according to the appearance but judge righteous judgment."

Jesus (Today):
Stop judging by what things look like on the outside.
Judge with truth. Judge with righteous judgment.

John 7:28-29 (KJV)

"Ye both know me, and ye know whence I am: and I am not come of myself, but he that sent me is true, whom ye know not. But I know him: for I am from him, and he hath sent me."

Jesus (Today):
You think you know Me, and where I come from.
But I'm not here on My own. The One who sent Me is real and you don't know Him. But I do, because I came from Him. He sent Me.

John 7:33-34 (KJV)
"Yet a little while am I with you, and then I go unto him that sent me. Ye shall seek me, and shall not find me: and where I am, thither ye cannot come."

Jesus (Today):
I'm only with you a little longer, then I'm going back to Him who sent Me. You'll look for Me and not find Me.
And where I'm going, you can't follow.

John 7:37-38 (KJV)
"If any man thirst, let him come unto me, and drink. He that believeth on me, as the scripture hath said, out of his belly shall flow rivers of living water."

Jesus (Today):
If you're thirsty, come to Me and drink.
Anyone who believes in Me, streams of living water will flow from deep inside them, just like the Scriptures said.

John 8

John 8:7 (KJV)
"He that is without sin among you, let him first cast a stone at her."

Jesus (Today):
If you're perfect, if you've never sinned, go ahead.
You throw the first stone.

John 8:10-11 (KJV)
"Woman, where are those thine accusers? hath no man condemned thee?" Neither do I condemn thee: go, and sin no more."

Jesus (Today):
Woman, where did your accusers go? Did no one condemn you?
Then neither do I. Now go, and don't live like that anymore.

John 8:12 (KJV)
"I am the light of the world: he that followeth me shall not walk in darkness, but shall have the light of life."

Jesus (Today):
I'm the Light of the World. If you walk with Me,
you won't live in darkness. You'll have the light that
gives life.

John 8:14 (KJV)
"Though I bear record of myself, yet my record is true..."

Jesus (Today):
Even if I testify about Myself,
what I say is still true. I know where I came from.
And I know where I'm going.

John 8:15-16 (KJV)
"Ye judge after the flesh; I judge no man. And yet if I judge, my judgment is true: for I am not alone, but I am he that sent me."

Jesus (Today):
If I do judge, My judgment is true. You judge by what you see on the outside. I don't judge like that. But when I do judge, I'm right, because I'm not doing it alone. I'm in full unity with the Father who sent Me.

John 8:18 (KJV)
"I am one that bear witness of myself..."

Jesus (Today):
I speak for Myself,
and My Father who sent Me backs Me up.

John 8:19 (KJV)
"Ye neither know me, nor my Father: if ye had known me, ye should have known my Father also."

Jesus (Today):
You don't know Me,
and you don't know My Father either.
If you knew Me, you'd already know Him.

John 8:21 (KJV):
"I go my way, and ye shall seek me, and shall die in your sins: whither I go, ye cannot come."

Jesus (Today):
I'm leaving soon. You'll look for Me,
but you'll die in your sin. Where I'm going, you can't follow.

John 8:23-24 (KJV)
"Ye are from beneath; I am from above: ye are of this world; I am not of this world. I said therefore unto you, That ye shall die in your sins: for if ye believe not that I am he, ye shall die in your sins."

Jesus (Today):
You're from below. I'm from above.
You're part of this world. I'm not.
That's why I told you, you'll die in your sins
unless you believe that I AM who I say I am.

John 8:25 (KJV)
"Even the same that I said unto you from the beginning."

Jesus (Today):
Who am I?
I've been telling you who I am from the start.

John 8:26 (KJV)
"I have many things to say and to judge of you: but he that sent me is true; and I speak to the world those things which I have heard of him."

Jesus (Today):
I've got plenty I could say and judge you for,
but I only speak what the One who sent Me gives Me to say.
And He is true.

John 8:28-29 (KJV)
"When ye have lifted up the Son of man, then shall ye know that I am he, and that I do nothing of myself; but as my Father hath taught me, I speak these things. And he that sent me is with me: the Father hath not left me alone; for I do always those things that please him."

Jesus (Today):
When you lift up the Son of Man, *then* you'll know I AM.
And you'll know I don't speak on My own.
Everything I say is what the Father taught Me.
He's with Me, He never left. Because I always do what pleases Him.

John 8:31-32 (KJV)
"If ye continue in my word, then are ye my disciples indeed, And ye shall know the truth, and the truth shall make you free."

Jesus (Today):
If you stay rooted in My word, you're truly My disciples.
Then you'll know the truth, and the truth will *set you free.*

John 8:34 (KJV)
"Verily, verily, I say unto you, Whosoever committeth sin is the servant of sin."

Jesus (Today):
Everyone who sins becomes a slave to it.

John 8:36 (KJV)
"If the Son therefore shall make you free, ye shall be free indeed."

Jesus (Today):
But if I set you free, you are truly, fully free.

John 8:37 (KJV)
"I know that ye are Abraham's seed; but ye seek to kill me, because my word hath no place in you."

Jesus (Today):
I know you are Abraham's children, but you want to kill me because my words have no place in you.

John 8:38 (KJV)
"I speak that which I have seen with my Father: and ye do that which ye have seen with your father."

Jesus (Today):
I'm speaking what I've seen firsthand from My Father.
You? You're doing what you've learned from your father.

John 8:39–40 (KJV)
"If ye were Abraham's children, ye would do the works of Abraham, But now ye seek to kill me, a man that hath told you the truth, which I have heard of God: this did not Abraham."

Jesus (Today):
If you were really Abraham's children,
you'd act like him. But instead, you're trying to kill Me,
just because I told you the truth I heard straight from God.
That's not Abraham behavior.

John 8:41 (KJV):
"Ye do the deeds of your father. Then said they to him, We be not born of fornication; we have one Father, even God."

Jesus (Today):
No. You're following your real father's ways.

John 8:42 (KJV)

"If God were your Father, ye would love me: for I proceeded forth and came from God; neither came I of myself, but he sent me."

Jesus (Today):
If God were truly your Father, you'd love Me.
I came from God. I'm not here on My own.
He sent Me.

John 8:43 (KJV):
"Why do ye not understand my speech? even because ye cannot hear my word."

Jesus (Today):
Why can't you understand what I'm saying?
Because you refuse to actually listen.

John 8:44 (KJV)
"Ye are of your father the devil, and the lusts of your father ye will do. He was a murderer from the beginning, and abode not in the truth, because there is no truth in him. When he speaketh a lie, he speaketh of his own: for he is a liar, and the father of it."

Jesus (Today):
You're children of your father, the devil. And you love doing what he does. He's been a murderer since the beginning. He doesn't stand in truth, because there's no truth in him. When he lies, it's his native language. He's the original liar. He's the father of lies.

John 8:45–47 (KJV)
"Because I tell you the truth, ye believe me not Which of you convinceth me of sin? And if I say the truth, why do ye not believe me? He that is of God heareth God's words: ye therefore hear them not, because ye are not of God."

Jesus (Today):
I'm telling you the truth, and you still don't believe Me.
Who here can prove Me guilty of sin?
If I'm telling you the truth, why won't you listen?

Whoever belongs to God hears what God says.
But you don't hear Me, because you don't belong to Him.

John 8:50 (KJV)
"I have not a devil; but I honour my Father, and ye do dishonour me."
Jesus (Today):
I don't have a devil. I honor my Father, but you dishonor me.

John 8:51 (KJV)
"Verily, verily, I say unto you, If a man keep my saying, he shall never see death."
Jesus (Today):
If you hold onto what I'm saying,
if you hold on to My words, you'll *never* see death.

John 8:54–55 (KJV)
"If I honour myself, my honour is nothing: it is my Father that honoureth me; of whom ye say, that he is your God: And ye have not known him; but I know him: and if I should say, I know him not, I shall be a liar like unto you: but I know him, and keep his saying."
Jesus (Today):
If I glorify Myself, it means nothing.
My Father is the One who glorifies Me,
the One you claim as your God. But you don't know Him.
I do. And if I said I didn't, I'd be lying, just like you.
But I know Him, and I do what He says.

John 8:56 (KJV)
"Your father Abraham rejoiced to see my day: and he saw it, and was glad."
Jesus (Today):
Your father Abraham was thrilled to see My day coming,
and he did see it, and he was filled with joy.

John 8:58 (KJV)
"Verily, verily, I say unto you, Before Abraham was, I am."
Jesus (Today):
Truly, truly, I tell you, before Abraham was born, I am.

John 9

John 9:4–5 (KJV)
"I must work the works of him that sent me, while it is day: the night cometh, when no man can work. As long as I am in the world, I am the light of the world."
Jesus (Today):
Neither this man nor his parents sinned, but this happened so that the works of God might be displayed in him. While I'm here in the world, I am the light of the world. As long as it's day, I have to do the work of the one who sent me, but night is coming when no one can work.

John 9:35 (KJV)
"Dost thou believe on the Son of God?"
Jesus (Today):
Do you believe in the Son of God?

John 9:37 (KJV)
"Thou hast both seen him, and it is he that talketh with thee."
Jesus (Today):
You've already seen Him,
and you're hearing Him right now.

John 9:39 (KJV)
"For judgment I am come into this world, that they which see not might see; and that they which see might be made blind."

Jesus (Today):
I came into this world to bring judgment,
to open the eyes of those who can't see,
and to expose the blindness of those who think they already can.

John 9:41 (KJV)
"If ye were blind, ye should have no sin: but now ye say, We see; therefore your sin remaineth."

Jesus (Today):
If you were truly blind, you'd be innocent.
But since you claim you can see,
your guilt is still on you.

John 10

John 10:1 (KJV)
"Verily, verily, I say unto you, He that entereth not by the door into the sheepfold, but climbeth up some other way, the same is a thief and a robber."

Jesus (Today):
If someone climbs in some other way instead of coming through the gate, they're not a shepherd. They're a thief.

John 10:2-5 (KJV)
"But he that entereth in by the door is the shepherd of the sheep. To him the porter openeth; and the sheep hear his voice: and he calleth his own sheep by name, and leadeth them out. And when he putteth forth his own sheep, he goeth before them, and the sheep follow him: for they know his voice. And a stranger will they not follow, but will flee from him: for they know not the voice of strangers."

Jesus (Today):

The true shepherd comes through the front gate.
The gatekeeper opens it for him, and the sheep know his voice.
He calls them by name and leads them out. They follow him because they know his voice. But they won't follow a stranger. They'll run, because they don't recognize that voice.

John 10:7 (KJV)
"Verily, verily, I say unto you, I am the door of the sheep."
Jesus (Today):
I'm the door for the sheep.

John 10:8 (KJV)
"All that ever came before me are thieves and robbers: but the sheep did not hear them."
Jesus (Today):
Everyone who came before Me were just thieves and liars. But My sheep didn't fall for it. They didn't listen to them.

John 10:9 (KJV)
"I am the door: by me if any man enter in, he shall be saved, and shall go in and out, and find pasture."
Jesus (Today):
I'm the door. If anyone enters through Me, they'll be saved. They'll come and go freely and find what they need.

John 10:10 (KJV)
"The thief cometh not, but for to steal, and to kill, and to destroy: I am come that they might have life, and that they might have it more abundantly."
Jesus (Today):
The thief only comes to steal, kill, and destroy. I came so you could have life, real life, overflowing.

John 10:11 (KJV)
"I am the good shepherd: the good shepherd giveth his life for the sheep."

Jesus (Today):
I'm the Good Shepherd. The Good Shepherd lays down His life for His sheep.

John 10:12-13 (KJV):
"But he that is an hireling, and not the shepherd, whose own the sheep are not, seeth the wolf coming, and leaveth the sheep, and fleeth: and the wolf catcheth them, and scattereth the sheep. The hireling fleeth, because he is an hireling, and careth not for the sheep."

Jesus (Today):
The hired worker isn't the shepherd. The sheep don't truly belong to him. So when he sees a wolf coming, he runs away, because he's just doing a job. And the wolf comes in, snatches some, and scatters the rest. That's the difference; he's not in it because he cares for the sheep.

John 10:14-15 (KJV)
"I am the good shepherd, and know my sheep, and am known of mine. As the Father knoweth me, even so know I the Father: and I lay down my life for the sheep."

Jesus (Today):
I'm the Good Shepherd. I know My sheep, and they know Me, Just like the Father knows Me, and I know the Father, I'm laying down My life for these sheep.

John 10:16 (KJV)
"And other sheep I have, which are not of this fold: them also I must bring, and they shall hear my voice; and there shall be one fold, and one shepherd."

Jesus (Today):
I've got other sheep too, they're not part of this flock yet. I've got to bring them in. They'll hear My voice, and together, we'll be one flock, with one Shepherd.

John 10:17-18 (KJV)
"Therefore doth my Father love me, because I lay down my life, that I might take it again. No man taketh it from me, but I lay it down of myself. I have power to lay it down, and I have power to take it again."

Jesus (Today):
My Father loves me because I lay down my life voluntarily and I have the power to take it back again. No one takes my life from me. I give it freely.

John 10:25-26 (KJV)
"I told you, and ye believe not. The works that I do in my Father's name, they bear witness of me."

Jesus (Today):
I already told you, and you didn't believe. The works I do in My Father's name, they speak for Me. But you don't believe, because you're not My sheep.

John 10:27-28 (KJV)
"My sheep hear my voice, and I know them, and they follow me. And I give unto them eternal life; and they shall never perish, neither shall any man pluck them out of my hand."

Jesus (Today):
My people know My voice. I know them, and they follow Me. I give them eternal life, and nothing can ever take them out of my hands.

John 10:29-30 (KJV)
"My Father, which gave them me, is greater than all; and no man is able to pluck them out of my Father's hand. I and my Father are one."

Jesus (Today):
My Father gave them to Me, and He's greater than anyone. No one can snatch them from His hand. *I and My Father are one.*

John 10:32 (KJV)
"Many good works have I shewed you from my Father; for which of those works do ye stone me?"
Jesus (Today):
I've shown you many good works from My Father,
which one are you trying to kill Me for?

John 10:34-36 (KJV)
"If he called them gods, unto whom the word of God came, and the scripture cannot be broken; Say ye of him, whom the Father hath sanctified, and sent into the world, Thou blasphemest; because I said, I am the Son of God?"
Jesus (Today):
If Scripture calls those people "gods" to whom God's word came and the Scripture can't be broken, then why do you say I am blaspheming when I say I am God's Son, whom the Father set apart and sent into the world?

John 10:37-38 (KJV)
"If I do not the works of my Father, believe me not. But if I do, though ye believe not me, believe the works: that ye may know, and believe, that the Father is in me, and I in him."
Jesus (Today):
If I'm not doing the works of My Father, don't believe Me.
But if I am, even if you don't believe Me, believe the works. So you'll know and understand: the Father is in Me, and I'm in Him.

John 11

John 11:4 (KJV)
"This sickness is not unto death, but for the glory of God, that the Son of God might be glorified thereby."
Jesus (Today):
This sickness won't end in death, it's happening so God's glory can be revealed, and so you'll know who I am.

John 11:7 (KJV)
"Let us go into Judaea again."

Jesus (Today):
Let's go back to Judea.

John 11:9-10 (KJV)
"Are there not twelve hours in the day? If any man walk in the day, he stumbleth not, because he seeth the light of this world. But if a man walk in the night, he stumbleth, because there is no light in him."

Jesus (Today):
Aren't there twelve hours of daylight? If you walk in the day, you don't trip, because you see the light. But if you walk at night, you stumble, because there's no light in you.

John 11:11 (KJV)
"Our friend Lazarus sleepeth; but I go, that I may awake him out of sleep."

Jesus (Today):
Our friend Lazarus has fallen asleep,
and I'm going to wake him up.

John 11:14-15 (KJV)
"Lazarus is dead. And I am glad for your sakes that I was not there, to the intent ye may believe; nevertheless let us go unto him."

Jesus (Today):
Lazarus is dead. And I'm glad I wasn't there, because what's about to happen will help you believe. Let's go to him.

John 11:23 (KJV)
"Thy brother shall rise again."

Jesus (Today):
Your brother will rise again.

John 11:25–26 (KJV)
"I am the resurrection, and the life: he that believeth in me, though he were dead, yet shall he live. And whosoever liveth and believeth in me shall never die. Believest thou this?"

Jesus (Today):
I am the resurrection and the life. If you believe in Me, even if you die, you'll live. And anyone alive who believes in Me will never really die. Do you believe this?

John 11:34 (KJV)
"Where have ye laid him?"

Jesus (Today):
Where did you lay him?

John 11:39 (KJV)
"Take ye away the stone."

Jesus (Today):
Move the stone.

John 11:40 (KJV)
"Said I not unto thee, that, if thou wouldest believe, thou shouldest see the glory of God?"

Jesus (Today):
Didn't I tell you, if you believe, you'll see God's glory?

John 11:41–42 (KJV)
"Father, I thank thee that thou hast heard me. And I knew that thou hearest me always: but because of the people which stand by I said it, that they may believe that thou hast sent me."

Jesus (Today):
Father, thank You for hearing Me. I know You always do, but I'm saying this out loud so everyone here will believe You sent Me.

John 11:43 (KJV)
"Lazarus, come forth."
Jesus (Today):
Lazarus, come out!

John 12

John 12:7 (KJV)
"Let her alone: against the day of my burying hath she kept this."
Jesus (Today):
Leave her alone. She saved that perfume for My burial.

John 12:8 (KJV)
"For the poor always ye have with you; but me ye have not always".
Jesus (Today):
You'll always have the poor among you, but you won't always have Me.

John 12:23 (KJV)
"The hour is come, that the Son of man should be glorified."
Jesus (Today):
The time has come. The Son of Man is about to be glorified.

John 12:24 (KJV)
"Verily, verily, I say unto you, Except a corn of wheat fall into the ground and die, it abideth alone: but if it die, it bringeth forth much fruit."
Jesus (Today):

If a grain of wheat doesn't die, it stays alone. But if it dies, it multiplies. That's what's about to happen.

John 12:25 (KJV)
"He that loveth his life shall lose it; and he that hateth his life in this world shall keep it unto life eternal."

Jesus (Today):
Whoever loves their life more than Me will lose it. But whoever hates their life in this world will keep it for eternal life.

John 12:26 (KJV)
"If any man serve me, let him follow me; and where I am, there shall also my servant be: if any man serve me, him will my Father honour."

Jesus (Today):
If you want to serve Me, follow Me. Where I am, that's where My servant belongs. And My Father will honor anyone who serves Me.

John 12:27-28 (KJV)
"Now is my soul troubled; and what shall I say? Father, save me from this hour: but for this cause came I unto this hour. Father, glorify thy name."

Jesus (Today):
My soul is heavy right now. Should I ask the Father to save Me from this hour? No, this is *why* I came. Father, glorify Your name.

John 12:30-32 (KJV)
"This voice came not because of me, but for your sakes. Now is the judgment of this world: now shall the prince of this world be cast out. And I, if I be lifted up from the earth, will draw all men unto me."

Jesus (Today):
This voice didn't come for me but for your sake. The judgment of this world is here, and the ruler of this world will be cast out.

And when I am lifted up from the earth, I will draw everyone to myself.

John 12:35–36 (KJV)
"Yet a little while is the light with you. Walk while ye have the light, lest darkness come upon you: for he that walketh in darkness knoweth not whither he goeth. While ye have light, believe in the light, that ye may be the children of light. These things spake Jesus, and departed, and did hide himself from them."

Jesus (Today):
The light's with you just a little longer. Walk while you've still got the light, so darkness doesn't overtake you. If you walk in the dark, you won't know where you're going. While you have the light, believe in it. Become children of light.

John 13

John 13:7 (KJV)
"What I do thou knowest not now; but thou shalt know hereafter."

Jesus (Today):
You don't understand what I'm doing right now, but you will soon.

John 13:8 (KJV)
"If I wash thee not, thou hast no part with me."

Jesus (Today):
If I don't wash you, you can't be part of Me.

John 13:10 (KJV)
"He that is washed needeth not save to wash his feet, but is clean every whit: and ye are clean,

but not all."

Jesus (Today):
If you're already clean, you only need your feet washed, the rest of you is good. And you are clean...but not all of you.

John 13:12-14 (KJV)
"Know ye what I have done to you? Ye call me Master and Lord: and ye say well; for so I am. If I then, your Lord and Master, have washed your feet; ye also ought to wash one another's feet."

Jesus (Today):
Do you understand what I have done for you? You call me Master and Lord, and rightly so, because that is who I am. Since I, your Lord and Master, have washed your feet, you should wash each other's feet too.

John 13:15 (KJV)
"For I have given you an example, that ye should do as I have done to you."

Jesus (Today):
I just set the example. Now go and do the same.

John 13:16 (KJV)
"Verily, verily, I say unto you, The servant is not greater than his lord; neither he that is sent greater than he that sent him."

Jesus (Today):
I tell you the truth, a servant is not greater than the master, and a messenger is not greater than the one who sent him.

John 13:17 (KJV)
"If ye know these things, happy are ye if ye do them."

Jesus (Today):
You know these things now. You'll be blessed *if you do them.*

John 13:18 (KJV)
"I speak not of you all: I know whom I have chosen: but that the scripture may be fulfilled, He that eateth bread with me hath lifted up his heel against me."
Jesus (Today):
One of you, who eats at My table, is about to turn on Me.

John 13:19 (KJV)
"Now I tell you before it come, that, when it is come to pass, ye may believe that I am he."
Jesus (Today):
I'm telling you this now, so when it happens, you'll know who I am.

John 13:20 (KJV)
"Verily, verily, I say unto you, He that receiveth whomsoever I send receiveth me; and he that receiveth me receiveth him that sent me."
Jesus (Today):
If someone receives the one I send, they receive me.
And if they receive me, they're receiving the one who sent me.

John 13:21 (KJV)
"Verily, verily, I say unto you, that one of you shall betray me."
Jesus (Today):
Listen carefully, one of you is going to betray Me.

John 13:26 (KJV)
"He it is, to whom I shall give a sop, when I have dipped it. And when he had dipped the sop, he gave it to Judas Iscariot, the son of Simon."
Jesus (Today):
It's the one I hand this bread to.

John 13:27 (KJV)
"That thou doest, do quickly."
Jesus (Today):
What you're about to do, do it quickly.

John 13:31–32 (KJV)
"Now is the Son of man glorified, and God is glorified in him. If God be glorified in him, God shall also glorify him in himself, and shall straightway glorify him."
Jesus (Today):
Now the Son of Man is glorified, and God is glorified through him. If God is glorified through him, God will glorify him in return and will do it soon.

John 13:33 (KJV)
"Little children, yet a little while I am with you. Ye shall seek me: and as I said unto the Jews, Whither I go, ye cannot come."
Jesus (Today):
I'm only with you a little longer. You'll look for Me, but where I'm going, you can't come. Not yet.

John 13:34–35 (KJV)
"A new commandment I give unto you, That ye love one another; as I have loved you, that ye also love one another. By this shall all men know that ye are my disciples, if ye have love one to another."
Jesus (Today):
I'm giving you a new command: love each other just as I have loved you. By this, everyone will know you are my followers if you love one another.

John 13:36 (KJV)
"Whither I go, thou canst not follow me now; but thou shalt follow me afterwards."
Jesus (Today):

Where I'm going, you can't follow Me *now*, but you'll follow Me later.

John 13:38 (KJV)
"The cock shall not crow, till thou hast denied me thrice."

Jesus (Today):
Before the rooster crows, you'll deny three times that you even know Me.

John 14

John 14:1 (KJV)
"Let not your heart be troubled: ye believe in God, believe also in me."

Jesus (Today):
Don't let your hearts be heavy. You believe in God, believe in Me too.

John 14:2-3 (KJV)
"In my Father's house are many mansions: if it were not so, I would have told you. I go to prepare a place for you. And if I go and prepare a place for you, I will come again, and receive you unto myself; that where I am, there ye may be also."

Jesus (Today):
There's plenty of room in My Father's house. I'm going there to prepare a place for you. And if I go, I'll come back for you. So you'll be with Me, where I am.

John 14:4 (KJV)
"And whither I go ye know, and the way ye know."

Jesus (Today):
You already know where I'm going, and you know the way.

John 14:6 (KJV)
"I am the way, the truth, and the life: no man cometh unto the Father, but by me."

Jesus (Today):
I *am* the Way. I *am* the Truth. I *am* the Life.
No one comes to the Father, except through Me.

John 14:7 (KJV)
"If ye had known me, ye should have known my Father also: and from henceforth ye know him, and have seen him."

Jesus (Today):
If you really knew Me, you'd know My Father too. From now on, you *do* know Him, because you've seen Him in Me.

John 14:9–10 (KJV)
"Have I been so long time with you, and yet hast thou not known me, Philip? he that hath seen me hath seen the Father; and how sayest thou then, Shew us the Father? Believest thou not that I am in the Father, and the Father in me? the words that I speak unto you I speak not of myself: but the Father that dwelleth in me, he doeth the works."

Jesus (Today):
Have I been with you so long, and you still don't know me? Anyone who has seen Me has seen the Father. So how can you say, "Show us the Father"? Don't you believe that I am in the Father and the Father is in me? The words I speak aren't my own; the Father living in me is doing his work.

John 14:11–12 (KJV)
"Believe me that I am in the Father, and the Father in me: or else believe me for the very works' sake. Verily, verily, I say unto you, He that believeth on me, the works that I do shall he do also; and greater works than these shall he do; because I go unto my Father."

Jesus (Today):

Believe me when I say I am in the Father and the Father is in Me. If you don't believe that, believe because of the works I do. I tell you the truth, anyone who believes in Me will do the same works I do and even greater works, because I am going to the Father.

John 14:13-14 (KJV)
"And whatsoever ye shall ask in my name, that will I do, that the Father may be glorified in the Son. If ye shall ask any thing in my name, I will do it."

Jesus (Today):
Whatever you ask in My name, I'll do it. So the Father will be glorified through the Son. If you ask anything in My name, I will do it.

John 14:15 (KJV)
"If ye love me, keep my commandments."

Jesus (Today):
If you love Me, then follow what I say.

John 14:16-17 (KJV)
"And I will pray the Father, and he shall give you another Comforter, that he may abide with you for ever; Even the Spirit of truth; whom the world cannot receive, because it seeth him not, neither knoweth him: but ye know him; for he dwelleth with you, and shall be in you."

Jesus (Today):
I'm going to ask the Father, and He'll give you another Comforter, who will never leave you. The Spirit of truth. The world cannot receive it because it does not see him or know him. But you know him because he lives with you and will be in you.

John 14:18 (KJV)
"I will not leave you comfortless: I will come to you."

Jesus (Today):
I'm not leaving you helpless. I'm coming back to you.

John 14:19 (KJV)
"Yet a little while, and the world seeth me no more; but ye see me: because I live, ye shall live also."
Jesus (Today):
Soon the world will not see me anymore, but you will see me. Because I live, you will live also.

John 14:20 (KJV)
"At that day ye shall know that I am in my Father, and ye in me, and I in you."
Jesus (Today):
When that day comes, you'll know I'm in the Father, and you are in Me, and I am in you.

John 14:21 (KJV)
"He that hath my commandments, and keepeth them, he it is that loveth me: and he that loveth me shall be loved of my Father, and I will love him, and will manifest myself to him."
Jesus (Today):
If you know my commands and live by them, you love me. And if you love me, my Father will love you, and I will reveal myself to you.

John 14:23-24 (KJV)
"If a man love me, he will keep my words: and my Father will love him, and we will come unto him, and make our abode with him. He that loveth me not keepeth not my sayings: and the word which ye hear is not mine, but the Father's which sent me."
Jesus (Today):
If anyone loves Me, they will obey my words. My Father will love them, and we will come to them and make our home with them.

But anyone who does not love Me does not obey My teachings. The words you hear are not Mine but come from the Father who sent Me.

John 14:26 (KJV)
"But the Comforter, which is the Holy Ghost, whom the Father will send in my name, he shall teach you all things, and bring all things to your remembrance, whatsoever I have said unto you."
Jesus (Today):
The Comforter, the Holy Spirit, whom the Father will send in My name, will teach you everything and remind you of everything I've said to you.

John 14:27 (KJV)
"Peace I leave with you, my peace I give unto you: not as the world giveth, give I unto you. Let not your heart be troubled, neither let it be afraid."
Jesus (Today):
I'm leaving you with peace, *My* peace.
Not like the world gives. Don't let your hearts be troubled.
Don't let fear move in.

John 14:28 (KJV)
"Ye have heard how I said unto you, I go away, and come again unto you. If ye loved me, ye would rejoice, because I said, I go unto the Father: for my Father is greater than I."
Jesus (Today):
If you truly loved me, you'd be glad that I'm going to the Father, because He is greater than I am.

John 14:29 (KJV)
"And now I have told you before it come to pass, that, when it is come to pass, ye might believe."
Jesus (Today):
I'm telling you all this before it happens, so when it does, your faith won't waver. You'll believe.

John 14:30–31 (KJV)
"Hereafter I will not talk much with you: for the prince of this world cometh, and hath nothing in me. But that the world may know that I love the Father; and as the Father gave me commandment, even so I do. Arise, let us go hence."

Jesus (Today):
I won't be talking with you much longer because the prince of this world is coming and he has no power over me. I do this so the world will know that I love the Father and I do exactly what the Father commands me. Let's go.

John 15

John 15:1 (KJV)
"I am the true vine, and my Father is the husbandman."

Jesus (Today):
I'm the true Vine. My Father is the Gardener.

John 15:2 (KJV)
"Every branch in me that beareth not fruit he taketh away: and every branch that beareth fruit, he purgeth it, that it may bring forth more fruit."

Jesus (Today):
If a branch connected to Me doesn't bear fruit, He removes it. But if it's growing and producing, He prunes it, so it can produce even more.

John 15:3 (KJV)
"Now ye are clean through the word which I have spoken unto you."

Jesus (Today):
You've already been cleaned, by the word I gave you.

John 15:4 (KJV)
"Abide in me, and I in you. As the branch cannot bear fruit of itself, except it abide in the vine; no more can ye, except ye abide in me."

Jesus (Today):
Stay connected to Me, and I'll stay connected to you. Just like a branch can't bear fruit by itself, you can't produce anything real without Me.

John 15:5 (KJV)
"I am the vine, ye are the branches: He that abideth in me, and I in him, the same bringeth forth much fruit: for without me ye can do nothing."

Jesus (Today):
I'm the Vine. You're the branches. If you stay in Me, and I in you, you'll bear much fruit. But apart from Me? You can't do anything.

John 15:6 (KJV)
"If a man abide not in me, he is cast forth as a branch, and is withered; and men gather them, and cast them into the fire, and they are burned."

Jesus (Today):
If someone disconnects from Me, they're like a dead branch; cut off, dried up, tossed out, and burned.

John 15:7 (KJV)
"If ye abide in me, and my words abide in you, ye shall ask what ye will, and it shall be done unto you.

Jesus (Today):
If you stay in Me, and My words live in you, ask whatever you want. It will be done.

John 15:8 (KJV)
"Herein is my Father glorified, that ye bear much fruit; so shall ye be my disciples."
Jesus (Today):
My Father gets glory when you produce fruit, and prove you're really My disciples.

John 15:9-10 (KJV)
"As the Father hath loved me, so have I loved you: continue ye in my love. If ye keep my commandments, ye shall abide in my love; even as I have kept my Father's commandments, and abide in his love."
Jesus (Today):
The same way the Father loves Me, that's how I love you. So stay rooted in My love. If you keep My commands, you'll remain in My love, just like I obey My Father and stay in His.

John 15:11 (KJV)
"These things have I spoken unto you, that my joy might remain in you, and that your joy might be full."
Jesus (Today):
I've told you this so My joy will live inside you, and your joy will be complete.

John 15:12-13 (KJV)
"This is my commandment, That ye love one another, as I have loved you. Greater love hath no man than this, that a man lay down his life for his friends."
Jesus (Today):
This is my command:
Love each other the way I've loved you. There is no greater love than this: To lay down your life for your friends.

John 15:14 (KJV)
"Ye are my friends, if ye do whatsoever I command you."

Jesus (Today):
You're My friends, if you live what I teach.

John 15:15 (KJV)
"Henceforth I call you not servants; for the servant knoweth not what his lord doeth: but I have called you friends; for all things that I have heard of my Father I have made known unto you."

Jesus (Today):
I'm not calling you servants anymore. Servants don't get let in on the plan. I've called you *friends*, because I've told you *everything* I heard from My Father.

John 15:16 (KJV)
"Ye have not chosen me, but I have chosen you, and ordained you, that ye should go and bring forth fruit, and that your fruit should remain: that whatsoever ye shall ask of the Father in my name, he may give it you."

Jesus (Today):
You did not choose me, but I chose you and appointed you to go and produce lasting fruit. Whatever you ask the Father in my name, He will give you.

John 15:17 (KJV)
"These things I command you, that ye love one another."

Jesus (Today):
I'm commanding you, love each other.

John 15:18-19 (KJV)
"If ye were of the world, the world would love his own: but because ye are not of the world, but I have chosen you out of the world, therefore the world hateth you."

Jesus (Today):
If the world hates you, remember it hated Me first. If you belonged to the world, it would love you. But I chose you out of it, so now it hates you.

John 15:20 (KJV)
"Remember the word that I said unto you, The servant is not greater than his lord. If they have persecuted me, they will also persecute you; if they have kept my saying, they will keep yours also."

Jesus (Today):
Remember what I told you: A servant isn't greater than their master. If they persecuted me, they will also persecute you. If they obeyed my teaching, they will obey yours as well.

John 15:22 (KJV)
"If I had not come and spoken unto them, they had not had sin: but now they have no cloak for their sin."

Jesus (Today):
If I hadn't come and spoken to them, they wouldn't be guilty. But now there's no excuse.

John 15:23 (KJV)
"He that hateth me hateth my Father also."

Jesus (Today):
If you hate Me, You hate My Father too.

John 15:26–27 (KJV)
"But when the Comforter is come, whom I will send unto you from the Father, even the Spirit of truth, which proceedeth from the Father, he shall testify of me: And ye also shall bear witness, because ye have been with me from the beginning."

Jesus (Today):
But when the Comforter comes, whom I will send to you from the Father, the Spirit of truth who proceeds from the Father, he will testify about me. And you will also testify because you have been with me from the beginning.

John 16

John 16:1 (KJV)
"These things have I spoken unto you, that ye should not be offended."
Jesus (Today):
I'm telling you all this so you won't fall away when it gets hard.

John 16:2 (KJV)
"They shall put you out of the synagogues: yea, the time cometh, that whosoever killeth you shall think that he doeth God service."
Jesus (Today):
They're going to kick you out of the synagogues. In fact, people will think killing you is doing God a favor.

John 16:3–4 (KJV)
"And these things will they do unto you, because they have not known the Father, nor me. But these things have I told you, that when the time shall come, ye may remember that I told you of them. And these things I said not unto you at the beginning, because I was with you."
Jesus (Today):
They'll do it because they don't know the Father, and they don't know Me. I'm telling you now, so when it happens, you'll remember I warned you.

John 16:5 (KJV)
"But now I go my way to him that sent me; and none of you ask me, Whither goest thou?
Jesus (Today):
Now I'm going back to Him who sent Me, and none of you are asking where I'm going.

John 16:6 (KJV)
"But because I have said these things unto you, sorrow hath filled your heart."

Jesus (Today):
You're filled with grief because of what I said.

John 16:7 (KJV)
"Nevertheless I tell you the truth; It is expedient for you that I go away: for if I go not away, the Comforter will not come unto you; but if I depart, I will send him unto you."

Jesus (Today):
But it's actually better for you that I leave, because if I don't go, the Advocate won't come. But if I do go, I'll send Him to you.

John 16:8-11 (KJV)
"And when he is come, he will reprove the world of sin, and of righteousness, and of judgment Of sin, because they believe not on me; Of righteousness, because I go to my Father, and ye see me no more; Of judgment, because the prince of this world is judged. :"

Jesus (Today):
When He comes, He'll expose the truth: what sin really is, what righteousness really means, and what judgment really looks like. He'll do this because people refuse to believe in Me, because I'm going to the Father, and because the ruler of this world is condemned.

John 16:12 (KJV)
"I have yet many things to say unto you, but ye cannot bear them now."

Jesus (Today):
I have so much more I want to tell you, but you're not ready yet.

John 16:13 (KJV)
"Howbeit when he, the Spirit of truth, is come, he will guide you into all truth: for he shall not speak of himself; but whatsoever he shall hear, that shall he speak: and he will shew you things to come."

Jesus (Today):
When the Spirit of Truth comes,
He'll guide you into all truth.
He won't speak on His own,
He'll speak what He hears and tell you what's coming next.

John 16:14–15 (KJV)
"He shall glorify me: for he shall receive of mine, and shall shew it unto you. All things that the Father hath are mine: therefore said I, that he shall take of mine, and shall shew it unto you."
Jesus (Today):
He'll glorify Me, because He'll take what's Mine and reveal it to you. Everything the Father has is Mine. That's why I said He'll take from Me and make it known to you.

John 16:16 (KJV)
"A little while, and ye shall not see me: and again, a little while, and ye shall see me, because I go to the Father."
Jesus (Today):
In a little while, you won't see Me. Then, in a little while, you'll see Me again.

John 16:20 (KJV)
"Verily, verily, I say unto you, That ye shall weep and lament, but the world shall rejoice: and ye shall be sorrowful, but your sorrow shall be turned into joy."
Jesus (Today):
You're going to cry and grieve, but your sorrow will turn into *joy*.

John 16:21-22 (KJV)
"A woman when she is in travail hath sorrow, because her hour is come: but as soon as she is delivered of the child, she remembereth no more the anguish, for joy that a man is born into the world. And ye now therefore have sorrow: but I will see you again, and your heart shall rejoice, and your joy no man taketh from you."

Jesus (Today):
A woman in labor experiences pain because her time has come, but once her child is born, she forgets the pain because of the joy a new life has arrived. You are sad now, but I will see you again, and your hearts will rejoice. A joy no one can take away.

John 16:23–24 (KJV)
"And in that day ye shall ask me nothing. Verily, verily, I say unto you, Whatsoever ye shall ask the Father in my name, he will give it you. Hitherto have ye asked nothing in my name: ask, and ye shall receive, that your joy may be full."

Jesus (Today):
On that day, you won't need to ask me anything. I tell you the truth, whatever you ask the Father in my name, He will give you. Until now, you have asked for nothing in my name. Ask and you will receive so your joy can be complete.

John 16:27 (KJV)
"For the Father himself loveth you, because ye have loved me, and have believed that I came out from God."

Jesus (Today):
The Father Himself loves you, because you loved Me and believed I came from Him.

John 16:28 (KJV)
"I came forth from the Father, and am come into the world: again, I leave the world, and go to the Father."

Jesus (Today):
I came from the Father into the world, and now I'm leaving the world and returning to Him.

John 16:31–33 (KJV)
"Do ye now believe? These things I have spoken unto you, that in me ye might have peace. In the world ye shall have tribulation: but be of good cheer; I have overcome the world."

Jesus (Today):
Do you believe now? I've told you these things so you can have peace in me. In this world, you will face trouble. But take heart. I have overcome the world.

John 17

John 17:1 (KJV)
"Father, the hour is come; glorify thy Son, that thy Son also may glorify thee:"
Jesus (Today):
Father, the hour has come. Glorify Your Son, so I can glorify You.

John 17:2–3 (KJV)
"As thou hast given him power over all flesh, that he should give eternal life to as many as thou hast given him. And this is life eternal, that they might know thee the only true God, and Jesus Christ, whom thou hast sent."
Jesus (Today):
You gave Me authority over all people,
to give eternal life to everyone You've given Me.
And this is eternal life: that they know You, the one true God,
and Me, Jesus Christ, the One You sent.

John 17:4–5 (KJV)
"I have glorified thee on the earth: I have finished the work which thou gavest me to do. And now, O Father, glorify thou me with thine own self with the glory which I had with thee before the world was."
Jesus (Today):
I glorified You on earth,
I finished the mission You gave Me.
Now, Father, glorify Me in Your presence
with the glory I had before the world even began.

John 17:6 (KJV)
"I have manifested thy name unto the men which thou gavest me out of the world: thine they were, and thou gavest them me; and they have kept thy word."

Jesus (Today):
I've revealed who You are to the ones You gave Me from the
world. They were Yours, You gave them to Me,
and they've kept Your word.

John 17:7-8 (KJV)
"Now they have known that all things whatsoever thou hast given me are of thee. For I have given unto them the words which thou gavest me; and they have received them, and have known surely that I came out from thee, and they have believed that thou didst send me."

Jesus (Today):
Now they know everything I have came from You.
I gave them the words You gave Me, and they believed.
They know I came from You. They believe You sent Me.

John 17:9 (KJV)
"I pray for them: I pray not for the world, but for them which thou hast given me; for they are thine."

Jesus (Today):
I'm praying for them, not for the world,
but for those You gave Me. They belong to You.

John 17:10 (KJV)
"And all mine are thine, and thine are mine; and I am glorified in them."

Jesus (Today):
Everything I have is Yours, and everything You have is Mine.
And I'm glorified in them.

John 17:11 (KJV)

"And now I am no more in the world, but these are in the world, and I come to thee. Holy Father, keep through thine own name those whom thou hast given me, that they may be one, as we are."

Jesus (Today):

I'm not going to be in the world much longer,
but they are. Holy Father, guard them by Your name, the name
You gave Me, so they'll be one, just like We are.

John 17:12 (KJV)

"While I was with them in the world, I kept them in thy name: those that thou gavest me I have kept, and none of them is lost, but the son of perdition; that the scripture might be fulfilled."

Jesus (Today):

I protected them while I was here.
I kept every one of them, except the one who chose destruction,
so Scripture would be fulfilled.

John 17:13 (KJV)

"And now come I to thee; and these things I speak in the world, that they might have my joy fulfilled in themselves."

Jesus (Today):

Now I'm coming back to You, and I'm saying this while I'm still
in the world so they'll have *My joy*, complete and full inside
them.

John 17:14–15 (KJV)

"I have given them thy word; and the world hath hated them, because they are not of the world, even as I am not of the world. I pray not that thou shouldest take them out of the world, but that thou shouldest keep them from the evil."

Jesus (Today):

I gave them Your word, and the world hated them for it.
They're not from this world any more than I am.
I'm not asking You to take them out of it,
but protect them from evil.

John 17:16-17 (KJV)
"They are not of the world, even as I am not of the world. Sanctify them through thy truth: thy word is truth."

Jesus (Today):
They are not of this world, just as I am not of this world. Make them holy through your truth; your word is truth.

John 17:18-19 (KJV)
"As thou hast sent me into the world, even so have I also sent them into the world. And for their sakes I sanctify myself, that they also might be sanctified through the truth."

Jesus (Today):
You sent Me into the world, and I'm sending them in the same way. I've set Myself apart for them, so they can be truly set apart too.

John 17:20-21 (KJV)
"Neither pray I for these alone, but for them also which shall believe on me through their word; That they all may be one; as thou, Father, art in me, and I in thee, that they also may be one in us: that the world may believe that thou hast sent me."

Jesus (Today):
I don't pray only for these, but also for those who will believe in me through their message. May all of them be one, just as you, Father, are in me and I am in you. May they also be one with us, so the world will believe that you sent me.

John 17:22-23 (KJV)
"And the glory which thou gavest me I have given them; that they may be one, even as we are one: I in them, and thou in me, that they may be made perfect in one; and that the world may know that thou hast sent me, and hast loved them, as thou hast loved me."

Jesus (Today):
And the glory you gave me, I have given them, so they may be one just as we are one. I am in them and you are in me, so they may be made perfect in unity. This is so the world will know

that you sent me and that you have loved them just as you have loved me.

John 17:24 (KJV)
"Father, I will that they also, whom thou hast given me, be with me where I am; that they may behold my glory, which thou hast given me: for thou lovedst me before the foundation of the world."

Jesus (Today):
Father, I want those you have given me to be with me where I am, so they can see the glory you have given me, because you loved me before the world was made.

John 17:25–26 (KJV)
"O righteous Father, the world hath not known thee: but I have known thee, and these have known that thou hast sent me. And I have declared unto them thy name, and will declare it: that the love wherewith thou hast loved me may be in them, and I in them."

Jesus (Today):
O righteous Father, the world has not known you, but I have known you, and these have known that you sent me. I have revealed your name to them and will continue to do so, so the love you have for me will be in them, and I will be in them.

Acts 1:8 (KJV)
"But ye shall receive power, after that the Holy Ghost is come upon you: and ye shall be witnesses unto me both in Jerusalem, and in all Judaea, and in Samaria, and unto the uttermost part of the earth."

Jesus (Today):
You will receive power when the Holy Spirit comes upon you. Then you will tell people about Me in your city, your region, and all the way to the ends of the earth.

"Power Released"

His last words before ascension. He commissions and empowers the movement that would carry His voice to the world.

Acts 1

Acts 1:4 (KJV)
"And, being assembled together with them, commanded them that they should not depart from Jerusalem, but wait for the promise of the Father, which, saith he, ye have heard of me."

Jesus (Today):
Wait for the Father's promise, which you heard me speak about.

Acts 1:5 (KJV)
"For John truly baptized with water; but ye shall be baptized with the Holy Ghost not many days hence."

Jesus (Today):
John baptized with water, but in a few days, you will be baptized with the Holy Spirit.

Acts 1:7 (KJV)
"It is not for you to know the times or the seasons, which the Father hath put in his own power."

Jesus (Today):
It isn't for you to know the times or seasons that the Father has set by his own authority

Acts 1:8 (KJV)
"But ye shall receive power, after that the Holy Ghost is come upon you: and ye shall be witnesses unto me both in Jerusalem, and in all Judaea, and in Samaria, and unto the uttermost part of the earth."

Jesus (Today):
You will receive power when the Holy Spirit comes upon you. Then you will tell people about Me in your city, your region, and all the way to the ends of the earth.

Acts 9

Acts 9:4–6 (KJV)
"Saul, Saul, why persecutest thou me?" I am Jesus whom thou persecutest: it is hard for thee to kick against the pricks. Arise, and go into the city, and it shall be told thee what thou must do. "

Jesus (Today):
Saul, Saul, why are you attacking Me? I am Jesus. The same Jesus you've been persecuting. You're only hurting yourself by trying to fight against Me. Get up and go into the city. You'll be told exactly what to do there.

Revelation

Revelation 2:3 (KJV):
"And hast borne, and hast patience, and for my name's sake hast laboured, and hast not fainted."
Jesus (Today):
You've endured, stayed strong, and kept going for My name. You didn't quit.

"The Final Word"
Jesus speaks from eternity. He warns, invites, and promises. These are the last recorded words from His mouth to ours.

Revelation 1

Revelation 1:8 (KJV)
"I am Alpha and Omega, the beginning and the ending, saith the Lord, which is, and which was, and which is to come, the Almighty."

Jesus (Today):
I am the Beginning and the End. The One who is, who always was, and who is coming again. I am the Almighty.

Revelation 1:11 (KJV)
"Saying, I am Alpha and Omega, the first and the last: and, What thou seest, write in a book, and send it unto the seven churches which are in Asia;unto Ephesus, and unto Smyrna, and unto Pergamos, and unto Thyatira,and unto Sardis, and unto Philadelphia, and unto Laodicea."

Jesus (Today):
I am the First and the Last. Write down everything you see in a book and send it to the seven churches in Asia:
Ephesus, Smyrna, Pergamum, Thyatira,
Sardis, Philadelphia, and Laodicea.

Revelation 1:17-18 (KJV)
"Fear not; I am the first and the last: I am he that liveth, and was dead; and, behold, I am alive for evermore, Amen; and have the keys of hell and of death."

Jesus (Today):
Don't be afraid. I'm the First and the Last.
I'm the Living One. I was dead, but look, *I'm alive forever.*
And I hold the keys to death and the grave.

Revelation 2

Revelation 2:1 (KJV):
"Unto the angel of the church of Ephesus write; These things saith he that holdeth the seven stars in his right hand, who walketh in the midst of the seven golden candlesticks;"
Jesus (Today):
Write this to the messenger of the church in Ephesus: This is from the One who holds the seven stars in His right hand and walks among the seven golden lampstands.

Revelation 2:2 (KJV)
"I know thy works, and thy labour, and thy patience, and how thou canst not bear them which are evil: and thou hast tried them which say they are apostles, and are not, and hast found them liars:"
Jesus (Today):
I see what you've done. Your hard work, your perseverance. You don't tolerate evil. You've tested those who claim to be apostles but aren't, and you've proven they're liars.

Revelation 2:3 (KJV):
"And hast borne, and hast patience, and for my name's sake hast laboured, and hast not fainted."
Jesus (Today):
You've endured, stayed strong, and kept going for My name. You didn't quit.

Revelation 2:4 (KJV)
"Nevertheless I have somewhat against thee, because thou hast left thy first love."
Jesus (Today):
But here's what I have against you,
you've walked away from your first love.

Revelation 2:5 (KJV):
"Remember therefore from whence thou art fallen, and repent, and do the first works; or else I will come unto thee quickly, and will remove thy candlestick out of his place, except thou repent."

Jesus (Today):
Remember how far you've fallen. Turn back and return to what you used to do. If you don't, I will come quickly and take your lampstand out of its place. Unless you repent.

Revelation 2:6 (KJV):
"But this thou hast, that thou hatest the deeds of the Nicolaitans, which I also hate."

Jesus (Today):
But you do have this going for you; you hate the actions of those who twist and corrupt My message to justify sin and compromise. I hate it too.

Revelation 2:7 (KJV)
"He that hath an ear, let him hear what the Spirit saith unto the churches; To him that overcometh will I give to eat of the tree of life, which is in the midst of the paradise of God."

Jesus (Today):
If you have ears, listen to what the Spirit is saying to the churches. To the one who overcomes, I will give access to eat from the tree of life in the center of God's paradise.

Revelation 2:8 (KJV):
"And unto the angel of the church in Smyrna write; These things saith the First and the Last, which was dead, and is alive;"

Jesus (Today):
Write this to the messenger of the church in Smyrna:
These are the words of the First and the Last.
The One who died and came back to life.

Revelation 2:9 (KJV):
"I know thy works, and tribulation, and poverty, (but thou art rich) and I know the blasphemy of them which say they are Jews, and are not, but are the synagogue of Satan."

Jesus (Today):
I see your struggle. Your suffering, your poverty.
But you are rich. And I know the slander coming from those who claim to be faithful, but aren't.
They belong to the synagogue of Satan.

Revelation 2:10 (KJV):
"Fear none of those things which thou shalt suffer: behold, the devil shall cast some of you into prison, that ye may be tried; and ye shall have tribulation ten days: be thou faithful unto death, and I will give thee a crown of life."
Jesus (Today):
Don't be afraid of what you're about to face.
The devil's going to throw some of you in prison to test you.
You'll suffer for a short time.
But stay faithful. Even if it costs your life,
and I'll give you the crown of life.

Revelation 2:11 (KJV):
"He that hath an ear, let him hear what the Spirit saith unto the churches; He that overcometh shall not be hurt of the second death."
Jesus (Today):
If you have ears, listen to what the Spirit is saying to the churches. Whoever overcomes won't be touched by the second death.

Revelation 2:12 (KJV):
"And to the angel of the church in Pergamos write;
These things saith he which hath the sharp sword with two edges;"
Jesus (Today):
Write this to the leader of the church in Pergamos:
This message comes from the One who holds the sharp,

double-edged sword, the truth that cuts deep and never misses.

Revelation 2:13 (KJV):
"I know thy works, and where thou dwellest,
even where Satan's seat is:
and thou holdest fast my name, and hast not denied my faith,
even in those days wherein Antipas was my faithful martyr,
who was slain among you, where Satan dwelleth."

Jesus (Today):
I see what you've done, and I know where you live, right where Satan has his throne.
Still, you've held tight to My name.
You didn't deny your faith in Me,
even when Antipas, My faithful witness, was killed there where Satan lives.

Revelation 2:14 (KJV):
"But I have a few things against thee, because thou hast there them that hold the doctrine of Balaam, who taught Balac to cast a stumblingblock before the children of Israel, to eat things sacrificed unto idols, and to commit fornication."

Jesus (Today):
But I've got a few things against you. You've let people stay who follow the spirit of Balaam, teaching others how to trip up My people. They lead believers into compromise, getting involved in things tied to idols and giving themselves away sexually without care.

Revelation 2:15 (KJV):
"So hast thou also them that hold the doctrine of the Nicolaitans, which thing I hate."

Jesus (Today):
And just like that, you've let in some who follow the

teaching of the Nicolaitans, people who twist grace into license. I hate it.

Revelation 2:16 (KJV):
"Repent; or else I will come unto thee quickly, and will fight against them with the sword of my mouth."

Jesus (Today):
Turn around. Now.
If you don't, I'll come quickly and go to war with them using the sword that comes from My mouth.

Revelation 2:17 (KJV)
"He that hath an ear, let him hear what the Spirit saith unto the churches; To him that overcometh will I give to eat of the hidden manna, and will give him a white stone, and in the stone a new name written, which no man knoweth saving he that receiveth it."

Jesus (Today):
Whoever has ears, let them hear what the Spirit says to the churches. To the one who overcomes, I will give some of the hidden manna. I will also give that person a white stone with a new name written on it, known only to the one who receives it.

Revelation 2:18 (KJV):
"And unto the angel of the church in Thyatira write; These things saith the Son of God, who hath his eyes like unto a flame of fire, and his feet are like fine brass;"

Jesus (Today):
Write this to the messenger of the church in Thyatira:
This is from the Son of God, the One whose eyes burn like fire and whose feet shine like polished bronze.

Revelation 2:19 (KJV):

"I know thy works, and charity, and service, and faith, and thy patience, and thy works; and the last to be more than the first."

Jesus (Today):
I see what you're doing. Your love, your service, your faith, your endurance. And I see how you're doing even more now than you did at the start.

Revelation 2:20 (KJV):
"Notwithstanding I have a few things against thee, because thou sufferest that woman Jezebel, which calleth herself a prophetess, to teach and to seduce my servants to commit fornication, and to eat things sacrificed unto idols."

Jesus (Today):
But I have this against you, you're letting that woman Jezebel do damage. She claims to speak for God, but she's leading My people into sin, teaching them to give their bodies away and compromise with idolatry.

Revelation 2:22 (KJV):
"Behold, I will cast her into a bed, and them that commit adultery with her into great tribulation, except they repent of their deeds."

Jesus (Today):
Look, I will throw her on a bed of suffering, and those who commit adultery with her will suffer greatly unless they repent of what they have done.

Revelation 2:24 (KJV):
"But unto you I say, and unto the rest in Thyatira, as many as have not this doctrine, and which have not known the depths of Satan, as they speak; I will put upon you none other burden."

Jesus (Today):
Now to the rest of you in Thyatira;
those who haven't followed this teaching
and haven't gotten into what they call "the deep things of Satan," I'm not putting anything else on you.

Revelation 2:25 (KJV):
"But that which ye have already hold fast till I come."
Jesus (Today):
Just hold on to what you've got, until I come.

Revelation 2:26 (KJV):
"And he that overcometh, and keepeth my works unto the end, to him will I give power over the nations:"
Jesus (Today):
To the one who overcomes and stays faithful to what I've asked until the very end, I'll give authority over the nations.

Revelation 2:27 (KJV):
"And he shall rule them with a rod of iron; as the vessels of a potter shall they be broken to shivers: even as I received of my Father."
Jesus (Today):
He'll rule them with strength, like iron in hand and break them to pieces like shattered clay, just like the authority My Father gave Me.

Revelation 2:28 (KJV):
"And I will give him the morning star."
Jesus (Today):
And I'll give him the morning star.

Revelation 2:29 (KJV):
"He that hath an ear, let him hear what the Spirit saith unto the churches."
Jesus (Today):

If you've got ears, then listen.
Hear what the Spirit is saying to the churches.

Revelation 3

Revelation 3:1 (KJV):
"And unto the angel of the church in Sardis write; These things saith he that hath the seven Spirits of God, and the seven stars; I know thy works, that thou hast a name that thou livest, and art dead."
Jesus (Today):
**Write this to the messenger of the church in Sardis:
This is from the One who holds the seven Spirits of God and the seven stars. I know your reputation. People think you're alive, but you're dead.**

Revelation 3:2 (KJV):
"Be watchful, and strengthen the things which remain, that are ready to die: for I have not found thy works perfect before God."
Jesus (Today):
Wake up. Strengthen what little you've got left before it dies too. Because what you've done so far, it hasn't measured up before God.

Revelation 3:3 (KJV):
"Remember therefore how thou hast received and heard, and hold fast, and repent. If therefore thou shalt not watch, I will come on thee as a thief, and thou shalt not know what hour I will come upon thee."
Jesus (Today):
Remember what you've heard and received. Hold onto it and

turn back. If you don't stay alert, I'll show up like a thief in the night, and you won't see Me coming.

Revelation 3:4 (KJV):
"Thou hast a few names even in Sardis which have not defiled their garments; and they shall walk with me in white: for they are worthy."
Jesus (Today):
There are a few in Sardis who haven't stained their clothes with compromise. They'll walk with Me, dressed in white, because they've proven themselves worthy.

Revelation 3:5 (KJV):
"He that overcometh, the same shall be clothed in white raiment; and I will not blot out his name out of the book of life, but I will confess his name before my Father, and before his angels."
Jesus (Today):
Everyone who overcomes will wear white, and I will never erase their name from the Book of Life. I'll personally speak their name in front of My Father and all His angels.

Revelation 3:6 (KJV):
"He that hath an ear, let him hear what the Spirit saith unto the churches."
Jesus (Today):
If you've got ears, use them. Listen to what the Spirit is saying to the churches.

Revelation 3:7 (KJV):
"And to the angel of the church in Philadelphia write; These things saith he that is holy, he that is true, he that hath the key of David, he that openeth, and no man shutteth; and shutteth, and no man openeth;"
Jesus (Today):
Write this to the messenger of the church in Philadelphia:

This comes from the One who is holy and true, the One who holds the key of David, the door I open, no one can shut. And when I shut it, no one can open it.

Revelation 3:8 (KJV)
"I know thy works: behold, I have set before thee an open door, and no man can shut it: for thou hast a little strength, and hast kept my word, and hast not denied my name"

Jesus (Today):
I see everything you've done. Look, I've opened a door for you that no one can shut. You don't have much strength,
but you've stayed faithful to My word and you haven't denied My name.

Revelation 3:9 (KJV):
"Behold, I will make them of the synagogue of Satan, which say they are Jews, and are not, but do lie; behold, I will make them to come and worship before thy feet, and to know that I have loved thee."

Jesus (Today):
Watch this, those who claim to be God's people but aren't, who lie and belong to Satan's crowd, I'll make them show up and bow down at your feet. And they'll know without a doubt that I've loved you.

Revelation 3:10 (KJV):
"Because thou hast kept the word of my patience, I also will keep thee from the hour of temptation, which shall come upon all the world, to try them that dwell upon the earth."

Jesus (Today):
Because you've held on to My call to stay faithful,
I'll protect you from the time of testing that's coming to shake the whole world and challenge everyone living on earth.

Revelation 3:11 (KJV)
"Behold, I come quickly: hold that fast which thou hast, that no man take thy crown."
Jesus (Today):
I'm coming soon. Hold on tight to what you've got, so no one takes your crown.

Revelation 3:12 (KJV):
"Him that overcometh will I make a pillar in the temple of my God, and he shall go no more out: and I will write upon him the name of my God, and the name of the city of my God, which is new Jerusalem, which cometh down out of heaven from my God: and I will write upon him my new name."
Jesus (Today):
Everyone who overcomes; I'll make them a permanent pillar in the temple of My God. They'll never be pushed out. I'll write on them the name of My God, the name of God's city, the New Jerusalem. Coming down out of heaven from Him. And I'll write on them My new name.

Revelation 3:13 (KJV):
"He that hath an ear, let him hear what the Spirit saith unto the churches."
Jesus (Today):
If you've got ears, listen. Hear what the Spirit is saying to the churches.

Revelation 3:14 (KJV):
"And unto the angel of the church of the Laodiceans write; These things saith the Amen, the faithful and true witness, the beginning of the creation of God;"
Jesus (Today):
Write this to the messenger of the church in Laodicea: This is from the Amen, the faithful and true witness, the One who began God's creation.

Revelation 3:15 (KJV):
"I know thy works, that thou art neither cold nor hot: I would thou wert cold or hot."
Jesus (Today):
I know what you've been doing. You're not cold, and you're not hot. I wish you were one or the other.

Revelation 3:16 (KJV):
"So then because thou art lukewarm, and neither cold nor hot, I will spue thee out of my mouth."
Jesus (Today):
But because you're lukewarm, not hot, not cold. I'm about to spit you out of My mouth.

Revelation 3:17 (KJV):
"Because thou sayest, I am rich, and increased with goods, and have need of nothing; and knowest not that thou art wretched, and miserable, and poor, and blind, and naked:"
Jesus (Today):
You say, "I'm rich. I've got everything I need."
But you don't even realize; you're wretched, miserable, poor, blind, and naked.

Revelation 3:18 (KJV):
I counsel thee to buy of me gold tried in the fire, that thou mayest be rich; and white raiment, that thou mayest be clothed, and that the shame of thy nakedness do not appear; and anoint thine eyes with eyesalve, that thou mayest see."
Jesus (Today):
Here's My advice: Come to Me and buy gold that's been refined in fire. The kind that makes you truly rich. Get white garments from Me so you can be clothed and no longer exposed in shame. And get salve for your eyes so you can finally see clearly.

Revelation 3:19 (KJV):
"As many as I love, I rebuke and chasten: be zealous therefore, and repent."
Jesus (Today):
Everyone I love, I correct and discipline.
So take it seriously. Get fired up, and turn back to Me.

Revelation 3:20 (KJV):
"Behold, I stand at the door, and knock: if any man hear my voice, and open the door, I will come in to him, and will sup with him, and he with me."
Jesus (Today):
I'm standing at the door, knocking. If you hear My voice and open the door, I'll come in and sit down with you. We will share the table together.

Revelation 3:21 (KJV):
"To him that overcometh will I grant to sit with me in my throne, even as I also overcame, and am set down with my Father in his throne."
Jesus (Today):
If you overcome, I'll give you a seat beside Me on My throne, just like I overcame and sat down beside My Father on His.

Revelation 3:22 (KJV):
"He that hath an ear, let him hear what the Spirit saith unto the churches."
Jesus (Today):
If you've got ears, listen. Hear what the Spirit is saying to the churches.

Revelation 22

Revelation 22:7 (KJV)
"Behold, I come quickly: blessed is he that keepeth the sayings of the prophecy of this book."
Jesus (Today):
I'm coming soon. Blessed are those who hold on to the words of this prophecy and live by them.

Revelation 22:12 (KJV):
"And, behold, I come quickly; and my reward is with me, to give every man according as his work shall be."
Jesus (Today):
Look, I'm coming soon. I'm bringing rewards with Me. Everyone will get what they've earned.

Revelation 22:13 (KJV):
"I am Alpha and Omega, the beginning and the end, the first and the last."
Jesus (Today):
I am the Alpha and the Omega, the beginning and the end, the first and the last.

Revelation 22:16 (KJV):
"I Jesus have sent mine angel to testify unto you these things in the churches. I am the root and the offspring of David, and the bright and morning star."
Jesus (Today):
I, Jesus, sent My angel to tell you all of this for the churches.
I am both the root and the descendant of David.
The bright and morning star.

Revelation 22:20 (KJV):
"Surely I come quickly."
Jesus (Today):
Yes. I'm coming soon.
Count on it.

www.ingramcontent.com/pod-product-compliance
Lightning Source LLC
Chambersburg PA
CBHW070749230426
43665CB00017B/2310